*The Rhetoric of Politics
in the English Revolution
1642–1660*

The Rhetoric of Politics
in the English Revolution
1642–1660

ELIZABETH SKERPAN

UNIVERSITY OF MISSOURI PRESS
COLUMBIA AND LONDON

Library of Congress Cataloging-in-Publication Data

Skerpan, Elizabeth Penley.
    The rhetoric of politics in the English Revolution, 1642–1660
Elizabeth Skerpan.
        p.   cm.
    Includes bibliographical references and index.
    ISBN 0-8262-0799-5
    1. Great Britain—Politics and government—1642–1660.
2. Rhetoric—Political aspects—Great Britain—History—17th century.
3. English prose literature—Early modern, 1500–1700—History and criticism.
4. Revolutionary literature, English—History and criticism. 5. Rhetoric—
1500–1800. I. Title.
DA406.S54   1992   91–36266
824′.409358—dc20   CIP

∞™ This paper meets the requirements of the
American National Standard for Permanence of Paper
for Printed Library Materials, Z39.48, 1984.

Designer: Elizabeth Fett
Typesetter: Connell-Zeko Type & Graphics
Printer and Binder: Thomson-Shore, Inc.
Typeface: Garmond No. 3

For
Ruth Skerpan
Alfred Lindsay Skerpan

In memory of
Alfred Andrew Skerpan
1914–1967

Contents

Preface

To evaluate the discourse of the English Revolution and, secondarily, the particular achievements of Milton and other notable writers, I adopt the framework of the rhetorical movement study. According to Leland M. Griffin, originator of the method, such a study attempts to "isolate the rhetorical movement within the matrix of the historical movement," focusing on specific ideas and techniques. The study traces these ideas from their inception to a moment of "crisis," at which point the audience must choose sides, and finally to the point of "consummation," when the ideas cease to be controversial, having been assimilated or rejected by the audience. Further, to judge the works of the movement, the study must employ the critical standards of the time to approximate the writers' and audiences' own perceptions of effective and appropriate writing.[1]

To follow this framework, I divide my study into an introduction and three parts. In the Introduction, I examine the potential audience of the revolutionary pamphleteers and seventeenth-century rhetorical theory. The parts that follow illustrate the practice of revolutionary rhetoric. Part I presents a sample of controversial discourse from the 1630s—an episode from the Laudian persecutions of 1637—as a point of departure for investigating a series of tracts from 1642. The 1642 tracts represent the responses of both royalists and parliamentarians to King Charles's attempt in January of that year to arrest five members of Parliament, one of the events that precipitated the first civil war. Part II centers on the regicide in 1649, inevitably the point of crisis in the revolution, and includes studies of two of Milton's works—*Eikonoklastes* and *The Tenure of Kings and Magistrates*. Part III follows the 1659–1660 debate over restoring the monarchy. Among the pamphlets I examine are Milton's *The Readie & Easie Way to Establish a Free Commonwealth* and several works by James Harrington. I begin each part with a historical introduction to provide what Quentin Skinner calls "contexts of meaning" for these "heteronomous works."[2]

---

1. "The Rhetoric of Historical Movements," in *Methods of Rhetorical Criticism: A Twentieth-Century Perspective*, 346–52.

2. "Hermeneutics and the Role of History," 226–27. The meaning of "heteron-

In addition, I employ several formal and generic constraints. Since Milton is my chief secondary focus, I have selected works from others that are comparable in intent to those of Milton that fall within the temporal restrictions. Thus, I examine prose responses to particular political events and issues, works pursuing specific arguments to definite conclusions. Also, since my primary concern is the overall rhetorical movement, I have excluded those of Milton's prose works that fall outside the historical framework—the antiprelatical and divorce tracts, for example. All the tracts in the study dated between 1642 and 1660 come from the Thomason Collection and are described in its catalog.

This study intends to shed some light on the activity of pamphleteering as a historically new part of the political process and to evaluate Milton's contribution to that process. Further, it investigates in a historical context a problem that became increasingly urgent to me during the 1980s and now into the 1990s: why the rhetoric of political positions that may be dangerous to the general public—the redefinition of "special interests" as the poor and the handicapped, the labeling of programs for minorities as "reverse discrimination," the use of the term "liberal" as a pejorative, for example—gains widespread popular acceptance, while the rhetoric of other positions becomes a target for ridicule. Then as now, the nature of a discourse—its use of conventions, cultural contexts, and presentation—frequently counts for more than its content, or even the day-to-day reality surrounding its audience. Such a discourse, in effect, creates its own reality and thereby may literally alter the course of events. Despite my hopes to the contrary, my reading of the tracts of Milton and his contemporaries within their contexts of meaning has led me to the conviction that the conventions and expectations of classical and seventeenth-century rhetoric favored conservatism to the detriment of any writer with radical ideas. For a radical writer to succeed in such circumstances, he would need to be aware of the conventions of political discourse *as conventions* rather than essential representations of political life. This awareness was precluded by his education.

With few exceptions, these tracts are true ephemeras. Most went through only one printing, often hurried. Few prompted any rejoinders; the majority are anonymous. To represent the characters of these tracts, I have retained their original punctuation, capitalization, italics, and spelling, including the common use of *i* for *j, v* for *u,* and *vv* for *w.* The long *s,* however, has been

---

omous" works depends upon their context—the full meaning exists outside the text. An "autonomous" text is self-contained and requires no contextual interpretation.

brought into accord with modern usage. Similarly, I follow New Style dating, with the year beginning January 1.

In *Areopagitica*, Milton defined controversial tracts as "the living labors of public men." This work is an account of those labors during the first revolution in modern times.

Acknowledgments

From growing up as a faculty child at Kent State University in the 1960s to teaching at a public university in the 1980s, I have always felt that it was impossible for me not to be interested in the relationship of language and politics. That my interest took the form of research in seventeenth-century English literature is the result of my undergraduate work at Miami University with Randolph L. Wadsworth, Jr., and John R. Romano. This project itself began at the University of Wisconsin–Madison with the assistance and encouragement of Raymond B. Waddington, A. B. Chambers, and Phillip Harth.

The manuscript and I benefited from the assistance of many people. Thomas O. Sloane read and commented on the Introduction. Sharon Crowley, Diane Parkin-Speer, Marion Tangum, and Richard Fralin read chapters and offered suggestions. Michael Hennessy and John Rumrich invited me to present materials to their graduate classes, the members of which stimulated me to greater clarity in my own rhetoric. John M. Wallace and the members of his 1984 National Endowment for the Humanities Summer Seminar for College Teachers at the University of Chicago provided an ideal environment for my research and writing. Since 1984, members of the South Central Renaissance Conference—James and Tita French Baumlin in particular—have been my sharpest and most attentive critics. Throughout this project I have appreciated the conversation and encouragement of Leah S. Marcus. Any shortcomings in the manuscript and argument are my responsibility.

Portions of several chapters have appeared elsewhere in slightly different form. Parts of chapters 2 and 5 were published as "Rhetorical Genres and the *Eikon Basilike,*" *Explorations in Renaissance Culture* 11 (1985): 99–111. An earlier version of the arguments pursued in chapters 8 and 9 appeared as "Writers—Languages—Communities: Radical Pamphleteers and Legal Discourse in the English Revolution," *Explorations in Renaissance Culture* 16 (1990): 37–56.

My final debt is personal. I thank my friends and colleagues Priscilla Leder, Miles Wilson, and especially Rebecca Bell–Metereau for everything they have done and who they have been for me during the last five years. No words can adequately express to them my affection, respect, and gratitude.

The Rhetoric of Politics
in the English Revolution
1642–1660

Readers and Rhetoric
in Seventeenth-Century England

This study investigates what happens to the discourse of a political community when the ideological assumptions forming that discourse are challenged. The political community of seventeenth-century England had been bound together by definite cultural, artistic, political, religious, and linguistic values since Tudor times. Those values—whether or not particular persons or groups shared them—defined the possible range of discourse, the background against which all ideas are judged.

Through many recent studies, we have come to recognize the assumptions that were held at the beginning of the seventeenth century. In 1600, art was a mirror held up to nature; human society was a hierarchy that reflected God's plan for the universe; Christianity, as expressed by some form of the Church of England, was the only true religion; monarchy was the only divinely approved form of government; meaning existed in signs not always accessible to the perceiver; and absolute truth was elusive, to be apprehended, but never fully understood, through rhetoric.[1] By 1699, some of these convictions had disappeared, while others, still held, were believed to need defending. The discourse of the community had changed.

For several reasons, seventeenth-century England provides particularly fertile ground for studying the alteration of the language of a political community under stress. First, the century is marked by the revolution— an incontrovertibly momentous period characterized by political, economic, and social violence.[2] Second, the period gave rise to a remarkable

1. Throughout this study, I follow Michel Foucault, *The Order of Things: An Archaeology of the Human Sciences,* in seeing a fundamental shift in Western thought occurring in the seventeenth century.

2. In current historiography the term *revolution* carries considerable significance, indicating the political orientation of the historian. For extended discussion of modern schools of thought, see Howard Tomlinson, "The Causes of War: A Historiographical

number of published works. Some twenty-two thousand items, acquired by contemporary bookseller George Thomason, are thoroughly cataloged and available in the British Library. Third, these published works are distinguished by their high quality and by the prominence of many of their authors, including John Milton, James Harrington, John Goodwin, and William Prynne. As well-crafted works, the tracts of the Thomason Collection lend themselves to systematic literary and rhetorical analysis.

Finally, these tracts emerged from a period in which writers were trained to be highly conscious of the power of language and its forms—the literary and rhetorical genres. As a result, we may find in the pamphlets of the English Revolution a means of defining the dynamic interaction of political events and the discourse that resulted from and shaped them—the relationship of form and ideology. Since the writer's ideology determined his perception of the audience and the kind of action he desired of it, that ideology also determined his choice of rhetorical strategy.[3]

Following Clifford Geertz's distinctions, I see during the revolution and afterward two fundamentally competing ideologies. One was essentially integrative, concerned with the form of society and government, and in this period was closely associated with supporters of the monarchy. The other ideology was distributive, concerned with the function of government, and became the dominant perspective of writers I broadly define as "radical"—those who to varying degrees opposed the formal, frequently organic vision of monarchy.[4] Monarchist writers increasingly shared a static view of the political community, a view in which each individual assented to a place and a role forever unchanging. This perception led them to integrative uses of rhetoric that persuaded their readers to identify with traditional forms and ideas. Radical writers, including Milton and Harrington, held a dynamic view of the community—a commitment to

Survey." I use the term not because of its political connotations but because of its implications for rhetoric. I believe the period is indeed revolutionary. Afterward, we see—and contemporaries themselves perceived—definite and irrevocable changes in public discourse. A revolution in political perception had taken place.

3. Because of the extremely low literacy rates for Englishwomen in this period and because of the language employed by the pamphleteers themselves, I am assuming the readers and writers of these tracts to be predominantly male.

4. *The Interpretation of Cultures,* 193–233. Briefly, integrative ideology unites a society while distributive ideology allocates resources. Neither has any specific associations with class or political orientation, although Geertz maintains that integrative ideology is easier to advocate rhetorically.

and a faith in change that required each individual to question himself and then to challenge and participate in public life. These writers adopted distributive uses of rhetoric, attempting to incorporate their transformed readers into the political process.

Writers of all political persuasions adapted their rhetoric by manipulating the genres of oratory. These genres—epideictic, forensic, and deliberative—resulted historically from the efforts of Greek and Roman orators to develop conventions for addressing various audiences in particular situations. By the seventeenth century, these conventions had become so well understood by educated readers and writers that they gave illocutionary force to written works, a force outside and in addition to the words or arguments themselves. The genres structured and therefore defined the possible relationships of writer and reader. The rhetoric thus reinforced and advanced the writer's ideology.[5]

In any time, the genres most closely associated with the dominant ideology carry the greatest illocutionary force—a normative force. Anything that can be expressed through those genres is part of acceptable public discourse. Anything outside may be readily rejected.[6] The task of the writer who would change society—certainly the goal of the seventeenth-century radicals—is therefore to manipulate the conventions of that society, the genres of its public discourse, so that they accommodate his arguments. When such a writer succeeds, his arguments and ideas transform the discourse and thus the actual structure of his society. When he fails, his discourse becomes marginal, his audience shrinks, and he persuades nobody outside his own group. To judge the achievement of that writer, then, we should look beyond both the texts he produces and the immediate reception of his ideas. We need to observe the degree to which his rhetoric enters into common use and becomes regarded as descriptive rather than argumentative. To have one's rhetoric accepted as reality is to change society at its most fundamental level.

On the pamphleteers of the English Revolution, Douglas Bush once remarked, "There probably never was a period in English history when the

---

5. See J. L. Austin, *How to Do Things With Words,* 116; the illocutionary speech act is one "producing consequences."

6. On the development of genres as conventionalized, institutionalized speech acts, see Tzvetan Todorov, *Les Genres du discours,* 47–54; Quentin Skinner, "Some Problems in the Analysis of Political Thought and Action," 294, and "Conventions and the Understanding of Speech Acts," 137.

heterogeneous battalion of minor political authors wrote so ably."[7] That they did so is beyond dispute, but how they did so is still largely an unexplored question. In this Introduction, I investigate the means by which seventeenth-century writers learned to write and, concomitantly, the ways in which they and the members of their potential audience learned to read. My aim is to establish both the heuristic contexts of the revolutionary pamphlets and the conventions that governed their reading. Further, I examine the role the oratorical genres, as understood by seventeenth-century educators and theorists, played in the composition and reception of written works.

The recent revival of interest in genre theory has firmly established the importance of genre to our understanding of particular texts. Essentially, theorists have concluded that genres—whether literary or oratorical—have a real existence at some level and that they exercise definite functions over reader, writer, and critic alike. Adena Rosmarin argues persuasively that the concept of genre is the "critic's heuristic tool" for understanding and interpreting any given work. The critic uses the idea of genre as long as it sheds light on a text and abandons or adapts it once its possibilities are exhausted. The genres are, then, models for interpretation, useful as pragmatic concepts but establishing neither descriptive nor prescriptive standards for literature.[8]

As Barbara Kiefer Lewalski points out, the structuralists have rediscovered genres as codes—"instruments of communication rather than classification." Moreover, these codes change over time and thus demand that the critic examine ideas and disciplines outside traditional literary history. The generic codes restrict the range of responses a reader may have to given texts and therefore restrict the range of meanings the texts may have at any given time. When the codes alter, the meanings of the text may alter as well. Jacques Derrida argues for this point when he explains that genres establish limits and norms and provide a means for the reader to identify the text.[9]

Treating the genres as codes allows them a powerful historical function. Through understanding the historical literary genres, the modern critic may gain insight into the contemporary meanings of the texts—and the

7. *English Literature in the Earlier Seventeenth Century, 1600–1660,* 271.

8. *The Power of Genre,* 25.

9. Lewalski, "Introduction: Issues and Approaches," 2; Derrida, "The Law of Genre," 56–57.

authors' intentions in writing them. Tzvetan Todorov indicates that the genres provide models for writers, bridges to their intended audiences. In addition, they establish expectations for those audiences: "Readers read as a function of the generic system, with which they are familiar through criticism, school, the distribution system for the book, or simple hearsay; it is not necessary that they be conscious of this system, however."[10] The genres give form to ideas. As a result, the genres themselves can communicate with the readers. A genre-conscious writer may then use the genres themselves—by which I mean the historical genres—as additional persuasive tools in constructing arguments or works of literature. As social, political, or cultural conditions change, the writer must adapt or change the genres to retain their persuasive power.

In seventeenth-century England the classical oratorical genres, applied by teachers to both written and spoken compositions, performed this powerful generative and persuasive function, and they did so chiefly because linguistic and rhetorical theories were undergoing profound changes during the period. Since rhetorical theory revived interest in genre, teachers and students were more likely to be profoundly aware then of the existence and employment of genre than in earlier periods. The flux in theory created—but only temporarily—a powerful combination of methods that joined political and religious convictions with consciousness of form to produce profoundly effective political rhetoric. Moreover, this special rhetoric was supremely adapted to the political and social conditions under which readers lived. Through the new rhetoric, writers gained the means to present strong political stands to their audiences.

Contexts: The Identity and Social Conditions of Seventeenth-Century Readers

To the seventeenth-century pamphleteer, the potential audience of his work must have seemed enormous. The early decades of the century saw growing numbers of people entering and remaining in some sort of school. The period also experienced an increase in inflation, which resulted in an increase in the numbers of men meeting the qualification for voting—a forty-shilling freehold. For the first time in living memory, the literate political community faced large additions and challenges to its ranks. As the historian Lawrence Stone comments, "It is surely more than a coincidence that the two great periods of English intellectual, cultural and politi-

10. "The Origin of Genres," 163.

cal activity [the seventeenth and nineteenth centuries] coincide with the two great waves of educational expansion."[11] These were the readers of the revolutionary arguments.

Literacy, defined by historians as the ability to sign one's name, increased significantly in the 1620s and 1630s. Since grammar schools taught writing later than reading, we may assume a larger group of readers than available statistics indicate. Judging from the surviving returns of the Protestation Oath of 1642, historians estimate average male literacy at the outbreak of the first civil war to have been around 30 percent, ranging from a low of 15–20 percent in the rural north and west to around 40 percent in and near London, and to a high of perhaps 60 percent in several large southern towns. From other sources, such as hearth-tax records, wills, marriage licenses, and other legal documents, we find that literacy was also associated with wealth, occupation, and gender. Gentlemen and clerics consistently ranked as the most literate, laborers and women the least. Among the "middle sort of people," yeomen, husbandmen, and tradesmen fell in the middle range of literacy, with yeomen at the head.[12]

During the 1620s and 1630s, the grammar school population increased, with the school generation of 1633 representing a prewar high in literacy. Both universities also grew. Cambridge enrollments reached a peak in the 1620s and Oxford in the 1630s, with Cambridge enrolling about four hundred students a year between 1610 and 1640.[13] The reading population swelled in the two decades before 1642, as the most highly literate groups also became most highly educated. More students than ever, therefore, received some formal instruction in reading and composition.

In the early seventeenth century, moreover, illiteracy did not mean exclusion from political discourse. In fact, the pamphleteers' labors drew nonreaders into public affairs. As the historian Thomas Laqueur comments, "The printed word formed the bond of political communication between disparate segments of the community." Reading itself became a public and often overtly political activity. Literate people often read to groups of nonreaders, and a printed proclamation itself frequently carried symbolic political significance. In January 1642, for example, the Trained

11. "Literacy and Education in England, 1640–1900," 137.

12. David Cressy makes this point in "Levels of Illiteracy in England, 1530–1730," 2; see also Richard T. Vann, "Literacy in Seventeenth-Century England: Some Hearth-Tax Evidence," 287; and David Cressy, *Literacy and the Social Order: Reading and Writing in Tudor and Stuart England*, 19–41.

13. Cressy, *Literacy and the Social Order,* 157–58, 164–72.

Bands of London carried copies of the Protestation Oath as they accompanied the Five Members, who were returning to Parliament after successfully evading Charles's attempt to arrest them.[14]

Above all, as Lawrence Stone shows, the growth of printing in the sixteenth century moved the whole of Europe "from an image-culture to a word-culture," especially in areas influenced by Protestantism. Properly, then, the "reading public" of the early seventeenth century included not only the educated and the literate but also anyone participating or interested in political activity.[15] The audience for political tracts grew faster than the rate of literacy. Religious and political conviction reinforced literacy, while interest in the written word encouraged political participation. In such an environment, readers or listeners were alert to the power of words and likely to be critical of what they read or heard.

Early seventeenth-century writers desperately needed such readers. Throughout the period, all written work was subject to strict censorship. Two recent studies argue that this fact is absolutely central to our understanding of the culture and discourse of the times. Christopher Hill believes that the relaxation of censorship in the 1640s and 1650s prompted an explosion of intellectual activity and encouraged participation in public life. Annabel M. Patterson sees a "hermeneutics of censorship," a conditioned proclivity to read between the lines, that developed during the period before the civil wars and continued regardless of actual laws. This habit of reading produced extremely critical minds, prepared to find significance even in silence.[16]

Shared by readers and public officials alike, the new, hypercritical practice produced tremendous respect for the power of the printed word. This respect—which occasionally became fear—persisted during the revolutionary period. Officially, there was never a completely free press. Freedom varied with the strength of the central government and the sympathies of local officials. In the three periods surveyed here—prewar, Common-

14. "The Cultural Origins of Popular Literacy in England, 1500–1850," 267, 257–65. The incident of the Trained Bands and the Protestation Oath is described by Edward Hyde, Earl of Clarendon, *The History of the Rebellion and Civil Wars in England Begun in the Year 1641*, 4:199.

15. "Literacy and Education in England," 77–79, 80–90, 100–102, 107–8, 111 (chart). Cf. Elizabeth L. Eisenstein, *The Printing Press as an Agent of Change: Communications and Cultural Transformations in Early-Modern Europe*, 43–159, 367–450.

16. Hill, *Some Intellectual Consequences of the English Revolution*; Patterson, *Censorship and Interpretation: The Conditions of Writing and Reading in Early-Modern England*, 44–119.

wealth, and Cromwellian—the licensing laws reflect a continuous battle between central authority and those who chose to defy it.

Until 1641, strict licensing was imposed on the press by the sovereign for two principal reasons. First, the existence of the Church of England made published religious dissent a potential challenge to the authority of the state. Second, the incorporation of the Stationers' Company as a monopoly in 1557 had made unlicensed printing a violation of trade law. Under the terms of the monopoly grant, the court and its officers were to approve all manuscripts before they were printed. The Stationers were held responsible for all printed matter. During periods of slackening official attention, the wardens of the company functioned as licensers and censors. Despite these provisions, unlicensed printing flourished and prompted two decrees from the court of Star Chamber: one in 1586, another in 1637.[17]

The Elizabethan decree proved counterproductive. It was enforced selectively, often for purely political ends, with the predictable result that readers expected political content in censored works. Robert Cecil used the decree with great success against the followers of the earl of Essex in 1599, suppressing all hidden avenues of support including satires, unauthorized plays and English histories, and madrigals. Throughout the reign of James I, printing was monitored so closely that early newspapers, often printed abroad and translated in London, rarely mentioned English news, since the censors found political implications everywhere.[18]

Since the bishops dominated the panels of censors, religious dissenters ran grave risks in publishing their tracts, as John Bastwick, Henry Burton, and William Prynne were to discover in 1637. These men became the most conspicuous victims of Archbishop Laud's vigorous exercise of his power as licenser in Charles's attempt to silence an increasingly hostile opposition. Charles and Laud held the laxities of the 1586 decree responsible for the continuous spread of "contentious" books. Thus, they proposed their own set of regulations. On July 11, 1637, five days after the public pillory-

17. Sir Walter Wilson Greg, *Some Aspects and Problems of London Publishing between 1550 and 1650*, 3–10, 43–51; William M. Clyde, *The Struggle for the Freedom of the Press from Caxton to Cromwell*, 1–47.

18. Edward Arber, *A Transcript of the Registers of the Company of Stationers of London, 1554–1640 A.D.*, 2:807–12; see also *Calendar of State Papers, Domestic Series, of the Reigns of Edward VI, Mary I, Elizabeth and James I*, vol. 190, article 48; Lillian M. Ruff and D. Arnold Wilson, "The Madrigal, the Lute Song, and Elizabethan Politics"; and Joseph Frank, *The Beginnings of the English Newspaper, 1620–1660*, 1–18.

ing of Prynne and his companions, the Star Chamber issued a severe decree to control the entire book trade in England.[19]

The new decree forbade the printing of English books abroad and prohibited foreigners, unless members of the Stationers' Company, from importing books. Printed matter could be imported into London alone. With a few exceptions, the bishops were to license all printed matter, including "all books and pamphlets and every title, epistle, preface, proem, preamble, introduction, table and dedication thereunto annexed." Further precautions were ordered to halt anonymous writing and printing. Owners of presses were required to give three-hundred-pound sureties not to print unlicensed materials. To the existing punishments of fines and imprisonments, the court added pillorying and whipping for "unallowed" printers.[20]

In this climate, writing, printing, and reading became political acts. Licensing laws and regulations gave heavy significance to every mildly political work, especially if that work was unlicensed and unsigned. Government censorship consequently failed to remove politics from publishing. As the Star Chamber created more martyrs, the reading public became more politically aware and more sensitive to written debate. By the outbreak of the first civil war, the pamphlet had established itself as a powerful vehicle for political action.

For pamphleteers and their audiences, the most crucial event of the revolution occurred long before the king fled Westminster. On July 5, 1641, the court of Star Chamber was abolished. Between then and January 29, 1642, when the Long Parliament issued the "Signature Order," the English press operated virtually free of restriction. With no means to enforce regulations, the Stationers' Company lost control over the printing craft. The ranks of printers swelled, while production of pamphlets exploded. In 1640, only twenty-two were printed; in 1642, the number increased to 1,966. To understand exactly how free the press was, we need only remember that the Signature Order commanded that nothing be printed without the author's consent. The Stationers' Company emerged as the principal champion of licensing for solid economic reasons: members' stock was being pirated, their trade ruined. Self-styled "wandering

19. *Calendar of State Papers, Domestic Series, of the Reign of Charles I, 1625–1649*, vol. 376, art. 15.

20. A summary of the 1637 Star Chamber decree appears in Clyde, *Struggle for the Freedom*, 295–97; quotations from arts. 2 and 20.

stationers" sold pamphlets in the streets, while journeymen agitated for their own shops. Between 1642 and 1649, the Long Parliament and later the army made seven attempts to regain control over the printing trade, each attempt but the last falling far short of its goal.[21]

Of the seven orders, three were major efforts at control. The first—the Licensing Order of 1643, against which Milton wrote the *Areopagitica*—attempted to suppress royalist propaganda and journalistic accounts of parliamentary activities, including "separates," published speeches alleged to have been delivered in Parliament. In essence, the order repeated Charles's regulations of 1637, requiring licensing and registration with the Stationers' Company, search and seizure of offending materials, and arrest and imprisonment of offending persons. The Long Parliament justified its action as a means of controlling rumors in wartime.

The war itself contributed greatly to the failure of the order. Many areas were war zones. The royalist "travelling press" defied both Parliament and the Stationers' Company, setting up in safe areas and moving as fortunes changed. In London, where the order naturally had the most strength, searchers often met with open physical resistance as they tried to seize papers, type, and presses. The order continued in effect for four years with declining success until superseded by the Order of September 30, 1647.

The new order reflected Parliament's campaign to suppress the news-books critical of its activities and produced by both royalists and Independents. Ten days before passage of the order, a bill transferred powers of enforcement to the Committee of the Militia of London. With the new enforcers commissioned, the order extended additional penalties to booksellers, stationers, and peddlers. This measure proved as ineffectual as its predecessor, even after a "flying squad" of twenty was appointed to aid in the search for clandestine printing.

As a result of these failures, there still existed few functioning controls on printing when Charles I was tried and executed in January 1649. Many inflammatory items slipped past the censors, including—incredibly—*Eikon Basilike*.[22] Printers and searchers continued their struggles until the spring, when Sir Thomas Fairfax, captain-general of the army, issued a warrant to the Militia of London to suppress the royalist and Presbyterian

21. Ernest Sirluck, Introduction to *The Complete Prose Works of John Milton*, 2:158–64. The figures come from Christopher Hill, *Milton and the English Revolution*, 65.

22. For examples, see David W. Petegorsky, *Left-Wing Democracy in the English Civil War: A Study of the Social Philosophy of Gerrard Winstanley*, 63–71.

press. The warrant was accompanied by a Treason Act that made it a capital crime to criticize the government.

On September 20, 1649, these activities were bolstered by a severe new Licensing Order. It mandated that all previous laws governing printing be put into execution; raised the fines levied on authors, printers, and sellers of proscribed books; and canceled all previous licenses, commanding that all books and pamphlets be licensed anew. It also set additional punishments for treasonable books and pamphlets, adding fines for buyers who concealed illegal books and arrest for sellers.[23] This order succeeded. Royalist printing was suppressed by the summer of 1650.

As the sequence of orders suggests, individuals and groups entered into the activities surrounding written political protest as never before. The process became at least as popular among radical sects as among the more mainstream members of the community. The outstanding, if temporary, success of the Levellers owed at least as much to their ability to print and circulate their ideas as to their flair for public demonstrations. John Lilburne's famed defiance of the House of Lords and direction of a protest rally from his cell in the Tower of London gained power from the almost simultaneous release of his pamphlets, often illustrated with his portrait, with prison bars drawn over it.[24]

Public acts corresponded to and depended upon their appearance in print. The tracts gave them permanence, an intellectual context, and a larger meaning—greater validity than those gestures alone would have possessed. Similarly, the tracts themselves took on the significance of political demonstrations. They not only documented and illustrated events— they *were* events.

In the 1650s, the fortunes of pamphleteering varied with the changes in the central government. Because of the success of the Licensing Order of 1649, the Commonwealth and Cromwellian periods saw few legislative efforts to control printing. Only two were truly significant—the Printing Act of January 7, 1653, and Cromwell's Orders of August 28, 1655. Essentially a revival of the Order of 1649, the 1653 Printing Act represented an effort to enforce the printing laws more systematically. It gave

23. "An Act against Unlicensed and Scandalous Books and Pamphlets, and for better regulating of Printing" [20 September 1649], in *Acts and Ordinances of the Interregnum, 1642–1660,* 2: 245. The complete text appears on 245–54.

24. C. V. Wedgwood, *The King's War, 1641–1647,* vol. 2 of *The Great Rebellion,* 580–99; see also Pauline Gregg, *Free-born John: A Biography of John Lilburne,* 124–25, 138–46.

the Council of State the authority to oversee printing and the power to regulate the trade. In a break from past practice, the act made the Stationers' Company a department of the government, ordered it to assist in the enforcement of the law, and empowered it to search all imported printed matter. Because of this division of authority and the overall weakness of the government, the act failed in six months.

A believer in freedom of religious debate, Oliver Cromwell issued his orders only after Penruddock's Rising, the royalist rebellion that precipitated the rule of the major-generals. In keeping with the thoroughness of the military administration, the orders laid out with great precision the scope and means of enforcing the new regulations. Cromwell ordered that the Council of State secure the names of all those involved in illegal printing, suppress all unlicensed printers and newsbooks, and send all offenders to Bridewell. So successful were these orders that between 1656 and 1658 even most unregistered books identified their author and printer.[25]

Effective regulation lasted as long as Oliver. Under Richard Cromwell and during the anarchy, the mechanisms of enforcement again collapsed. Throughout the 1650s, controls on the press depended largely on local and national officials' willingness and ability to enforce the laws. With periodic suspension or interruption of one or the other, authors continued to circulate their works with relative ease. Especially in the localities, popular dissent and criticism flourished—provided that writers agreed with local sentiments.

The sequence of acts and orders illustrates the constant battle between authority and pamphleteers. Failures though the laws were, they prove that the printed word was taken very seriously indeed. All writers and readers knew this and therefore knew the limits of political discourse. The entirety of an individual tract—not just the words—needed to carry the burden of argumentation to evade censorship. As a result, the mere appearance of a tract guaranteed that it would be read politically, and read with close attention. As Patterson shows, the circumstances of censorship politicized form as well as content. Particular genres began to carry partisan significance.[26] Significantly, the audience was unusually well prepared for this transformation in public discourse. Midcentury readers had been prepared by teaching methods that emphasized form as a means of under-

25. David Underdown, *Royalist Conspiracy in England, 1649–1660*, 127–58.
26. On the politicization of literary genres, see Patterson's discussions of lyric, romance, and epistle in *Censorship and Interpretation*, 120–58, 159–202, 203–32.

standing argument. Any attempt to control communications to this audience was destined to fail.

Conventions: The Theory and Practice of Rhetoric in the Seventeenth-Century Classroom

The rhetoricians and teachers of the first half of the seventeenth century based their ideas on their understanding of the theory and practice of classical oratory. They possessed and used in the classroom both ancient treatises on rhetoric and actual surviving speeches. From these texts came the models for student speeches and compositions and hence the students' notion of the formal speech and writing of public men. Through their teachers' instruction, students came to regard genre not only as an aid to invention but also as a heuristic device to help them understand authorial intention. Genre was thus regarded as a bridge of convention uniting writer and audience. From the treatises, Renaissance theoreticians learned that ancient conceptions of genres of oratory were fluid and practical, and that genres could be, and often were, mixed.

As described by ancient writers, the oratorical genres arose out of practical needs. As a result, classical explanations of those genres—whether in Plato, Aristotle, Cicero, Quintilian, or the *Rhetorica ad Herennium*—depend more on external circumstances than on internal cohesion, or as Thomas O. Sloane indicates, probability rather than conviction.[27] Analyses of classical speeches include the audience and the immediate political context, as well as, in some cases, the conditions under which they were published. The end of any speech was persuasion—to move an audience—by means of the conventions of the community. As the *Rhetorica ad Herennium* explains, "The task of the public speaker is to discuss capably those matters which law and custom have fixed for the uses of citizenship, and to secure as far as possible the agreement of his hearers" (1.2.2).[28] The nature of the audience determines the nature of the speech.

Further, as Cicero explains in *Partitiones oratoriae*, the orator's success depends on the audience: "The prudent and cautious speaker is controlled by the reception given by his audience—what it rejects has to be modified" (4.15). To his projected speech, the orator may adapt any style or organization, any digression or proof, according to his interpretation of the circum-

27. *Donne, Milton, and the End of Humanist Rhetoric,* 119–20.

28. Except as noted, I have used the Loeb Classical Editions of Greek and Roman texts and traditional divisions.

stances under which he speaks. The classical oration then becomes a dynamic association between speaker and audience.[29] Moreover, the process of invention becomes the process of discovering the nature of that association.

As the ancient rhetoricians understood them, the genres were tools of the process of invention. They were points of departure rather than ends. As the orator discovered his relationship with his audience, he began to structure his discourse accordingly, finding arrangement and style suitable to the situation. Conversely, as he gave form to his speech, he further comprehended his audience and his task. In the *"Art" of Rhetoric*, Aristotle defines three kinds of hearers: those who judge a recommended future action; those who judge a past action; and those who listen to be entertained and evaluate a speaker's performance and thereby judge a present action. To each of these audiences corresponds a genre: deliberative, forensic, or epideictic (1.3.1–6).[30]

As described in both Greek and Roman texts, the three genres are broken into six species: deliberative into hortatory and dissuasive oratory; forensic into accusatory and defensive; epideictic into laudatory and vituperative. While in theory the species have their own distinguishing features, in practice they overlap and may be used separately or jointly. The genres, in fact, share several topics and methods of proof. These common grounds permit the mixing of genres. Any one can be subordinated to and incorporated into another. Ancient authors frequently mixed genres when they described speeches, sometimes using the same oration to provide examples of different genres. As there is no pure situation, so there is no pure genre. Situation and genres act reflexively to give form to experience.[31]

The process of discovery continues as the orator arranges his material. The ancient rhetoricians claimed that each genre had its proper form, but upon examination we see rather that it is the idea of the speech that has a specific form, with four parts common to all the genres—the introduction or exordium, the narration, the proofs, and the conclusion or peroration.[32]

29. See also Cicero, *Brutus*, 49.185, and *Orator*, 21.69.

30. Cf. Cicero, *De Oratore*, 1.31.141, and *Partitiones oratoriae*, 4.11; *Rhetorica ad Alexandrum*, 1427b12–15; Quintilian, *Institutio oratoria*, 3.4.9.

31. On mixed genres, see Aristotle, *"Art" of Rhetoric* (abbreviated hereafter as *Rhetoric*), 1.3.3, 2.18.2–5; Quintilian, *Institutio*, 3.4.9; *Rhetorica ad Alexandrum*, 1421b18–1427b31, 1427b35–1428a11.

32. Examinations of arrangement can be found in Aristotle, *Rhetoric*, 3.13.3; *Rhetorica ad Alexandrum*, 1436a28–40; *Rhetorica ad Herennium*, 1.2.2–3, 5; Cicero, *De Inventione*, 1.14.19, and *Partitiones*, 8.27; and Quintilian, *Institutio*, 4.1–6.1.

It is the special adaptation of each part to suit the audience that creates the distinct appearance of the genre.

The exordium is the part most directly connected to the circumstances under which the speech is given. Aristotle suggests that the epideictic exordium resembles the openings used in flute playing—it presents the main theme and the keynote. The forensic exordium begins like a dramatic prologue or epic exordium, attempting to predispose the audience to the speaker's point of view. The deliberative exordium borrows from the forensic but eliminates the explanation of the situation, assuming the hearers already know it.[33]

The narration is especially important to the forensic oration. An advocate must state the facts of the case, discuss the characters of the contending parties, and make his accusations. The *Rhetorica ad Alexandrum,* however, states that the narration belongs to all public cases, whether forensic or deliberative. Cicero explains that narration is frequently not needed in deliberative speaking, especially when the orator wants to arouse emotions. Epideictic narrations can, as Aristotle says, be "disjointed," covering anything from a person's own deeds to his genealogy and the actions of remote ancestors.[34]

Each genre adapts proofs according to its need for facts. Because it depends upon impressions more than facts, the epideictic oration has the simplest proofs. The orator confirms merely by amplifying his subject. The deliberative oration employs examples, logical proofs, and evidence, since the orator must show the consequences of the position he is urging. The forensic oration requires the most detailed proofs and relies most heavily on the enthymeme—the syllogism in which the premises are generally, rather than absolutely, true.[35]

Ancient writers generally do not distinguish distinctive forms for the

33. See for example Cicero, *De Inventione,* 1.14.20–18.26; Quintilian, *Institutio,* 4.1.40–75; and Aristotle, *Rhetoric,* 3.14.1–12.

34. Definitions of narrations appear in *Rhetorica ad Alexandrum,* 1438a40–1438b29; Cicero, *Partitiones,* 9.31, and *De Inventione,* 1.19.27; *Rhetorica ad Herennium,* 1.8.12–13; and Quintilian, *Institutio,* 4.2.1–24. For instructions about when to omit the narration, see Cicero, *Partitiones,* 4.12. Aristotle's remarks on the narration in epideictic speaking occur in *Rhetoric,* 3.16.1.

35. Cicero, *De Inventione,* 1.24.34; *Rhetorica ad Alexandrum,* 1445a30–1445b23; Aristotle, *Rhetoric,* 3.17.1–17; see also Quintilian, *Institutio,* 5 (contains a detailed discussion of legal proofs and bases); *Rhetorica ad Herennium,* 2.20.31–29.46 (for faults in proofs); Cicero, *De Inventione,* 1.29.44–42.77, and *Partitiones,* 9.33–43.

peroration. They agree that no matter what the genre, the peroration includes summation of the arguments, an attempt to move the emotions of the audience, and an effort to make the subject seem attractive. The four major parts of the oration should blend so that they lead logically and emotionally to the conclusion. Cicero explains simply that narration and proof procure belief while exordium and peroration appeal to feeling, regardless of the genre of the oration.[36]

Style is the final part of rhetoric that contributes to the overall definition of the genre. More than any other ancient author, Cicero focuses on the three styles of discourse—the *genera dicendi*—grand, plain, and middle. As his distinct contribution, Cicero associates the *genera dicendi* with the *genera oratoriae* and gives each particular political significance. The grand style belongs to deliberative oratory and as such is the one he most closely identifies with himself. It is the style of the public man, upon whose oratorical skill a free state must depend. As A. E. Douglas shows, Cicero's greatest treatise in defense of the grand style—the *Brutus*—is also a plea for Brutus to retain his republican ideals.[37] Cicero associates the middle style with epideictic oratory, regarding it as a style for sophists, while the plain style is the language of the courts and forensic oratory. He sees the plain style as private language—the discourse of his own political opponents.

In classical theory, then, the genres of oratory give form to the dynamic relationship of speaker and audience. Their chief function is to structure invention, to shape the process of discovery. The practice of mixing genres assures that any experience can be structured and therefore expressed. Politically, classical rhetoric shows orator and listener alike the range of relationships possible within the existing governmental and societal structures. Classical rhetoric works when speaker and listener share basic assumptions about the principles and functions of their government and society. Criticism of that rhetoric thus becomes a serious matter. Cicero himself understood the real issue at stake when in the *Brutus* he identified his enemies' attack on deliberative oratory as an attack on the republican government it supported: "It is a source of deep pain that the state [under

36. Aristotle's discussion of the peroration appears in *Rhetoric*, 3.18.19. For Cicero's distinction between belief and feeling in the oration, see *Partitiones*, 8.27. Cf. Quintilian, *Institutio*, 6.1; *Rhetorica ad Herennium*, 2.30.47–31.50; Cicero, *De Inventione*, 1.52.98, and *Partitiones*, 15.52.

37. Introduction to *Brutus*, xii–xx. On style, see Aristotle, *Rhetoric*, 3.2–8.1; Cicero, *De Oratore*, 3.4.211, and *Orator*, 5.30, 9.37–13.40. Cf. *Rhetorica ad Alexandrum*, 1434a35–1436a14; *Rhetorica ad Herennium*, 4; Quintilian, *Institutio*, 8.

the dictatorship of Caesar] feels no need of those weapons of counsel, of insight, and of authority, which I had learned to handle and to rely upon,—weapons which are the peculiar and proper resource of a leader in the commonwealth and of a civilized and law-abiding state" (2.7). The uncivilized and lawless state, he implies, has no need of rhetoric. To Cicero, rhetoric was an integral part of the government he valued. An attack on that government had to come as a challenge to its public discourse.

Rhetoric, skepticism, and political loyalty were the legacy the ancient world left to the sixteenth-century northern humanists. As Sloane observes, "In that humanism, there is little impulse to reform or change things, but much to increase diversity and human possibility within preexistent boundaries."[38] The political status quo is the assumption out of which all humanist rhetoric proceeds. English Ciceronian rhetoric—like its classical predecessor—describes a circular process by which all invention begins and ends with the audience and the established social structure.

Rhetoric based on these principles characterizes what Wilbur Samuel Howell describes as the "scholastic" period in English rhetorical theory.[39] This period begins with Desiderius Erasmus and his associates and ends with Sir Thomas Wilson's *The Arte of Rhetorike* (1553) and Richard Rainolde's *A Booke called the Foundacion of Rhetorike* (1563). Writers belonging to this period accept Cicero's division of rhetoric into the five parts of invention, arrangement, style, memory, and delivery. As Sloane shows, theoreticians of this period emphasize forensic rhetoric—the genre that best typifies the principle of infinite variation within the boundaries of an existing system, the legal system.

By the end of the century, humanist rhetoric faced a major challenge from the followers of the French logician and rhetorician Peter Ramus (Pierre de la Ramée). Howell dates the height of Ramism from 1574 to 1600. Ramus's method removed invention, arrangement, and memory from the province of rhetoric and assigned them to logic. Rhetoric became simply a matter of style and delivery. For the circular relationship of audience and invention, the Ramists substitute a linear one of idea and form. As Sloane rightly observes, Ramist rhetoric is properly not rhetoric at all. It is a method for unfolding "truth" to the audience—a method that is intuitive rather than persuasive.[40]

---

38. *End of Humanist Rhetoric*, 285–86.
39. *Logic and Rhetoric in England, 1500–1700*, 6–11.
40. *End of Humanist Rhetoric*, 137–44. Recent scholarship has effectively challenged

The school generation that grew up to be the revolutionary pamphleteers faced a third approach to discourse, one that I believe should be labeled "Neo-Ramist."[41] Essentially Ciceronian-influenced Ramism, this rhetoric began at the turn of the century and reached a peak in the 1620s and 1630s. Its innovation was to replace the Ramist, linear association of idea to form with a triangular one that reintroduced the audience, by way of the oratorical genres, into the process of composing. While the theory of the Neo-Ramists was not highly innovative, it arose out of a very real need to address problems inherent in both scholastic and Ramist rhetoric. Further, it became abundantly practical, creating a discourse the humanists did not envision, eminently suitable for its times.

The scholastic rhetorics of the sixteenth century emphasized the process of invention, frequently seeing it perform an explicitly social function. As Wilson comments in the preface to the second edition of *The Arte of Rhetorike* (1560), eloquence was given by God, lost by man, and restored by God to repair the effects of the Fall by enabling orators—defined as statesmen and preachers—to persuade people to accept order and social responsibility. Rainolde describes oratory as a service to the commonwealth, attributing the greatness of Rome to the eloquence of the Caesars (a statement that would have shocked Cicero).[42]

Like their ancient models, the scholastics recognized the oratorical genres and perceived them as arising out of the process of invention and the orator's understanding of his situation. For readers and writers alike, the genres are the conventions of discourse. Neither Wilson, Rainolde, nor the early sixteenth-century rhetorician Leonard Cox ever defines "genre" or

---

earlier interpretations of the impact of Ramism, although all maintain that, for Ramists, "rhetoric" meant "style." See Kees Meerhoff, "Pédagogie et rhétorique ramistes: le cas Fouquelin," and *Rhétorique et poétique an XVIe siècle: Du Bellay, Ramus el les autres;* James J. Murphy, Introduction to *Peter Ramus, Arguments in Rhetoric Against Quintilian: Text and Translation in Peter Ramus's Rhetoricae Distinctiones in Quintilianum;* Nelly Bruyère-Robinet, *Méthode et dialectique dans l'oeuvre de la Ramée: Renaissance et age classique;* and Marc Fumaroli, *L'Age de l'éloquence: Rhétorique et 'res literaria' de la Renaissance au seuil de l'époque classique.*

41. Howell's term is "Neo-Ciceronian," since the authors accept the five-part division of rhetoric, but in practice the theory is essentially Ciceronian method grafted onto a Ramist foundation: Ciceronian-influenced Ramism.

42. Wilson, *Arte of Rhetorike,* 6 (sig. Av) and 9–12 (sigs. A3–A4v); Rainolde, *Foundacion of Rhetorike,* sigs. Av–A2. The abbreviation *sig.* indicates "signature number" in both the notes and the text; unless otherwise noted, all other parenthetical documentation in the text is to page numbers.

states that genres may be mixed. Throughout their works, however, they describe the three genres and see more than one at work in each of the speeches they present as examples. As the genres are bridges to the audience, so mixed genres become tools for adapting discourse to a variety of audiences. Wilson illustrates his discussion of the deliberative genre by printing in full Erasmus's encouragement of marriage. In many places, the work may be read as an encomium of the institution, especially when Erasmus amplifies by including such subjects as "Mariage among trees," "Mariage among precious stones," and "Mariage betwene the firmament and the earth." In *The Arte or Crafte of Rhethoryke* (circa 1532), in fact, Cox uses the speech as an example of epideictic oratory.[43]

In general, the scholastics paid little attention to the relationship of genre and arrangement. Only Cox imitates the classical theorists by describing how the genres adapt each of the parts of the oration. Instead, they evaluate arrangement as part of the process of judgment. Wilson says that the decorum produced by judgment is essential to the rhetorician, since the speaker must insure that his words and behavior suit his audience and occasion. One must exercise judgment at every point in the creation of a speech. Form and structure are relatively unimportant to these theoreticians. Both are subordinate to invention and are regarded as rhetorical in nature, to be adjusted to circumstances and audience; they have no independent existence. The crucial question these rhetoricians ask is not "Does my material fit the genre?" but "Does my selection of genres move my audience and advance my position?"[44]

From Cox to Wilson, the scholastic rhetoricians reveal declining interest in form and genre. Increasingly, they shift their attention to style, a subject that readily illustrated the process of invention, clearly adapted to the dynamic relationship of audience and writer, and carried the endorsement of Erasmus, whose treatise on style, *De duplici copia verborum ac rerum commentarii duo* (1512), furnished a generation of English schoolmasters with advice on teaching composition. The most prominent scholastic stylebook, Richard Sherry's *A Treatise of Schemes & Tropes* (1550), ignores the classical correspondence of *genera oratoriae* and *general dicendi*. Sherry draws examples from forensic speeches to illustrate each style.

43. Wilson, *Arte of Rhetorike,* 43–80 (sigs. D4–I2v). For Cox's reference to Erasmus's praise of marriage, see *Arte or Crafte,* 66 (sig. C8).

44. Cox, *Arte or Crafte,* 66–71 (deliberative oratory), 71–87 (forensic oratory); Wilson, *Arte of Rhetorike,* 21–22 (sigs. B–Bv).

Yet elements of the old associations occur in Sherry's assignments. As examples of the grand style, he cites Cicero's Verrine orations, Catilinaria, and speeches for Milo and against Piso. All are primarily forensic speeches, but all are noted for their strong political content. Some of these orations were in fact delivered before the Roman Senate. There was, therefore, a deliberative character to these works that is absent in the speech for Roscius, for example. Similarly, Sherry identifies as a representative of the middle style Cicero's deliberative speech for the Manilian law. The reason for the identification becomes clear when we recognize that the speech contains an extensive praise of Pompey that Renaissance rhetoricians frequently cite as an example of epideictic oratory. The middle style, of course, corresponds to that genre. Sherry, then, relies on the situation to provide a guide for the selection of style. Rather than use genre as the starting point for selecting style, Sherry sees the kinds of style as responses—the answer to the question of what kind of effect the writer wants to produce. Style, to Sherry, is part of the process of discovery rather than an attribute of form.

The emphasis on discovery and variation reveals a fundamental problem with the humanist rhetoricians. Their approach leaves no room for stepping outside a political or religious system to question or examine fundamental principles. As a result, it preempts certain kinds of political and religious controversy since it cannot reach an audience that listens with a different set of assumptions. By its very nature, political rhetoric cannot be a means of discovering or investigating truth. It presumes that it possesses the truth, as does religion. The humanists themselves, for example, never used their rhetoric to question the premises of their society. Their principles worked as long as they accepted some principles dogmatically. That dogma defined the possible range of relationships with the audience so that, ultimately, those definitions restricted the range of discourse. When the dogma itself becomes the subject to be argued, Ciceronian rhetoric fails.

By assigning invention and arrangement to the province of logic, Ramist theory abandoned concern for genre. Form was an attribute of truth, just as truth was inherent in form. Hence, form could be apprehended logically and was independent of audience. For the circular process of discovery, the Ramists substituted the linear process that began with ideas and mobilized rhetoric—that is to say style—to serve them. The audience disappears from the process of invention. It needs no special treatment to see truth, once that truth is revealed. In the words of the Ramist rhetorician

Dudley Fenner, rhetoric is mere "garnishing." As a result, Ramist rhetorics are, like Sherry's early work, treatises of schemes and tropes—classified lists of rhetorical figures. As the Ramists saw it, when rhetoric is used poorly, as by "sophists" and "papists," it obscures the truth. When it is used well, it enhances the truth. In either case, however, truth was absolute and revealed itself through form.[45]

While effective in religious controversy, the Ramist method could not adapt itself fully to political debate. To its adherents, a particular religion is truth, beyond the realm of debate. Thus, a speaker or writer may unfold that truth by following Ramist method—exposition by dichotomy. But by definition, political questions concern audiences and some kind of communal discussion. While political ideology presumes itself to be true, it also assumes some need to persuade. The Neo-Ramists met the problem by reviving the classical means for constructing bridges to audiences—the oratorical genres. In fact, unlike their sixteenth-century counterparts, the Neo-Ramists focused extensively on genres, including mixed genres. To these theoreticians the genres, after all, were forms. By adding attention to genre to a Ramist foundation, the seventeenth-century rhetoricians developed a means of accommodating audiences to form.

Four textbooks brought these ideas to the early seventeenth-century classroom. These were Thomas Vicars's *Cheiragogia sive manductio ad artem rhetoricam* (1619), Thomas Farnaby's *Index rhetoricus* (1625), Charles Butler's *Oratoriae libri duo* (1629), and John Clarke's *Formulae oratoriae* (1629). We can judge their popularity from their use. In *A Consolation for Our Grammar Schools,* John Brinsley recommends Farnaby's and Vicars's books as guides for the study of rhetoric. In *A New Discovery of the Old Art of Teaching Schoole,* Charles Hoole lists the works of Butler and Farnaby as handbooks for rhetoric and those of Farnaby and Clark for theme writing. Donald Lemen Clark shows that in Milton's time the masters at St. Paul's School may have used Butler's book and those of Farnaby and Vicars. In fact, Farnaby was a friend of the younger Alexander Gil, while the elder Gil, headmaster, quoted him in the first edition of *Logonomia Anglica.*[46]

45. *The Artes of Logicke and Rhethorike,* sig. Dv. Other popular Ramist books included Henry Peacham, *The Garden of Eloquence* (1577); Abraham Fraunce, *The Arcadian Rhetorike* (1588); and Charles Butler, *Rhetoricae libri duo* (1598). Butler's work was extremely popular, mentioned by John Brinsley in *Ludus Literarius* (1612), sig. Dd2v, and *A Consolation for Our Grammar Schools* (1622), sigs. L3–L3v; and by Charles Hoole, *A New Discovery of the Old Art of Teaching Schoole,* 174–75.

46. Brinsley, *Ludus,* sig. Dd2v, and *Consolation,* sigs. I4–K2, L3–L3v; Hoole, *New*

These rhetoricians of the 1620s wrote with an altered perception of invention and the genres of oratory. As they saw it, genre exists outside the process of invention. Before invention can begin, the orator must identify the form of his situation. The genre gives a general definition of the audience. Invention makes that definition specific. To the classical orator, experience can have structure; to the Neo-Ramist, experience needs structure and in fact does not exist without it. Building on this foundation, and true to their Ramist roots, the seventeenth-century rhetoricians tried to identify many kinds and groups of situations for which a writer could use similar methods of argument and arrangement.

The need to find a form for every situation led the Neo-Ramists to devote extensive attention not only to genre but to the conceptual possibility of mixed genres. Mixing the genres enabled orators to adapt any situation to a generic framework. Therefore, the textbooks take pains to define genres, their attendant subgenres, and formulas. Vicars carefully divides the genres, emphasizing the wide range of situations to which they correspond. He explains that the epideictic genre includes praises and vituperations as well as narrations or descriptions of countries, mountains, rivers, buildings, parades, banquets, and journeys. The deliberative genre entails persuasion and dissuasion, as well as exhortations, dehortations, petitions, consolations, commendations, deliberations, and all other functions by which something is urged or opposed. In the judicial or forensic genre, the speaker is concerned with accusations and defenses, followed by expostulations, purgations, complaints, deprecations, and invectives.[47]

Butler classifies his genres and their variations by situation.[48] For example, epideictic oratory becomes all oratory that praises. A speech of praise delivered to a public, popular gathering is an Encomion, while one delivered to a huge, public, and solemn assembly is a Panegyric. If a speech of vituperation is more than usually violent, it is an Invective. If that speech also attacks a particular leader, it is a Philippic. To Butler, then, each situation may be defined according to a particular form. Understanding that form precedes all invention, which becomes a process of examining forms and formulas and arranging them appropriately.

To the Neo-Ramists, composing means arranging forms. As Hoole

---

Discovery, 174–75, 208–11; Clark, *John Milton at St. Paul's School: A Study of Ancient Rhetoric in English Renaissance Education,* 147–52; Gil the elder, *Logonomia Anglica,* 1:158–59, 216–17, n. 37

47. Vicars, *Cheiragogia,* sigs. B2–B2v (definitions).

48. Butler, *Oratoriae,* sigs. H4–H4v; Clarke, *Formulae,* sigs. B3–B4.

notes, students should "learne how to prosecute the severall parts of a theme more at large, by intermixing some of those Formulae Oratoriae, which Mr. Clarke and Mr. Farnaby have collected, which are proper to every part [of an oration]." Invention means proceeding from the forms. Clarke's *Formulae* corresponds to Butler's grouping of subgenres according to situation and shows students how each part of oratory may be adapted to a particular genre. As Clarke defines them, all formulas are to be used for narration and they come together for declamations, in which we apply formulas of entreating, insinuating, and restraining. All orations begin with comprehension of the circumstances of time, place, and persons.[49]

Farnaby lists similar "species" and yet removes some of them from any associations with a particular genre. He identifies them as separate forms, giving as examples "old" and "new" panegyrics, epithalamiums, birthday speeches, funeral orations, and expressions of thanks. Also, there are categories of companionable, valedictory, and travel compositions, as well as compositions of warning, swaying, encouraging, consoling, consulting, petitioning, and others, which appear more frequently in poetry and letters than in orations. As Farnaby understands composing, each oration must begin with a definition of purpose and form. Without form, no invention is possible.

Adapting Ciceronian definitions to the Ramist method of dichotomy, Farnaby reduces invention to a tool of persuasion, not a means of discovery in itself. The duty of rhetoric is to delight, teach, and move. Its material is whatever can persuade, and its topics are either simple or complex questions. Further, there are three genres for either hypothetical or definite questions: epideictic, which concerns praise or blame; deliberative, which involves debate on a future provision; and judicial, which defends or attacks a past act. There are two general means of persuading—by nature and by art. Invention and arrangement are aspects of persuasion by art.

Invention, for these rhetoricians, is the process of thinking out arguments that are appropriate for persuasion. To invent, an orator must consider the audience and its experiences. Farnaby recommends that orators consider the forms of government under which their audiences live, since each form has its own topics. In a republic, the orator should reflect on liberty; in a democracy, the teaching of laws; in an aristocracy, riches; and in a monarchy, the care of the prince.[50] Such an orator must decide on

49. Hoole, *New Discovery,* 210; Clarke, *Formulae,* sigs. A10v–A11.
50. Farnaby, *Index,* sigs. A8, A5–A5v.

a dominant purpose for his speech by judging the main reason for the audience to have assembled, thereby determining the principal genre of his oration. He must then invent arguments by continuing his analysis of that audience.

After invention, the Neo-Ramists turn to what for them is the far more important question of arrangement. Here, they explain in detail how to adapt invention to genre. Vicars and Farnaby in particular give detailed descriptions of the parts of an oration, with Vicars supplementing each step with references to classical speeches that illustrate the techniques under discussion. Both writers provide general definitions of each part, followed by special instructions for adapting that part to a particular genre. Farnaby organizes by sequence of parts; Vicars, by genre. Both authors also accept the classical number and order of parts: exordium, narration, division, confirmation, confutation, and peroration.[51]

Vicars explains that an exordium must prepare the audience for listening by making it favorably disposed, attentive, and teachable. To accomplish this end, the speaker must be brief and lucid. Farnaby suggests that an epideictic oration be opened with an example, fable, saying, or similar simple illustrative statement, while a deliberative speech should begin with the forensic techniques of accusation or defense, or with amplification, diminution, or ornamentation. In a forensic speech, the orator should begin with his own character and then address the matter at hand, the judges, the audience, and his opponents. Vicars states that in some situations, a forensic orator may need to draw attention away from his client, while in others, such as Cicero's speech for the poet Archias, the speaker may borrow from the epideictic genre and praise him.

Narration and its accompanying parts, proposition and division, are more easily handled. The narration, defined by Farnaby as a rehearsal of deeds which is designed to persuade, can be omitted in deliberative orations and, both authors agree, should be omitted in forensic speeches when that information would be prejudicial to one's client. Vicars adds that the information contained in the narration of an epideictic speech may be scattered throughout the confirmation instead of occupying a separate section.

According to Farnaby, proposition and division can appear in any speech. Vicars leaves them out of his discussion of forensic oratory but

51. The following discussion is summarized from Vicars, *Cheiragogia*, sigs. B3–D2; and Farnaby, *Index*, sigs. B–B4.

assigns them an important role in deliberative. Vicars outlines two methods of division in the epideictic genre—by enumeration of a person's character traits and by exposition of a situation. He believes that Cicero used a version of the first in the praise of Pompey section of his primarily deliberative speech for the Manilian law, and a version of the second in his forensic defense of Marcellus.

All three genres share the need for confirmation, while epideictic oratory alone may do without confutation. Confirmation requires arguments, and each genre has argumentative methods particularly suited to it. According to Farnaby, the use of enthymeme is the primary instrument for argument in the forensic genre, amplification in the epideictic, and examples in the deliberative. Vicars adds that the forensic confirmation also depends upon the *status* of the principal legal question of the case.

Despite these distinctions, a situation may demand that the orator introduce a confirmation that properly belongs to another genre. Vicars shows how forensic confirmations appear outside courtroom oratory. Cicero's eighth *Philippic* against Marcus Antonius contains an example of a confirmation *in statu definitivo,* which asks the nature of the crime committed. His speech for King Deiotarus employs a confirmation *in statu conjecturali,* the question of what was done. The subject of the eighth *Philippic* concerns the nature of Antonius's actions against Rome—whether he is an "adversary" or an "enemy." The speech for King Deiotarus is one of Cicero's Caesarian orations—matters of a criminal nature that were argued before Caesar because of their political and international ramifications. Both speeches thus arise from mixed occasions, with an audience assembled for more than one purpose.

Epideictic confirmations generally follow the life of the person praised, after giving attention to his country, locality, heritage, and other extrinsic factors associated with him. Again, Vicars shows how the techniques of the epideictic confirmation may be translated into other genres. "Lauditory confirmations" appear in Cicero's forensic speech for the poet Archias and in his deliberative speech for the Manilian law. The oration for Marcellus, Vicars adds, has a confirmation by example, a technique normally assigned to deliberative oratory.

The confutation, of course, depends upon refutation of an opponent's arguments, anticipation of objections, and counterarguments. Long confutations do not suit the epideictic speech, warns Vicars. A speaker would draw attention away from his goal—praise or blame—if he spent too much time even mentioning possible objections. Sometimes, however, the orator may need to excuse or uncover an event in his subject's life that cannot be hidden. Farnaby gives a list of situations when an opponent's arguments ought to be addressed: if one point does not agree with the others; if we know a point to be false; if, from points conceded, one is denied to follow logically; if against a firm argument another equally or more firm may be drawn; and if, serious responses not being readily available, we may make light of or reproach the opponent's statements.

Similarly, the techniques of the peroration are frequently theatrical and antilogical. Farnaby suggests that a forensic orator use irony in his final attempts to arouse indignation or pity. The epideictic oration must also work on the audience to produce admiration and enjoyment. The deliberative speech alone may make further use of examples and lists of good or evil effects.

To the Neo-Ramists, the genres provided a means of structuring arguments. Mixed genres adapted the structures, causing a creative exchange between writer and audience. When a writer began composing, he first identified the genres appropriate to the relationship he desired with his audience. Thus, the way he interpreted a situation politically—ideologically—determined his choice of genres, and hence, in the Neo-Ramist scheme, his rhetoric. Choice of genre could therefore signal political orientation to a genre-conscious reader.

Early seventeenth-century pedagogy virtually insured that even moderately educated men would be such readers. As numerous studies of Renaissance schooling have shown, the average curriculum was grounded in rhetoric to such a degree that contentiousness virtually became the mark of education. Walter J. Ong observes: "A rhetorically dominated education gave a boy no training whatsoever in uncommitted, 'objective,' neutral exposition or narrative. . . . Rhetoric is the art of persuasion, and the orator who exemplifies its training is a committed man, one who speaks for a side."[52]

In the 1620s and 1630s, with rhetoric came instruction by attention to genres. A teacher trained students to compose letters, themes, and orations by having them observe various situations in their models, most frequently drawn from classical and historical sources. Cicero's epistles, philosophical essays, and orations appear regularly in school curricula as the best models for study. Neo-Ramist practice assumed genres to be the starting points for

52. "Tudor Writings on Rhetoric," 50.

the exploration of topics. Consequently, as they approached a model, students would have begun any analysis by determining its genre.

Understanding a speech meant understanding its context. Sixteenth- and seventeenth-century educators regularly recommended a course of study focusing on classical historians and public figures and culminating in examinations of Greek and Roman orators. Reconstructing a typical curriculum, Donald Lemen Clark outlines a progress through the lower forms ending with the writing of simple Latin epistles and themes. In the upper four forms, pupils began to study Latin poetry and oratory.

In Milton's time, Clark believes, serious introduction to Cicero began in the sixth form with the reading of the *Epistles* and *Offices*. The seventh form probably studied the *Orations*, while the eighth increased its knowledge of oratory by reading Isocrates and possibly Demosthenes. This pattern corresponds to those of several other grammar schools, including those at Norwich; Blackburn, Lancashire; and Rotherham. Certainly, Hoole describes such a curriculum in his *New Discovery*.[53]

Attention to genres began in the fourth form when students studied the epistle.[54] Recommended by Hoole, John Clarke's *Formulae* presents its letters according to genre. Clarke first distinguishes letter writing from the oration, reminding readers that the audience of the letter is removed from the writer—not in his presence—so that the entire success of the composition relies on the written word. An epistle must avoid ornate language: "Odiosa in *Epistolis* garrulitas." When we write letters, we must consider both the condition of the composition—including methods of beginning, ending, and dating—and its genre.

As in oratory, there are three genres of epistle writing. Each has several subgenres. In the epideictic genre, Clarke lists eight species of epistles: narrative; lamentatory; appreciatory; gratulatory, in which we exaggerate our happiness; obligatory; disputatory, in which we ask for something; laudatory; and deprecatory. The deliberative genre also has many subgroups of letters, including suasory, hortatory and dehortatory, petitionary, commendatory, consolatory, responsory, monitory, accusatory, reconciliatory, and unitive, in which we solicit support. The judicial genre is least complex, containing only five groups: accusatory, defensory, expostu-

53. *John Milton at St. Paul's School,* 109–24.

54. For Renaissance educators' comments on epistle-writing, see Hoole, *New Discovery,* 182–98; Brinsley, *Consolation,* sig. H3, and *Ludus,* sigs. Y3v–Z2. For the quotation from Clarke, see *Formulae,* sig. L7. The following paragraph is based on sigs. L7–L10.

latory, reproachful, and purgatory or excusatory. Each possible situation has its appropriate genre and attendant structure and style.

After epistle writing came theme writing.[55] While the epistles taught genres and their uses, themes taught technique. The theme, like the epistle, was to be composed following the oratorical parts of invention, arrangement, and style; it was often regarded as practice for the oration, since it could be declaimed. In *Ludus Literarius,* Brinsley suggests that Cicero's shorter orations—in particular the Catilinaria—be used as models for the declamations, which are no more than extempore themes. According to Brinsley, the theme itself, like the oration, must be persuasive: "The principal end of making Theams, I take to be this, to furnish schollars with al store of the choisest matter, that they may therby learne to vnderstand, speake or write of any ordinary Theame, Morall or Poeticall, . . . so as to work in themselves a greater loue of the vertue and hatred of the vice, and to be able with soundnesse of reason to draw others to their opinion."[56]

The basic textbook for instruction in the writing of themes was Aphthonius's *Progymnasmata* in a Latin translation of the Greek. Reflecting patterns established in Quintilian's day, the themes formed a series of graduated exercises ending in legislation—compositions for or against a particular law. Brinsley cautions that teachers use Aphthonius only as a starting point for instruction, allowing pupils to write from their own experiences, which could be drawn from their history assignments.[57] Clarke's list of topics for declamation follows similar lines. He includes such topics drawn from history as "whether Alexander owed more to his teacher, Aristotle, than to his father, Philipp." Many more present theoretical questions concerning government and philosophy.

Grammar-school pupils understood the importance of genre and rhetorical context before they began to study oratory. That culmination of grammar-school education reinforced and extended the early lessons. To many schoolmasters, oratory provided a means for teaching both history and what today we would call "citizenship." Hoole says, "I would have this Form [the fifth] to learn some lively patterns of Oratory, by the frequent and familiar use whereof and the knowledge of the Histories themselves, to

55. Renaissance discussions of themes appear in Hoole, *New Discovery,* 210–11; Brinsley, *Consolation,* sig. K2, and *Ludus,* sigs. Z2v–Aa4. For statements comparing the theme to the oration, see Brinsley, *Consolation,* sig. K2v. The quotation comes from Brinsley, *Ludus,* sigs. Z3v–Z4.

56. *Ludus,* sigs. Z3v–Z4

57. *Ludus,* sigs. Aa4v–Bb3v.

which they relate; they may at last obtain the Artifice of gallant expression, and some skil to mannage future affairs." John Brinsley expresses the same concern in *Consolation,* when he recommends "the diligent studie of the famous and ancient Grecian or Roman history, & their noble warres; to help the better to perserue, and defend your natiue countrey."[58]

To stress the importance of history, Brinsley gives a list of English translations with which to stock the school library. He includes Sir Clement Edmunds's of Caesar's commentaries; Philemon Holland's of Livy's Roman history; Sir Henry Savill's of Tacitus' Roman history; and Florus' Roman history, dedicated to the Lord Marquis of Buckingham, which covered the period from the founding to the emperor Trajan. No matter to what degree the student had mastered Latin, he was expected to know the historical contexts of the orations he studied. When he read them, the seventeenth-century student would have been able to identify speakers and their opponents, other figures mentioned in the speeches, and the historical significance of events surrounding delivery of the orations. The student was taught to regard the classical orations not as artifacts from a dead past, but as living, practical examples of public men in action.

Under such circumstances, the study of oratory by means of genre—as recommended by such Neo-Ramists as Thomas Vicars—could accomplish two ends at once. It gave students a method by which to analyze materials for their own compositions, and it reinforced their historical readings by drawing attention to the purposes and contexts of the classical orations.[59] Vicars underscores this point in his book, designed to be a manual for teachers. *Cheiragogia* concludes with a long section of "analyses"—the word is Vicars's own—of three Ciceronian speeches. As Vicars defines it, analysis is the methodical exploration of something written or advised, called "unraveling" because this exercise unravels the fabric of a speech just as Penelope unraveled her weaving. It explains the method of the orator and the parts of the oration.

Each of the speeches chosen illustrates a genre. *Pro Archias* exemplifies epideictic oratory, *Pro Lege Manilia* deliberative, and *Pro Milone* forensic.[60]

58. Hoole, *New Discovery,* 201; Brinsley, *Consolation,* sig. C3v. Described in the following paragraph, Brinsley's list of recommended histories appears on sigs. I4v–K.

59. This principle had sound, humanist origins. See Desiderius Erasmus, *De Ratione studii ac legendi interpretandique auctores,* 679–80. For Vicars's comments on analysis, see *Cheiragogia,* sig. F3.

60. Vicars's selection of illustrations was traditional by his time. For other discussions of the speech, see Cox, *Arte or Crafte,* sig. B8 (narration as praise), sigs. D2–D2v

In each case, the "analysis" begins by identifying the main subject of the oration and the corresponding genre. Vicars starts his examination of *Pro Lege Manilia,* for example, with a series of simple statements: "Whether Pompeius ought to be made commander for the Asian war. That is what Cicero advises. Therefore this matter belongs to the deliberative genre." Determination of genre occurs outside Vicars's investigation of "artificium" in the speech and is presumed, given the nature of the principal topic, to be self-evident.

The analysis proper first identifies the parts of the oration—in this case exordium, narration, partition, confirmation, confutation, and peroration—and then, by means of questions and answers, explains Cicero's technique in each part. Vicars recognizes that Cicero has two objectives— to show that the Asian kings Mithridates and Tigranes are pushing on Rome a dangerous and serious war, and to argue that Pompeius is the one general best able to conduct the Roman offensive. Hence, while his principal purpose is to advise, Cicero must also praise. As Vicars sees it, the speech has a laudatory confirmation that uses the *topoi* of epideictic oratory—life history, patriotism, and personal characteristics—to commend Pompeius. Because Cicero advises by praising and praises by advising, *Pro Lege Manilia* is a speech of mixed genre.

By the time they came to compose full-fledged orations in their last year in grammar school and in the university, seventeenth-century students had been taught to recognize and write according to genres. They had read political history and the words of prominent participants. They had studied classical oratory, which was almost inseparable from politics, and in doing so they had learned to analyze an oration according to its genre and rhetorical intent. The ancient orator, they learned, could only rarely speak in a "pure" genre. Mostly, those orations needed to reflect political reality—the fact that influential men were involved in most governmental decisions and many legal cases and that a speech commemorating or attacking such men inevitably reverberated in the public sphere. Mixed genres provided the flexibility an orator needed to manipulate his words into a composition that could fit both audience and political situation.

The pamphleteers of the English Revolution not only possessed the rhetorical skills to present cogent, effective arguments in volatile times, but

---

(narration as deliberation); Richard Sherry, *A Treatise of Schemes & Tropes,* sig. B4v (example of middle style); and Peacham, *Garden of Eloquence,* sig. D4v (example of hyperbole).

they also faced an audience specially equipped to receive those arguments. As we have seen, the reading public of the early seventeenth century was a particularly well defined group. When a pamphleteer set out to construct arguments, he could be fairly certain who could and would read them. He also knew that he and his readers shared a language of public discourse and assumptions about how to read. Any literate person knew the "hermeneutics of censorship" and was fully prepared to read between the lines, to look for nontextual meaning in published work. Moreover, anyone with a grammar-school education knew the expressiveness of oratorical genres. Readers and writers alike understood the generic conventions.

Literacy, censorship, and the oratorical genres—these were the contexts of meaning for political discourse in the mid–seventeenth century. The genres were closely tied to ideology, to the writer's way of perceiving his audience. To the Neo-Ramist rhetorician and his students, perception of genre was epistemic: it completely structured the manner in which the writer argued and determined both how he perceived his audience and how that audience could respond to his argument. Conversely, political and ideological shifts appeared in generic terms—in the kind of discourse the writer selected.

As we shall see, from 1642 to 1660 English political discourse underwent a profound change. What began as a common language with minor generic variations depending on political orientation gradually broke down. First generically and then thematically, the language of each competing side distinguished itself from the other. By 1659 and 1660, monarchists and radicals were formally speaking different languages. The monarchists successfully adopted and adapted the language of the parliamentary opposition of 1642. The radicals, including even John Milton, evolved a language that effectively isolated them. Their choice of genres insured their inability to persuade their audience, or what their audience had become. In theory, pedagogy, and practice, genre determined the limits of what it was possible to say. The genres themselves adapted quickly to the times. The writers, however, led by their ideology to select particular genres, sometimes proved less flexible than seventeenth-century rhetoric enabled them to be.

I.

The Language of Controversy
before the Revolution

ONE

Prologue: Politics, Society, and the Reading Public under the Early Stuarts

In early seventeenth-century England, the practical result of censorship, licensing, and careful rhetorical training was a climate in which anything, properly viewed, could take on political meaning. Indirectly, forms of entertainment and both the literary and the oratorical genres adopted special and extended significance. On the stage, historical dramas presented examinations of kingship, governance, and the role of the subject. Music often had political content, especially when performed for its usual patrons—landed aristocrats. Published satires and panegyrics drew on long traditions of complaint and advice literature, while religious and political controversialists debated in prose, writing both general analyses like *New Atlantis* and specific polemics like the Marprelate and *vox populi* tracts.

Literary historians now recognize that many works of the period are indeed what Quentin Skinner calls "heteronomous." That is, their full meaning depends on the reader's awareness of specific political contexts. Moreover, the works themselves played a far more important role than has been supposed in affecting the course of contemporary events. Scholars such as Jonathan Goldberg and Stephen Orgel dispel the idea that court masques of the early Stuart period were merely trivial entertainments and show how literary works of all kinds figured in public debate. Leah S. Marcus argues that promulgation of the Book of Sports in the 1630s immediately politicized both traditional entertainments and poetry written about them. In 1637, John Bastwick, Henry Burton, and William Prynne found themselves mirroring events in their own books as they went on trial for published opposition to Archbishop Laud.[1] Throughout the

---

1. Goldberg, *James I and the Politics of Literature: Jonson, Shakespeare, Donne, and Their Contemporaries*; Orgel, *The Illusion of Power: Political Theater in the English Renaissance*; Mar-

period preceding the civil wars, writers depended on informed readers to supply the most important meanings of both literary and nonliterary works.

As many historians of literacy in the seventeenth century note, the burgeoning pamphlet trade both before and during the civil war era indicates a growing audience willing and able to read political arguments. Literacy in turn depended upon social and economic forces and upon the influences of Puritanism. Recent research suggests that the audience of Bastwick, Burton, Prynne, and the pamphleteers of 1642 in no way presented a monolithic form of organized opinion, and that it was in fact abnormally varied and large. Readers and potential voters increasingly came from groups no longer strongly affiliated with the local aristocracy or gentry, and as J. H. Plumb remarks, "Large electorates require more care in management, more cajolery, more argument than tiny bodies of twenty or thirty."[2]

At the outbreak of the first civil war, then, pamphleteers faced the task of persuading a "general public" of diverse backgrounds and interests, a group perhaps more alert to rhetorical forms and persuasive skills than to particular ideas. Unlike the classical orator, the seventeenth-century pamphleteer could not immediately characterize his audience.

The early seventeenth century saw a marked shift in the economic, social, and political character of the electorate. Owing to a series of bad harvests, Continental wars, and outbreaks of disease, many areas were in moderate to severe economic trouble in the 1620s and 1630s. The textile industry was especially hard-hit, leaving, as Peter Clark demonstrates, "major pockets of distress" even in otherwise prosperous counties.[3] By 1649, the political difficulties of the crown contributed to further depression in international trade, which in turn particularly affected London.

The economic problems of the 1620s and 1630s, coupled with an increase in the population, precipitated the dislocation of many groups. The "middle sort" of society—tradesmen, craftsmen, yeomen, and small merchants—were experiencing what historians describe as great economic mobility. Many moved up into the lower ranks of the gentry. Still more moved down, some even becoming wage laborers.

Movement into the upper ranks occurred in part due to widespread

---

cus, *The Politics of Mirth: Jonson, Herrick, Milton, Marvell, and the Defense of Old Holiday Pastimes;* and numerous "New Historical" studies published since 1985.

2. "The Growth of the Electorate in England from 1600 to 1715," 99.

3. *English Provincial Society from the Reformation to the Revolution: Religion, Politics and Society in Kent, 1500–1640,* 353–56; see also Brian Manning, *The English People and the English Revolution, 1640–1649,* 99–111.

economic decline of the old landed families. As Lawrence Stone shows, early seventeenth-century aristocrats frequently sold off their holdings to raise ready money, and their property often ended up in the hands of well-to-do merchants and tradesmen. Landowners, both aristocratic and royal, also increasingly exploited their remaining properties to raise funds, thereby uprooting many in the lower classes. Enclosure, fen-drainage projects, deforestation, and rack-renting displaced tenants and small farmers who depended on the free use of common lands.[4]

One result proved damaging to towns—a significant increase in the numbers of subsistence migrants, poor people looking for the bare means of survival, crowding into urban areas, overtaxing the local systems of relief. Thus, the years before the civil war were economically unstable, and many people, no matter what their class or wealth, felt with good reason that their position and well-being were easily threatened.

Economic problems led naturally to social ones. There was an important, though temporary, shift in the traditional power structure that continued into the revolution and the Protectorate. The declining fortunes of the aristocracy, combined with its new exploitative practices in estate management, alienated large segments of local electorates from their traditional leaders. With this loss of old allegiances, authority shifted to the upper ranks of the "middle sort" and brought with it increased participation of the middle class in public affairs.

In many areas, the influx of poor people prompted the consolidation and overhauling of local governments, which were gaining influence as aristocrats lost control of them. Such governments sometimes developed into oligarchies as officials were called upon to pay the additional money needed to operate the civic administration out of their own pockets. In depressed towns, this process was aggravated as the demand for relief grew and wider gaps appeared between the comfortable and the poor.

The tensions were exacerbated by the actions of the crown. During the Personal Rule, Charles's efforts to finance his policies—most notoriously through the exacting of ship-money—fell heaviest on the very men who managed local governments. His associations with the Merchant Adventurers and the London trade in general abandoned provincial industry and

---

4. Stone, *The Crisis of the Aristocracy, 1558–1641,* 156–98; see also Christopher Hill, *The World Turned Upside Down: Radical Ideas during the English Revolution,* 39–56; and Peter Clark, "'The Ramoth-Gilead of the Good': Urban Change and Political Radicalism, 1540–1640."

contributed to the depression in the counties. Paradoxically, Charles's need for a mechanism to collect funds further activated local governments through the Book of Orders, issued in 1630. The crown's policies thus alienated the middle classes just as they were gaining social and political power.[5]

The shift in the power structure was mirrored by changes in political organization. Plumb indicates that the English electorate greatly increased in the sixteenth and seventeenth centuries, largely because of inflation, as more and more people's property became valued at forty shillings—the minimum qualification for voting. Then, in 1604, the House of Commons won Goodwin's Case, which gave it the power to rule on the legality of elections and to determine the right of membership in the House.[6] The Commons thus could strengthen itself by extending the franchise and altering election laws, which it did between 1621 and 1628. These changes crippled the court's efforts to nominate its own candidates for Parliament and opened the field for the opposition: in the election of the Long Parliament, more than 70 of the 259 seats were contested.

In the two decades preceding the civil war, the electorate extended increasingly downward, including in most areas the middle class. The year 1642 saw a large electorate, more varied than ever, under the influence of gentry and local governments rather than the court. Moreover, there was something different about the new voters. They were motivated by political and religious issues. For the moment, controlled patronage was dead. Interest in issues prompted political awareness and involvement.[7] People represented ideas as well as interests, ideas which often found their origins in Puritanism and religious radicalism. Opposition to the court materialized from groups that had recently gained real electoral power and possessed the ideology to make the most of it.

5. I follow Stone's definition of "middle classes," which includes everyone above wage-earners and below the peerage but which concentrates on the greater merchants, lesser gentry, professionals, and country elite (*Crisis of the Aristocracy,* 51–52). On the Personal Rule, see Kevin Sharpe, "The Personal Rule of Charles I"; and Esther S. Cope, *Politics Without Parliaments, 1629–1640.*

6. Plumb, "Growth of the Electorate"; see also Derek Hirst, *The Representative of the People? Voters and Voting in England under the Early Stuarts,* 132–37; see also Mark A. Kishlansky, *Parliamentary Selection: Social and Political Choice in Early Modern England,* 225–30.

7. David Underdown, *Revel, Riot and Rebellion: Popular Politics and Culture in England, 1603–1660,* 1–145.

The ideology of the opposition is variously characterized as "urban" or "committed," but most historians agree that it stems from the concept of "godliness" current among the middle classes, prompted in part as a reaction to abuses in the Church of England. "Godliness" as a value— sobriety, industry, moral uprightness, and other attributes now identified as the Protestant ethic—was primarily a middle-class ideology through which its adherents distinguished themselves from the upper and lower classes. It was truly an alternate worldview, not an imitation or adaptation of aristocratic tastes. The godly saw themselves as standing outside the traditional order of things.

Michael Walzer suggests that this sense of "estrangement" produced an ideology of commitment among the "saints"—one made a conscious choice to be a saint out of deeply felt disagreement with the establishment, both church and state. Tracing the feeling of alienation to the Marian exiles, Walzer argues that ministers and other leaders of the godly wanted a voice in government from the first, and at the same time turned away from the court as a focus for their careers. Yet their strong beliefs and personal commitment led not to quietism but to local and national activism: "Wounded honor was satisfied in the duel; injured conscience led to political opposition."[8]

Godly gentlemen, especially the educated, began to believe themselves called to public affairs, the governing of the city. Peter Clark identifies this sense of public vocation as "urban ideology." Focused on the city, the attention of these men was directed toward reform. They often took the initiative for establishing schools and libraries, and their activities in trade linked them to like-minded men in other towns, solidifying among them a sense of genuine opposition to the ruling order. This belief in civic duty may easily be seen in the composition of the House of Commons in 1642: most members of the Long Parliament were Puritans of various persuasions.[9]

The religious identity of these public-spirited citizens was a major source of their power. The creation of a state church by Henry VIII had greatly weakened the independent economic and political power of the church, while the distribution of church lands gave new families what

8. *The Revolution of the Saints: A Study in the Origins of Radical Politics,* 254, 232–57; and Richard M. Douglas, "Talent and Vocation in Humanist and Protestant Thought."

9. Clark, "Ramoth-Gilead," 181; J. H. Hexter, *The Reign of King Pym,* 77–89; D[oug-las] Brunton and D. H. Pennington, *Members of the Long Parliament,* 38–52.

Christopher Hill terms a "vested interest in Protestantism."[10] Meanwhile, the church became a major tool of the state, a condition that caused no widespread trouble until the Stuarts started to use it to coerce the gentry within their own counties. Also, the succession of Laud and other High Church clergy renewed old distrust of Roman Catholicism along with new fears of continental absolutism. As Brian Manning argues, Puritans and other radical Protestants were the most conspicuous opponents of Roman and Anglo-Catholicism and thus the logical choices as leaders of religious opposition. Further, in many counties, Puritans and others had already initiated reforms where the established church had neglected to do so. They not only wanted to fill the gap created by the decline of the church and aristocracy, but they also were the most likely to be accepted as the appropriate leaders. Everywhere, Separatists urged all to participate in both church government and politics.

The reading public of 1637 and 1642 constituted a potent political force. Likely to suffer from some form of economic dislocation and spiritual discomfort, the civic-minded individual also participated in public life, equipped with an ideology that suggested that doing so was a spiritual imperative. Alienated from local aristocrats and the court, he often took power into his own hands and conceived of political struggles in terms of specific issues.

There was a redefinition of the ideas of "public life" and "public men" in the early seventeenth century. The older ideal of civic humanism and Christian princes broadened and altered to include individuals committed to the maintenance of a godly commonwealth, men who felt a calling to serve and guide their fellow citizens.[11] Extension of the electorate meant that many more who were called were also chosen—that is, more people could participate in government and contribute their voices directly to it.

A large electorate, eager participation, and specific issues demanded public argument. That argument appeared in the growing pamphlet literature. And as never before, there needed to be a public language to serve debate. An author could not assume that his audience could be extensively characterized. Especially among the opposition, a man might be a reform-motivated member of the Church of England or a religious radical, a local

10. *Puritanism and Revolution: Studies in Interpretation of the English Revolution of the 17th Century*, 44, 32–49, and "Parliament and People in Seventeenth-Century England."

11. Jerrold E. Seigel, *Rhetoric and Philosophy in Renaissance Humanism: The Union of Eloquence and Wisdom, Petrarch to Valla*, xi–xvi, 3–30; Annabel M. Patterson, "The Civic Hero in Milton's Prose."

magnate or a London apprentice. When issues are important but the audience diverse, the form of an argument may have more power to unify than the content.

As political conflict intensified in the 1620s and 1630s, three varieties of composition became increasingly popular: the tract of religious persecution, the published speech, and the petition. They are distinguished from other prose tracts by being specific in both topic and event, as well as being frequently addressed to particular persons. As vehicles for expression, these varieties were especially well suited to the times, as their authors had been trained since childhood in the writing of politically engaged argumentation.

Characteristic of the new pamphlets was their aggressive contentiousness. While the preceding generations of rhetoricians had assigned to oratory the ceremonial function of affirming the commonly held values of the society, leaving to logic the burden of challenge to authority, the new pamphleteers often advanced values contradictory to certain established opinions. They strove not only to persuade individuals but also to shape current events. Defiance of the king in January 1642 led to his execution in January 1649. The last step, since it was a collective act and not that of an individual, could not have been taken without the first, and the pamphlets of 1642 established many themes and techniques for debates upon which later arguments were built.

In 1637, under Charles's Personal Rule, Bastwick, Burton, and Prynne wrote to an audience powerless to act on a national scale. In describing their own experiences with persecution for their faith, they cast their arguments in language and techniques that already possessed deep significance for English readers—discourse adapted from John Foxe's *Acts and Monuments,* or the *Book of Martyrs.* Their opponent—Archbishop Laud—won his case but lost popular appeal by employing the language of the law courts in his attack on these pamphleteers. In 1642, under the Long Parliament, pamphleteers could call to arms. These writers chose forms of discourse long associated with the language of political participation—the parliamentary speech and the petition. Such discourse lent legitimacy to political arguments emanating from outside the House of Commons. Before the civil wars began, pamphleteers and readers alike were accustomed to argumentation by means of established forms.

TWO

1637: Laud and His Victims

In 1637, in the name of Charles I, Archbishop of Canterbury William Laud set out to suppress religious dissent by enforcing censorship. Laud wanted, in effect, a "show trial," during which he could warn his enemies that he would not tolerate their attacks on his and Charles's alterations in the worship service of the Church of England. He found his targets in John Bastwick, a physician; Henry Burton, a clergyman; and William Prynne, a lawyer already notorious for his published attacks on current fashions, acting, and "innovations" in religion.[1] All had published tracts denouncing Laud, and, technically, it was the books—not the authors—that stood trial before the Star Chamber on June 14.

The trial itself consisted of various members of the Star Chamber "descant[ing]" on and "vent[ing] much bitternes" against the books, while the members prohibited the accused authors from speaking in their own defense. As Bastwick reportedly described it to the court, "They take away our weapons (our Answers) by vertue of your Authority, by which we should defend our selves, and yet they bid us fight." Instead of being allowed to reply, the three had to listen to Laud deliver a specially prepared speech against their books, after which they were sentenced to lose their ears in the pillory, pay fines of five thousand pounds each, and spend the

---

1. The books in question were John Bastwick's *The Letany of John Bastwick, Doctor of Phisicke,* an unidentified Latin work attributed to Bastwick (probably *Praxeis ton episkopou sive Apologeticus ad Praesules Anglicanos*), Henry Burton's *An Apology of an Appeale to the Kings Most Excellent Majestie,* and two anonymous pamphlets—*Newes from Ipswich* and *A Divine Tragedy Lately Acted*—both charged to Prynne but neither identified in court as his work. Paul Christianson, *Reformers and Babylon: English Apocalyptic Visions from the Reformation to the Eve of the Civil War* attributes *A Divine Tragedy* to Burton (14), although the Star Chamber accusation never established authorship. See John Bastwick, *A Briefe Relation of Certaine Speciall and Most Materiall Passages, and Speeches in the Starre-Chamber, Occasioned and Delivered the 14th Day of Iune, 1637,* sigs. A3, B3, C; and *Documents Relating to the Proceedings Against William Prynne, in 1634 and 1637,* 75–76.

remainder of their lives in prison. In addition, Prynne, committing his second major offense, was condemned to be branded on the face with the letters *S.L.* ("seditious libeller"). As the prisoners' sympathizers watched, the mutilations were carried out on June 30.[2]

Despite Laud's intentions, he had created martyrs to the cause of the opposition. In the following days, crowds of supporters turned out at Chester when Prynne passed through that town on his way to prison. The scene repeated itself for Burton at Coventry. Nor was the persecution forgotten once the victims were jailed. The Short Parliament heard petitions for their release, and, finally, on November 28, 1640, the newly freed Prynne and Burton made a triumphal entry into London, with Bastwick following a few days later, an event not matched until the Five Members returned to Parliament in January 1642.[3]

Encouraged by the example of Bastwick, Burton, and Prynne, others became bolder in their attacks on the prelates, while the government hesitated to prosecute. Clarendon remembers:

> All pulpits were freely delivered to the schismatical and silenced preachers, who till then had lurked in corners or lived in New England; and the presses [were] at liberty for the publishing the most invective, seditious, and scurrilous pamphlets that their wit and malice could invent. Whilst the ministers of the State, and judges of the law, like men in an ecstasy, surprised and amazed with several apparitions, had no speech or motion; as if, having committed such an excess of jurisdiction, as men upon great surfeits are enjoined for a time to eat nothing, they had been prescribed to exercise no jurisdiction at all.[4]

Although Charles and Laud had law and authority behind them, clearly the power had shifted to their opposition.

The Laudian persecutions of 1637 reveal nothing less than a reversal of power through rhetoric. Brought to trial because of their books, the pamphleteers were already known to many. Those who had not previously read the books could study published accounts of the trial, as well as Laud's own speech, printed separately. No matter who each writer explicitly addressed, that second audience—the elusive general public—existed as a significant part of the background. As Charles, Laud, and their supporters

2. Bastwick, *Briefe Relation,* sigs. A3, B3, C; *Documents Relating to . . . Prynne,* 75–76.
3. William M. Lamont, *Marginal Prynne, 1600–1669,* 39–41; Edward Hyde, Earl of Clarendon, *History of the Rebellion and Civil Wars in England Begun in the Year 1641,* 3:64.
4. *History of the Rebellion,* 3:65.

realized too late, this audience possessed considerable power. Its sympathies could, and did, strengthen whichever group managed to mobilize them. And they were most effectively rallied not through public speaking, but through print and the culture that print had created.

Laud misjudged the need to address the "second audience." Falsely secure in his position as archbishop, he chose to speak chiefly to the members of the Star Chamber. His speech is a model of forensic oratory. With the law on his side, as he sees it, he selects a genre that excludes general readers who do not understand the intricacy of the issues involved. Logical and self-assured, he relies on his own authority and the facts of the case to prove his argument. He makes no effort to unify his audience, assuming that all that truly counts is the Star Chamber, which shares his interpretation of events.[5] To Laud, the issue is simple: the law had been flagrantly broken by men who did so explicitly to interfere with his reforms in the Church of England and hence to provoke religious strife. He is shocked that these men should be so bold as to attack the church. His policies need defending, so defensive he becomes. Laud's rhetoric creates a figure of authority in retreat.

In contrast, their very interpretation of the issues at hand gave the pamphleteers a distinct rhetorical advantage. While Laud kept his focus narrow, on a few of the specific, published attacks, the pamphleteers presented a broad-based challenge to the fundamental powers of the prelates of England. They recalled that, since late in James's reign, the government had been passing laws to restrict the activities of Puritan preachers and writers, while giving a free hand to Arminian clergy. Moreover, they knew that with the rise of Laud came a strengthening of the claim that the bishops possessed power directly from God—*jure divino.* This position distressed not only Presbyterians but also many members of the Church of England, who argued that since the sovereign was the head of the church, bishops ruled *jure humano.* William Prynne was only one of many who believed the prelates' appropriation of *jure divino* to be both a challenge to the king and a disguise for Roman Catholicism.[6]

Bolstering these suspicions were the prelates' actions, which included encouraging ritual at the expense of preaching and making several sus-

---

5. This is not to say that forensic oratory is inherently nonintegrative. When effectively mixed with other genres, notably epideictic, it can unify an audience. Cf. Emile Zola's "J'Accuse."

6. Godfrey Davies, *The Early Stuarts, 1603–1660,* 73–76.

picious changes in the Book of Common Prayer. Among these changes was the removal of the king, queen, and their children from the catalog of the elect, a move called "horrid treason" by *Newes from Ipswich,* one of the books brought to trial with the pamphleteers. Further changes included the omission of a prayer for Lady Elizabeth, the king's sister and Protestant heroine, and the elimination of a clause in the first collect praising God for delivering his people from superstition and idolatry. This last act, the *Newes* suggested, appeared to pave the way for increased ritual, "so we may walke on in romish hellish darknesse, serving and honouring the Pope and Devill in stead of God" (sig. A4).

To Bastwick, Burton, and Prynne, each one of these matters, perhaps trivial by itself, was not simply a "reform" but part of a hidden agenda to subvert the foundations of the Church of England, and indeed, England itself. Thus, the pamphleteers could present themselves as both religious and patriotic defenders of Christian and national interest. Fortunately for them, choosing this stance enabled the pamphleteers to express their positions through a form of discourse already validated by their culture. That form—originated by and continued through the new print culture—carried persuasive power and prepared readers for a sympathetic reaction to any writer employing it.

Originating with John Foxe's *Acts and Monuments* and the accession of Queen Elizabeth, this discourse—simultaneously Protestant and patriotic—enabled writers to protest abuses by linking them with foreign and often explicitly Catholic conspiracy. Complaining of his own troubles through this discourse allowed the writer to represent himself as a spokesman for many, since it made his experiences not unique but exemplary. From this stance, the writer could protest vociferously while implying his basic loyalty to church and crown. Joan Webber identifies this public, generalized "I" as Puritan, but historians have seen it at work in political discourse as well. By the late sixteenth century, public speech invoked nationalism by depicting England as a "beleaguered isle," constantly in danger from foreign threats.[7] Bastwick, Burton, and Prynne inherited a discourse in which personal suffering assumed a patriotic dimension. In fact, in this discourse, suffering confirmed patriotism and noble intentions.

Foxe's *Acts and Monuments*—or, popularly, the *Book of Martyrs*—was,

---

7. Webber, *The Eloquent "I": Style and Self in Seventeenth-Century Prose,* 8, 11–12, 53–79; Carol Z. Weiner, "The Beleaguered Isle: A Study of Elizabethan and Early Jacobean Anti-Catholicism."

next to the Bible, one of the first notable achievements of English print culture. It was so successful that it imprinted itself on the collective mind of English readers so that it could provide a subtext to any subsequent pamphlet that employed its perspective and techniques. The historian William M. Lamont calls it "quite simply, the best monarchist propaganda that a Protestant Englishman had ever written."[8] Briefly, its achievement was to adapt a Roman Catholic genre—the saint's legend—to a political, millenarian, and anti-Catholic end.

As presented by Foxe, the accession of Queen Elizabeth represented a victory over the Antichrist, and as such deserved the support of all loyal Protestants. Further, Foxe wanted to encourage fellow Protestants to see themselves and their beliefs confirmed in the conduct of his martyrs, so that they would stand together against inevitable future acts of violence against themselves and their church. To explain recent persecutions, he placed them within the context of the entire history of the church, from the earliest martyrs to Wyclif and the Lollards and Martin Luther. As thorough as it was, Foxe's presentation of ecclesiastical history became the official truth for subsequent polemicists.[9]

Part of the later power of the *Book of Martyrs* came from its simple accessibility. From 1563 to 1641, it went through eight folio editions. Officially printed by the Stationers' Company, the book found its way into most English churches, where preachers used it to provide material for sermons. As a result, most English people knew the stories and their polemical perspective in much the same way that Catholics knew the patterns of their saints' legends. Further, just as the saints' legends gave their readers and listeners a firm sense of themselves as Catholics, Foxe's audience received an idea of themselves as Protestants. As Foxe intended it, his *Book of Martyrs* would tell the true stories of the church, to counter and defeat the lies of its opposite number, the *Legenda aurea.* The *Book of Martyrs* is a book to defeat a book.

Foxe's perspective leads him to make several noteworthy changes in his method of presenting the stories of his martyrs. In the *Legenda,* time is cyclical, and each martyr's experience is a variation on a never-ending

8. *Richard Baxter and the Millennium: Protestant Imperialism and the English Revolution,* 13.

9. Among important studies arguing for the enormous influence of Foxe are Christianson, *Reformers and Babylon;* Katharine R. Firth, *The Apocalyptic Tradition in Reformation Britain, 1530–1645;* Lamont, *Richard Baxter and the Millenium;* and William Haller, *Foxe's Book of Martyrs and the Elect Nation.*

pattern. In the *Book of Martyrs,* time is linear. Each martyr's death is a marker on the road to the apocalypse. In the *Legenda,* the subject—whether martyr or saint—is an intercessor with God, an extraordinary person whose special nature is revealed through specific acts before death and miracles after. If the life is illustrated, it is probably depicted by stock pictures. Throughout the narration, the emphasis falls on the subject's suffering.[10]

In the *Book of Martyrs,* the subject is a witness to the injustice and cruelty of the Antichrist. Also, Foxe repeatedly stresses that his subject is an ordinary person who could be a representative of any good Christian. In place of acts, Foxe underscores character, frequently printing as fully as possible the subject's letters, speeches, and even transcripts of examinations before the ecclesiastical courts. When an episode is illustrated, the picture is usually quite carefully detailed and almost always accompanied by a full, explanatory caption. Most important, the emphasis in Foxe's book is not on deeds but on speech, especially the words of the martyrs themselves. The words become the martyr's chief justification, the suffering simply an additional proof of sincerity.[11]

Foxe's new perspective demonstrated five distinct features that later writers could use to invoke Foxe and his arguments. The first is a self-conscious narrative voice that provides the religious and political context for interpreting events. Foxe is always present in his descriptions, intervening in the narrative to cry out against "a spectacle wherein the whole world may see the Herodian crueltie of this gracelesse generation of Catholique tormentors, Ad perpetuam rei infamiam" (745). This committed voice easily modulated into the vehement first-person narratives of later Puritans, as they both reported and commented on their experiences.

Foxe also persuades through sheer bulk and depth of examples, as well as by extended quotation. His catalogs of specific, detailed accounts, carefully verified and strengthened whenever possible by dates, places, and names of witnesses, insist on the veracity of his arguments. The quotation

10. On Roman Catholic martyr-writing, saints, and saints' lives, see Peter Brown, *The Cult of the Saints: Its Rise and Function in Latin Christianity,* 65–66, 79–82; and Sherry L. Reames, *The "Legenda aurea": A Reexamination of Its Paradoxical History,* 44–70.

11. As Reames, *"Legenda aurea,"* 101–14, indicates, many speeches and dialogues appear in the *Legenda,* but with this crucial difference: in context, these dialogues are nondramatic. They do not characterize the speakers. Rather, they are discussions on points of faith and doctrine, lifted out of time and space and designed primarily to educate the reader.

of the martyrs' own words as direct testimony gives readers a full sense of the martyrs as real people like themselves. Further, the quotations turn Foxe's account into a direct conversation with the readers. Narrator and readers become witnesses themselves to the apocalyptic struggle of God's church.

An apocalyptic perspective within the historical narrative is the fourth feature of Foxe's presentation. He continually urges readers to see the continuity of Protestant and proto-Protestant faith throughout time. History of this kind inevitably directs readers toward the future, providing them with a guiding principle through which to evaluate current events. This perspective gives readers a common language that immediately adds a particular historical, religious, and political context to any event it describes.

The last feature grows out of the fourth. Foxe places all past events within this apocalyptic context, but he also encourages readers to do the same with present and future conflicts. From the beginning of his undertaking, Foxe insists that there shall be no final edition of his work until the church triumphs on earth. He concludes, "The elder the World waxeth, the longer it continueth, the neerer it hasteneth to his end, the more Sathan rageth, giving still new matter of writing Bookes and Volumes" (1026).[12] From year to year, from edition to edition, Foxe took seriously his own charge, adding new examples as he uncovered them. So strong was Foxe's vision that after his death subsequent editions not only reprinted Foxe's own narratives but added others as recent proof of the truth of his argument. In 1632, the seventh edition continued accounts to 1621 and included the Gunpowder Plot. In 1641, the eighth edition included a portrait and biography of Foxe himself.[13] Such was the impact of Foxe's work that a generation after the first edition readers readily and literally cast current events into chapters for the *Book of Martyrs*.

In both their writings and their lives, Bastwick, Burton, and Prynne accommodated themselves to Foxe's model. While we can never determine to what extent their imitation was conscious, we can observe that their techniques do recall those of the *Book of Martyrs*. Certainly, their interpretation of events is similar to Foxe's, and they do deliberately invoke Foxe to defend their own arguments. Throughout their works, they subordinate their personal struggles to their vision of the millennium. Further, they

12. The impressive bulk of the *Book of Martyrs* comes from its extensive reproduction of such letters and transcripts.

13. Christianson, *Reformers and Babylon,* 47–92, 100–106.

present their criticisms of Laud and his supporters in patriotic as well as religious terms. As was the case with Foxe, this approach was an accurate barometer of their actual views. Of the three, only Burton had Independent leanings, while Prynne would remain a royalist and a supporter of ecclesiastical hierarchy throughout the coming revolution. Like Foxe, the pamphleteers portrayed themselves as defenders of England and Protestantism. This combination gave them, as we shall see, their enormous popular appeal.

Foremost among the pamphleteers' concerns is the establishment of their loyalty and devotion to the king. In so doing, they use remarkably similar techniques. First, they rhetorically separate the prelates from the king and the "lordly" prelates from the others. Through this maneuver, the pamphleteers can oppose what they perceive to be abuses without criticizing the basic institutions of the Church of England. This process enables them to present themselves as defenders of both God and king, while accusing the prelates of un-English innovation. Second, the pamphleteers need to characterize the innovations as both repulsive and dangerous— ritualistic, meaningless, mindless, and therefore "popish." Last, and most important from the point of view of their opposition in the Star Chamber, they focus their attacks on the behavior and personality of Archbishop Laud, attributing to him, either directly or indirectly, all the worst qualities of absolutist, foreign princes and bishops.

By publicly contending that Laud abuses his power in the prerogative courts, the pamphleteers make their boldest challenge, implying that Laud is striving with Charles for supreme power in England and thus committing treason. To Laud, then, these pamphleteers were particularly offensive, and yet he had more than personal reasons for fearing their influence. The process of rhetorical separation is inextricably tied to that of redefinition. In the pamphlets, Laud is contending with Bastwick, Burton, and Prynne to define the role of the prelate. Oddly, Laud, by claiming ecclesiastical power *jure divino,* himself separates bishops from the king and the loyalty the king commands, while the pamphleteers, defending *jure humano* and the king's power, undermine their audience's unquestioning acceptance of both institutions.

The pamphleteers aim at putting distance between their readers and the prelates to counter any loyalty the readers might have to hierarchy for its own sake. To accomplish this end, they appeal to their readers' higher devotion to the king. In the dedicatory epistle to his *Letany,* Bastwick contends that he, his wife, and his children have been suffering great hardships "for my maintaining the religion established by publick author-ity, & the Kings most excellent maietys prerogatiue royall" (sigs. A2v, A3). In fact, he continues, the prelates' cry of "no Bishop, no King" is an affront to Charles, implying that he rules by their grace rather than they by his. *Jure divino* Bastwick defines as "one of the solecisms of the Beast," urging all God-loving people to force the prelates away from the king, since many monarchies have been ruined by bishops.

Newes makes similar accusations of treason, noting that Laud and his fellows, by altering the Prayer and Fast Books, "robbed [Charles] both of [his] Gods and peoples loves, and pulled [his] Crowne off [his] Royall head, to set it on their own trayterous, ambitious pats, by exercising all ecclesiasticall power, yea Papall jurisdiction over [his] Subjects in their own names, and rights alone" (sig. A4v). *Newes* reminds its readers that the king has issued two declarations in which he promises to allow no innova-tions, idolatry, or errors. Thus, the prelates defy their sovereign's explicit orders and bring the wrath of God on England, evident in the visitation of the plague.

Burton makes his *Apology* directly to the king, pleading for help to defend himself against the prelates, who are accusing him of seditious preaching. Referring to himself as a "faithfull and vigilant Servant," Bur-ton reminds both his readers and the king that the prelates commit innova-tions against laws, statutes, and royal proclamations (sig. A3). As *Newes* and Bastwick do, he stresses the nature of the prelates' actions—all, as he sees them, defying basic principles of English ecclesiastical and civil law. All three set the king above the bishops and imply that the prelates aspire to invert the order of both lay and church government. The pamphleteers thus present themselves as truly patriotic and religious, their opponents ambitious and proud.

In characterizing the changes in the worship service as foreign and dangerous, the pamphleteers deliberately invoke Foxe, equating their mis-sion with his. In criticizing the Book of Sports, *A Divine Tragedie Lately Acted* is also modeled on Foxe. Like the *Book of Martyrs*, it is chiefly a catalog of examples of God's punishment of Sabbath-breakers. Moreover, the intro-duction to *Divine Tragedie* discusses what it holds to be traditional English practice by quoting and describing the *Book of Martyrs* and drawing analo-gies between contemporary events and the Marian persecutions. Through this historical survey, bolstered by Foxe, *Divine Tragedie* argues that the bishops traditionally opposed recreation on the Sabbath. Further, it lists two statutes, two acts, and numerous homilies, articles, injunctions, and canons, as well as the Book of Common Prayer, in support of its position and indicates that both James and Charles believed the plague to be a punishment for Sabbath-breaking (sigs. A2v–A4). The prelates themselves seem to confirm the threat to the country, prohibiting sermons on the fast day in London, its suburbs, and other infested areas. Like Foxe, *Newes* agrees with *Divine Tragedie* in seeing foreign influence at work, contending that these activities prove the prelates "desperate Archagents for the Divell, and the Pope of *Rome*" (sigs. A2v–A3).

Bastwick proposes that it is time for a new *Book of Martyrs* to record the latest challenge to God's church. As he sees contemporary events,

> It seeme they would faine be at their old occupation againe, a butchering of vs at smithfield; and that is the thing indeed which their feirce and bloud-thirsty ambition aspires to; for why otherwise should they make such complaints in publicke, and vse such expressions? Without doubt, if they had once obtayned their desire in that, they would then make as great hauock of the Church of God as euer bloody Bonner or Gardinier did. (sig. A4)

Using this perspective, Bastwick and the others can suggest that opposition to the bishops reflects traditional English patriotism, while Laud's innovations foreshadow brutality and danger to the freedom of the English people—another reign of Bloody Mary. The pamphleteers thus proclaim themselves new Foxes with an equally serious commitment to their faith.

In support of their arguments, these pamphleteers draw another technique from the *Book of Martyrs* by presenting vivid pictures of the new rituals and the bishops' behavior, carefully calculated to disgust an English reader—especially one of Puritan inclinations. In the mildest of the pamphlets, Burton declares that the bishops attempt to silence him to prevent his preaching against Arminianism. He catalogs their objectionable practices, all smacking of Catholicism—changing communion tables into altars, bowing to them, putting crucifixes on them, banning sermons on Sunday afternoons, and asking the catechism without explaining the meaning of the answers (sig. A2v). To this list of grievances, Bastwick adds the bishops' requirement that their parishioners perform "CAPPING, DVCKING, STANDING AND KNEELING" while church officials note failures to conform (sig. C2).

Both Bastwick and *Divine Tragedie* decry the eviction from their livings of ministers (including Burton) who refuse to comply with the innovations, while *Divine Tragedie* sees in the Book of Sports a plot "to teach inferiours rebellion to their Superiours, and in a word hasten the pulling down of vengeance from heaven upon the Land" (sig. Fv). The pamphleteers use the bishops' behavior as proof of these suspicions. According to *Newes,* Bishop Pocklington "boast[ed]" that bishops were *"lineally descended"* from the pope (sig. A4). Burton concentrates on the persecution of ministers by the ecclesiastical courts, which distort established legal procedures in order to attack their enemies. If the standard forms do not apply to a victim, charges Burton, the ecclesiastical lawyers "put in Additionals, and Additionals upon Additionals contrary to the course of Iustice in all other your Majesties Courts within the Realme" (sig. B3).

Fusing Foxe's self-conscious, committed narrator with the martyr he describes, Burton cites irregular procedures in his own case—the appearance before a single commissioner at a private house; the exclusion of Burton's friends from the hearing; the ex officio oath forced upon him; his suspension; and the charge of sedition, which is not an ecclesiastical offense and therefore beyond the jurisdiction of the Court of High Commission, which had been trying him (sigs. B3v–C). Bastwick recalls Foxe's vivid descriptions when he attacks Laud. He envisions the archbishop on his way to the Star Chamber, accompanied by men who clear his way by pushing children and women aside and knocking stalls of produce into the river: "The noyse of the Gentleme*n* crying roome, & cursing all that meet them . . . & on the other side seeing the wayling mourning and Lamentation the women make crying out saue my puddings, save my codlings for the Lords sake, the poore tripes and apples in the meane tyme swimming like frogs about the Thames making way for his Grace to goe home againe" (sig. A4v).

Above all, these pamphleteers make themselves the chief focus of their complaints. Burton and Bastwick explicitly discuss themselves, while *Newes* and *Divine Tragedie* echo Foxe with their vigorous, individualistic narration. Each author presents his story as only an example of a pattern of episcopal abuses. Each writer relies on his audience to recognize and understand his method so that each reader will see the greater significance of the illustration. Sincerity is the principal proof of rightness. Bastwick depicts himself "In *Limbo Patrum,*" dying of a fever, and begging his jailer to release him to see his wife and children. Coming from a fever, his words are visionary. Hence, he writes "Limbo Rhetorick" to "vindicate my liberty" and to "demonstrate, that those whom you terme reuerend fathers, and the apostles successors, deserve no such magnificant titles" (sig. B2v).

Burton makes a similar plea. His pamphlet addresses the king, declaring that, since Burton has been denied justice in every other quarter, he must appeal "unto Cesar. *And blessed bee God, that I have such a Christian Cesar to appeale unto*" (i–ii). As part of his effort to clear his name, Burton warns Charles (and readers) that he writes in self-defense, hoping that the prelates "will . . . excuse me, when they shall reflect upon how they have provoked mee, by their calling mee forth upon the stage, and by their strange molesting, and prosecuting of me, as if I were a fellon, or a traitor" (iii). Just as Foxe reports on the trials of his martyrs, so Burton lists the actions against him, framing his tract as a formal appeal, describing in detail the nature and date of each abuse and the reasons such abuses violate his rights as an Englishman. These reasons justify an address to the king as symbol and arbiter of the law.

Their words, rendered in familiar form, made Bastwick, Burton, and Prynne popular heroes before their lives imitated their art. Their sentence merely added weight to their status as martyrs. On June 30, 1637, an observer recorded, tremendous crowds gathered "with tender affections to behold those three renowned soldiers and servants of Jesus Christ, who came with most undaunted and magnanimous courage [to the pillory], having their way strawed with sweet herbs . . . with all the honour that could be done unto them." Speaking from the pillory, Bastwick defined the potential power of the printed word: "If the presses were as open to us as they formerly have been, we would shatter [Laud's] kingdom about his ears."[14] Bastwick's words took root in the minds of many opponents of both Laud and the king. Fittingly, in the days before Charles's attempt to arrest the Five Members, Parliament discussed an "Act for the reversing of the illegall proceedings in the starre-chamber" against Laud's victims.

The fame and impact of these pamphleteers would have been impossible without their writings. Others had publicly suffered before, many Puritans and writers, but rarely had any been greeted with the reception accorded Bastwick, Burton, and Prynne. Such a response came from an audience prepared by its culture to value certain kinds of conduct and interpretation. The pamphleteers benefited from their ability to make their protests in culturally acceptable ways. In their writings were enough parallels to Foxe and conventional political discourse to insure wide appeal. They could make their arguments—and thus themselves—part of an already existing rhetorical community. As a result, their audience was predisposed to give them a favorable hearing.

14. Nehemiah Wallington, "Historical Notices," 47–48; in the second quotation the pronoun *his* may refer to either Laud or the pope.

The pamphleteers' rhetorical stance proved to be one of the most effective of the revolution. The monarchists would put it to amazingly successful use in *Eikon Basilike*. Ironically, Prynne's publication of Laud's journal elicited sympathy for the archbishop during his trial, providing the ethos he sorely needed in 1637.[15] In that year, however, Laud revealed little capacity for introspection. Nor did he understand the necessity of reaching the audience outside his circle of power. The speech he delivered in the Star Chamber—when seen in conjunction with the pamphleteers' works—marks him as rigid, vindictive, and self-righteous. His public stance intensified his reputation for arbitrary cruelty and confirmed the accusations against him.

Although he had his speech printed, understanding some need to reach beyond court circles, Laud addresses the king as a fellow ruler and dismisses the criticism of his adversaries.[16] Ignoring the fact that most of the pamphleteers' attacks consist of bitter commentary on his own and other bishops' arrogant and pontifical behavior, Laud singles out for his response the complaints against "innovations" in the worship service, especially those in *Newes*—charges that he can easily refute before a sympathetic audience. By refusing to answer the more significant accusations, however, he fails to justify himself to the growing audience of critics outside of Westminster. Ultimately, by addressing only his own party, Laud loses the ability to evaluate the power of his challengers or understand the fragility of his own position. Reasoned, balanced, and articulate as his speech may be, its tone and his insistence on points of theology reveal his detachment from the fears of his opponents' audience. He refuses to join their community.

Laud begins the printed version of his speech with an epistle dedicated to the king. In the beginning of the epistle, the archbishop identifies his interests with Charles's, remarking that he goes to print only at the king's command, at inconvenience to himself. Further, he asks for royal protection from those who will inevitably write against his speech. Laud argues that the pamphleteers attack the king through the bishops and try to alienate the people's natural loyalty. He comments, "I must humbly beseech your Majesty to consider that 'tis not we only, that is, the Bishops,

15. Lamont, *Marginal Prynne*, 119–38.

16. William Laud, "A Speech Delivered in the Starre-Chamber at the Censure of J. Bastwick, etc.," in *The Works of the Most Reverend Father in God, William Laud, D.D.: Sometime Lord Archbishop of Canterbury* 6.1. According to the *Short Title Catalogue*, the speech was printed three times in 1637.

that are struck at, but, through our sides, your Majesty, your honour, your safety, your religion, is impeached" (38).

In what proves to be a prophetic vein, he indicates that a king cannot retain the love of his people if he allows changes in their religion or permits his bishops to do so. Without mentioning the question of *jure divino* powers, Laud threatens his opposition in words that royalists would echo in 1649—he reminds readers that blaspheming God and slandering his anointed king are "joined together." Here, Laud attempts to deflect his opponents' attack and make it hit the king, denying its relevance to himself by simply ignoring its particulars. He challenges their initial and crucial premise—that the bishops as a group are separate from the king—by issuing a flat statement to the contrary.

Having shifted the subject of his epistle from a defense of himself to a defense of the king, Laud concludes by clearing the "three professions" of law, divinity, and medicine of suspicions of disloyalty and praising Charles's "clemency," "since . . . you might have justly called the offenders into another court, and put them to it in a way that might have exacted their lives, for their stirring . . . of mutiny and sedition" (40). He finally warns Charles that even the best governments need to change when threatened by disaffected individuals who urge "a parity in the Church or commonwealth." According to Laud, then, he and the other bishops are not the true targets of Bastwick's, Burton's, and Prynne's writings. He suggests that the pamphleteers conceal treasonous intent when they attack *jure divino* episcopacy.

Subtly, without responding to the pamphleteers' accusations, Laud manipulates the assumptions of *jure humano* powers. If the pamphleteers believe in *jure humano* themselves, then they must surely believe that the bishops are merely agents of the king. Therefore, they must believe that "superstitious" changes in religion result from the king's pleasure. Thus, charges Laud, his opponents directly challenge the head of the church—the king—by implying that he wishes to betray his people to a foreign power, the pope. In this context, Laud's own behavior and that of his bishops mean nothing, *jure divino* episcopacy protects religion, and charges of innovation are treasonous.

His patriotism established by the prefatory letter, Laud can appear as the defender of both God and king against three petty, misguided malcontents. He commits a logical fallacy here—shifting the grounds of argument—and his explication of the ramifications of *jure humano* strikes one as sophistry. He intends to show absurdity in the other side's accusations, but he runs the risk of having unsympathetic readers see trickery and a suggestion of insincerity in his words when compared to the forthrightness of his opponents. Sensing their popularity, Laud denies their apparent kinship with Christian martyrs. The martyrs, he declares, never "libel[ed] the governors" of the church (41).

Ranking himself with King David and Saint Jerome, Laud makes his own claims for martyrdom by affirming his determination to withstand the accusations against him and to be proud of doing good by upholding the worship services of the church. He and all bishops, he says, merely maintain traditions established in "the Apostles' times" by claiming their calling *jure divino.* Moreover, bishops are confirmed "both in their power and means, by Act of Parliament," so that any challenge to a bishop's actions is a criticism of the laws of England. Yet the English people, always zealous in their love of their religion, are not uniformly educated about the traditions of worship and governance within their church. The three pamphleteers, in their desire to cause sedition, exploit their readers' ignorance and zeal by writing vicious lies about the bishops and alluding constantly to "Romish superstition." In so doing, they hurt the king and jeopardize the safety of the church, about which they express so much concern (42–43).

In a model of the forensic genre, Laud offers a point-by-point refutation of the substance of his opponents' arguments. Appealing to statutes and history, sometimes resorting to ridicule, he evaluates separately each charge of innovation that appears in *Newes* with an occasional glance at Burton's and Bastwick's works. In each case, Laud states the charge, explains why it is groundless, and maligns the motives of the one who made it.

Against the accusations concerning changes in the Prayer and Fast Books during that season, Laud responds that the elimination of sermons during the plague—although indeed contrary to normal practice in a fast—was ordered by the king's council to prevent the spread of infection. Changes in prayers were ordered left to the discretion of local ministers. Several changes in the practice of worship were not recent innovations, but traditions standing since Elizabeth's time. As for the change of "in the name of Jesus every knee shall bow" to "at the name . . ." Laud simply derides suspicions that it was counter to the act of Parliament: "This can make no innovation. For 'in the name,' and 'at the name of Jesus,' can make no essential difference here. And Mr. Pryn (whose darling business it hath long been to cry down the honour due to the Son of God, at the mention of His saving name Jesus) knows the grammar rule well, 'In a place, or at a place' " (51).

After a series of similar refutations, the archbishop ends by briefly giving thanks to the members of the Star Chamber for their sympathy for him and excusing himself from personally censuring the defendants, since they have singled him out for abuse. The refutation is a reductio ad absurdum of not only the pamphleteers' but also many readers' concerns. The explanations of church practices are insignificant, since to the readers tradition is whatever they remember or think they remember. And the question remains: If "in the name" and "at the name" are synonymous, then why was the phrase changed? Laud's response to the accusations is logical and rational but fails in emotional impact.

Laud's prefatory letter and speech attempt to unite king and bishops in the public mind by appealing to patriotism and deference to authority. Taken objectively, his reasoning is persuasive, and yet in each answer to a charge of "innovation" he addresses facts rather than the fears of his audience. Prayers for the navy and protection against superstitious practices may indeed have no tradition or law to uphold them. Nevertheless, in an atmosphere of growing official tolerance for ritual and Arminian clergy, people did have grounds for fearing what they perceived to be alterations in public religious policy. Laud's suggestion that the English people were ignorant and needed to be guided was not likely to win over a person who had recently read Bastwick's or Prynne's descriptions of "lordly" prelates who wish to control parishioners as a Roman Catholic priest leads his flock. The archbishop's attempts to discredit the pamphleteers' sincerity fail horribly in the face of both their previous suffering and their later conduct on the pillory. While it convinced the already converted, Laud's speech did nothing to stop the burgeoning opposition to both himself and the entire court party.

The archbishop and the pamphleteers speak different languages and address separate audiences. Nothing in Laud's speech effectively answers the charges against him. Logical, self-assured, and contemptuous of his accusers, he ignores their pivotal argument—that he himself is the source of all the disturbances in church and state. His logical fallacy of shifting the grounds of argument by concentrating on the king proves to be a rhetorical miscalculation. To have his speech succeed, Laud needs to convince readers that his analysis of the nature of the pamphleteers' charges is correct. But the three men have effectively undermined his credibility—his ethos—for large numbers of readers. Laud does not know how many.

For his own supporters, Laud presents an adequate response. Knowing and agreeing with him, they do not question his motives because they believe his interpretation from the outset. The audience of the printed speech is another question, however. To this group, Laud has become a hated symbol of pride, arbitrary rule, and wickedness—a symbol outlined and dramatized in the pamphlets of Bastwick, Burton, and Prynne. Laud shifts the grounds of argument—the pamphleteers have warned that he is tricky. He makes a joke at Prynne's expense—they have said that he is arrogant. He offers legal proof that the charges are false—they have suggested that he and his party misuse the law. He condemns the three men to the pillory—they have argued that he is vindictive and cruel. Every action he takes confirms those readers' suspicions. To this audience, he needs to humble himself, confess possible errors, and declare his dedication to their values. Instead, Laud gambles on their weakness and insignificance, and he eventually loses.

The rhetoric of 1637 reveals several points that will recur in my discussion of the revolution. Even before the king actually raised his standard, English public discourse had bifurcated. We find in 1637 two distinct audiences with different kinds of discourse. One is the audience immediately concerned with a particular matter—in this case, the Star Chamber. The other audience is the larger political community—one that includes not only voters and elected officials but also anyone who follows public life, reads or listens to pamphlets, or participates in public spectacles and demonstrations. More and more, it was the latter community that needed to be addressed and persuaded.

For this latter community, the tradition of public discourse established by Foxe proved in 1637 to be integrative. Diverse members of this amorphous group responded favorably to writers employing aspects of Foxe's rhetoric. It drew them together in common agreement, whether the readers were anonymous members of the group that watched the pamphleteers on the pillory or the members of Parliament who introduced bills for their relief. The combining of private "confession" with public issues produced powerfully persuasive arguments—a point that royalists would remember in 1649.

Laud's signal failure was his misjudgment of audience. By publishing his speech, he attempted to reach a larger group, but the rhetorical techniques—and, indeed, the principal genre—he selected effectively eliminated broad, popular appeal. By choosing forensic rhetoric, he chose a genre recognized by both Cicero and seventeenth-century rhetoricians to be essentially private in nature. The audience of such rhetoric must share the fundamental assumptions of the speaker or writer. The members of the

Star Chamber were such an audience, but they were not the ones who needed persuading; the political community could not be safely presumed to share the convictions of the Star Chamber. The two groups constituted separate discourse communities. Employing the discourse of one inevitably marginalized the writer with the other. Such a problem would reappear for Milton and other radical pamphleteers in 1649 and again in the years 1659 and 1660.

In rhetorical battles such as this one, victory belonged to those whose understanding of their audience led them to integrative discourse. Bastwick's, Burton's, and Prynne's understanding of their conflict enabled them to move a large general audience. Laud's did not. In 1642, addressing an event in Parliament, writers on both sides of the issue addressed the same audience. Yet, within that boundary, fundamental differences in the pamphleteers' ways of perceiving their government and the roles of its officers led them to diverge in their methods of argumentation. And, ominously, this difference in discourse appeared not between two communities—a court party and a group of religious dissenters—but within one, the center of the political nation.

THREE

1642: King and Parliament

On November 22, 1641, the great list of complaints against the crown known as the Grand Remonstrance passed the House of Commons by the margin of only eleven votes. Supporters of the king believed they saw the coming dissolution of their opposition. Yet, in fewer than two months, Charles was to flee London with his family and the first civil war was to begin. Between the adoption of the Grand Remonstrance and January 10, 1642, the date he abandoned Whitehall, Charles committed several major blunders that alienated many of his followers, not only in the two houses of Parliament but also in the city of London.

The defection of the citizens, beginning in December 1641, enabled parliamentary leader John Pym to regroup his party and finally, on January 5, 1642, saved Pym, four other members of the House of Commons, and Viscount Mandeville from the king's last attempt before the outbreak of the war to regain the powers he had been steadily losing since the first assembly of the Long Parliament. This action of the king, rapidly named the attempt on the Five Members, was the last in a series of episodes that galvanized Londoners into an opposition that marked a significant departure from previous political conflicts. As Perez Zagorin remarks, "The intervention that preserved the revolution was the work of the politically conscious populace, not of the civic government."[1] The political consciousness of the citizens was both reflected and encouraged by the hoards of anonymous pamphleteers unleashed by the abolition of the Star Chamber. The credit for establishing the attempt on the Five Members as a pivotal event in the revolution largely belongs to those pamphleteers. Empowered by print and through symbolically significant political demonstration, they determined the conventions of common political discourse at the beginning of the revolutionary debate.

1. *The Court and the Country: The Beginnings of the English Revolution*, 282.

The attempt on the Five Members came at the end of two weeks of intense activity in court, Parliament, and city, beginning on December 21, 1641, with the election to the London Common Council of men favorably disposed toward the Puritan opposition. Fearing the London mobs, Charles appointed the unpopular royalist Sir Thomas Lunsford as lieutenant of the Tower of London and answered the Grand Remonstrance, supporting the rights of the bishops to sit in the House of Lords. Six days later, Charles bowed to pressure and replaced Lunsford while the Commons received news from Ireland that the king was laying plans for Catholic toleration. A mob attacked Westminster. On the following day, the twenty-eighth, most of the bishops absented themselves from the House of Lords while, as Clarendon recalls, "many dissolute and profane people went into the abbey at Westminster, and would have pulled down the organs and some ornaments of the church; but being resisted, and by force driven out, they threatened they would come with greater numbers, and pull down the church."[2]

Under these circumstances, a motion was presented in the Lords declaring that Parliament was not free; that is, not free to deliberate and vote since it was under threat of mob violence. This action provoked suspicion in the Commons, since similar tensions between the two houses had developed during the trial of Strafford the previous spring. Although the motion failed by four votes on the twenty-ninth, the bishops kept the issue alive by protesting to the king their right to sit in the House of Lords and urging that he register the protest. He did so the next day, thereby challenging the authority and independence of the Lords, which then joined with the Commons to impeach the twelve bishops who had signed the protest.[3]

On December 31, the Commons adjourned until January 3 and resolved to meet in the interim as a committee of the whole at Guildhall, where it was decided to impeach the queen. In anticipation of this move, George, Lord Digby, suggested that Charles impeach the impeachers, selecting as the leaders John Pym, John Hampden, Denzil Holles, Sir Arthur Haslerigg, and William Strode. Consulting with only the attorney general, Sir Edward Herbert, the king and Digby added to the list Viscount Mandeville, referred to in the documents of impeachment by his title, Lord

2. *History of the Rebellion and Civil Wars in England Begun in the Year 1641*, 4:113. All references to Clarendon in this chapter are to vol. 4, and will hereafter be cited in the text by page numbers.

3. Valerie Pearl, *London and the Outbreak of the Puritan Revolution: City Government and National Politics, 1625–1643*, 109, 112–46.

Kimbolton. When Parliament reassembled on January 3, Herbert presented the impeachment to the Lords, who, asked to sacrifice one of their own number, opposed it. Meanwhile, in the Commons, Pym, Holles, and Hampden revealed that their studies, trunks, and private papers had been sealed, declaring this action to be a breach of parliamentary privilege. The sergeant at arms, under the king's order, attempted to arrest the Five Members, whereupon the Commons refused to yield them, and the members of the Lords stated that the action usurped their right to order arrests. The Lords then ordered the seals on the members' studies to be broken and joined the Commons' request for a guard to be placed outside the Parliament building.

This united front prompted the king's tremendous blunder—his attempt to arrest the Five Members personally. On January 4, Charles went to Parliament accompanied by the Elector Palatine and three to four hundred armed men, eighty of whom followed the king and prince into the lobby of the Commons. His targets having escaped before his arrival, the king quickly left, but not before his retinue had made threatening gestures toward the assembly. These actions horrified the members. Sir Simonds D'Ewes believed

> the designe was to have taken out of our Howse by force and violence the saied five members if wee had refused to have delivered them upp peaceblie and willinglie which for the preservation of the priviledges of our howse wee must have refused. And in the taking of them away, they weere to have sett upon us all if wee had resisted in an hostile manner. It is verie true that the plott was soe contrived as that the King should have withdrawen out of the howse and passed thorough the lobbie or little roome next without it before the massacre should have begunn upon his passing thorough them: but tis most likely that those Ruffians . . . being armed all of them with swords and some of them with pistols, readie charged were soe thirstie after innocent bloud as they would scarce have staied the watchword if those members had been ther but would have begunn ther violence assoon as they had understood of our deniall.[4]

With this action, the king lost not only the support of Parliament but also the loyalty of the City of London. Cries of "privilege of Parliament" answered Charles the next day when he went to Guildhall to arrest the Five Members. By January 7, when Charles proclaimed the six impeached men

4. *The Journal of Sir Simonds D'Ewes from the First Recess of the Long Parliament to the Withdrawal of King Charles from London*, 382–83.

guilty of treason, the Commons' committee of the whole had voted that the impeachment was illegal. The lord mayor of London—himself a supporter of the king—refused to have Charles's proclamation read in the city.[5]

The following days, from the eighth to the eleventh, brought consolidation of the opposition, largely accomplished through symbolic acts and the printed word. On the tenth, during the meeting of the committee of the whole in which the popular Philip Skippon was appointed sergeant major general of the Trained Bands, several delegations representing various groups made formal offers of support to Parliament. The seamen and mariners declared that they would defend the houses of Parliament. The men of Southwark volunteered to guard their own side of the Thames. The apprentices asked to march as a group in the next day's procession, whereupon they were assigned to guard the city of London. Clarendon notes that the impeached member John Hampden announced the impending arrival of a protest march composed of several thousand of his constituents from Buckinghamshire carrying with them petitions in defense of the Five Members (200). These petitioners met the returning members at the House of Commons the next day.

The return was a spectacle. The members traveled by water, accompanied by a decorated fleet of small boats and followed on land by the Trained Bands. The printed word figured prominently in the march as well. Clarendon remembers:

> There was one circumstance not to be forgotten in the march of the city that day, . . . that the pikemen had fastened to the tops of their pikes, and the rest in their hats or their bosoms, printed papers of the Protestation which had been taken and enjoined by the House of Commons the year before for the defence of the privilege of parliament; and many of them had the printed votes of the King's breaking their privileges in his coming to the House and demanding their members. (199)

As never before, printed pamphlets would play a role in political conflict.

The pamphlets brought to the reading public the debate occurring at the center of the political nation. There, each side—royalist and parliamentarian—struggled to establish its interpretation as the true version of the conflict between the king and Parliament. As both sides surely knew, the one that prevailed would win more than a rhetorical victory. That side could have all subsequent debate framed in its terms and consequently hold the upper hand in any argument. Also, since language forms thought,

5. Godfrey Davies, *The Early Stuarts, 1603–1660,* 118–23.

the winners could define not only what it was possible to say but also what it was possible to think. In one way or other, the conventions established in the pamphlet wars of the early 1640s governed the political language of the revolution.

The documents of the Thomason Collection reveal that in 1642 the pamphleteers responding to the attempt on the Five Members chose forms that conveyed legitimacy by allying the writers to the established discourse of the political community—petitions, public declarations, and parliamentary speeches. The petitions are from several counties and groups, and they protest to the king his treatment of the Five Members. The declarations include reproductions of the Articles of High Treason brought by the king against the members, formal questions of the Commons to the attorney general, and declarations of support for the members. The greatest number of tracts, however, are "separates"—copies of individual speeches purportedly delivered in Parliament.[6] Most of those dated between January and March 1642 are attributed to the Five Members and Mandeville—two to Denzil Holles, one each to the others. Finally, one tract is the published speech of the king himself.

Except for the king's speech of January 4, all the separates follow the form of a parliamentary speech. They address "Mr. Speaker," consider the deliberations of the Commons and events unfolding outside, and urge a course of action. All break into very definite sections and most are written in plain, declarative sentences. Some offer motions. Most cover no more than six printed quarto pages. Underlying each tract are the questions of the proper relationship between the king and Parliament, the rightness of both sides' impeachments, and the best means of dealing with the current crisis.

The multiple purposes of the separates make them difficult to classify generically. All speakers urge a course of action, whether conciliation or resistance. This end suggests that the pamphlets have a primarily deliberative nature. Appropriate to this genre are the themes of devotion to

6. Samuel Rawson Gardiner, *History of England from the Accession of James I to the Outbreak of the Civil War, 1603–1642*, 10:135, argues conclusively from internal evidence that the speeches attributed to the Five Members and Mandeville are written by somebody else and circulated in their names. The British Museum's *Catalogue of the Pamphlets, Books, Newspapers, and Manuscripts Relating to the Civil War, the Commonwealth, and Restoration, Collected by George Thomason, 1640–1661* attributes these pamphlets to anonymous authors.

country and criticism of alternate solutions, both of which appear regularly in the separates. Borrowing from the epideictic genre to praise or blame individual persons as part of a call to action suits the deliberative end. Defense and accusation of the members and the king necessarily form a major part of the arguments of each separate.

The particular circumstances, however, make additional demands on the speech. The king produces Articles of Impeachment and accuses the Five Members of high treason. In response, and to gain support of readers, the members must refute the charges and defend themselves. Hence, these speeches also borrow two important aspects of the forensic oration—the formal refutation and the attention to definitions. Four of the speeches examined below—those attributed to Pym, Haslerigg, Mandeville, and Strode—list all the articles and refute them point by point, either by claiming the action was justified or by denying that it was treasonous. One speech—Haslerigg's—continues to answer the charges by declaring lack of treasonous intent, a defense typically reserved for criminal trials.

In all these speeches, the insistence on defining enemies and actions points to legal precedent. Which version of the event will the judge or jury accept? Did the defendant commit an offense? If so, what kind was it? In effect, the audience is placed in the position of jury. It must evaluate the validity of the charges and the culpability of the members. But the audience performs a deliberative function as well—it must decide which course of action to follow. To agree to support the cause of the Five Members (a deliberative end) a reader must first agree that they are innocent of the charges against them (a forensic end). The use of both genres together draws the reader into the argument and involves him in the writer's outrage and protest.

Both sides represented in the pamphlets employ the same genres. The common forms of discourse indicate that the writers share the same basic understanding of the political nation. Royalists and monarchists alike assume that they can invite their readers to deliberate about current events and evaluate the innocence or guilt of the Five Members. Each writer seeks to redefine the chief issues within the existing formal structure of government and society. To succeed in doing so is to gain legitimacy for one's position. From that point onward, any statement of that position will appear natural and right. It will have become the conventional expression of certain political ideas. Furthermore, any argument employing those conventions will have power beyond its mere words. Present in the arguments defending the Five Members is language that eventually would enable both the execution of Charles I and—ironically—the restoration of Charles II.

The issue at stake in the controversy over the Five Members is the fundamental question of primacy: which comes first—king or Parliament? In the pamphlets, two visions of order compete for the sympathies of the audience. The debate centers on the definition of national enemies, the nature of English kingship, and the nature of parliaments. While both are yet within the bounds of traditional discourse, the languages of royalists and parliamentarians diverge enough to prevent ready seeking of common grounds.

The principal focus of debate in these tracts is the nature of the enemy. Who is responsible for the present discord between king and Parliament? Sir Edward Hales, member for Queenborough and supporter of the king, describes opponents of royal policy as deliberate spreaders of discord. Together, he argues, Parliament and the king have recently settled many of the problems, religious and political, that had been facing the kingdom. For reasons unknown, however, some oppose these achievements.

The opponents, by "subtle and wily practices," have "sofarre prevailed that they have raised such distempers and distractions in the State that laying aside the former affayres we had in hand, we have beene forced against our desires and reall intentions to certifie all things amisse both in Church and State, to bend all our endeavours to prevent eminent danger now in agitation both against the Parliament and the whole State, and to remove the impediments that have hindered the same."[7] Attempting to minimize the current crisis, Hales links present troubles with "impediments," diminishing their importance and suggesting that they are serious but momentary blocks to the normal flow of business in the Commons, the regulation of great matters of Church and State. Rhetorically, Hales unites himself and his faction to the idea of the well-ordered state ruled by the king through the power he justly wields. He turns his opponents into an isolated clique of obstructionists, not serious critics of royal policy.

The opposition accepts the essential message of Hales's speech—that there is a group of men allied to the king and supporting his actions. These writers, however, see great danger in this alliance. The king has been acting malevolently, they charge, but he does so only because he bases his decisions upon the "informations of ill minded persons, buzzing in his Maj-

7. Sir Edward Hales, in his speech annexed to *To the Kings most Excellent Majestie: The Humble Petition . . . Glocester,* sig. A4. Full titles and Thomason Catalogue numbers of pamphlets may be found in the Bibliography.

esties eares." They are "disaffected Spirits" who have misled the House into giving them high honors, proof that they are self-serving and ambitious.[8] "Delinquents and Malefactors in the State," the "evill Councillors" wish in fact to subvert the laws of the land. The common laws and acts of Parliament depend upon each other, so "he that breaks the Priviledges of the one, subverts the other." Parliament thwarts the designs of "dissolute and disaffected persons" who must in turn try to influence the King to use his power in their favor. "Under the colour of Loyalty," this faction commits "flat abuses" against the country.

As an example, the parliamentarian pamphleteers present the case of attorney general Herbert, leader of the royalists. He is respected because of his position. He did not need to be "ambitious, or malitious," but "his heart was not right." Indeed, this personal quality characterizes all the defenders of the king. Pretending to be disinterested, they attack the members of Parliament who are most likely to vote against them, "but their hearts disagreeing with their outward qualities, being not upright and perfect, have at least shewed themselves in their perfect colours, and brought themselves to shame and dishonour."[9]

The parliamentarian writers see their opponents as simply using the pretense of supporting royal prerogative to attack the rights, privileges, and actions of Parliament. The royalists therefore jeopardize the rights and liberties of all subjects. While Hales defines the source of the troubles as self-serving malcontents stirring up the state, the parliamentarians see self-serving malcontents using the king to destroy it. They believe that the king's party puts pretended loyalty to Charles above real loyalty to the state so that the party itself separates and isolates him from his people. For this reason, the royalists must be stopped. Otherwise, such royalists "will incourage ill affected Cavaliers and Commanders about the Court, to attempt any mischief against both Houses of Parliament or particular members thereof, upon the least opportunity that shall be offered them, thinking thereby they shall doe the King good service."[10]

8. *Master Hollis His Speech . . . January,* sig. A3v; *Master Hollis His Speech . . . March,* sig. A3. The remaining quotations in the paragraph come from *Sir Arthur Haslerigg His Speech in Parliament,* sigs. A3, A2v; and *Right Honourable the Lord Kimbolton His Speech in Parliament,* sig. A3v.

9. *Mr. Glyn, His Speech in Parliament,* sigs. A3–A3v; *Master Hollis His Speech . . . March,* sig. A3v.

10. *Right Honourable the Lord Kimbolton His Speech in Parliament,* sig. A3v. See also *Mr. Glyn, His Speech in Parliament,* sigs. A3–A3v.

An ominous note sounds in the last statement. Already, certain writers affirm that the royal party tries to please the king by hurting Parliament. These efforts suggest to them that Charles himself wishes Parliament hurt. In their attempts to characterize the "evil persons," both sides reveal their assumptions about the true nature of current events. Both divide king from country and king from Parliament, acknowledging the rift between the two. The chief difference between the two groups lies in the perception each has of the proper relationship between king and Parliament. Royalists define the country as the king, aided by Parliament, while parliamentarians see the Parliament as the embodiment of the country.

To counteract the royalist vision, the parliamentarian writers offer their own interpretation of the political nation. They characterize it as the interrelationship of God, King, and Country. The principal function of Parliament, they note, is to defend God—that is, the Church of England, "without which we are nothing, being no lesse then meer Atomes to the World, and the just Antipothes to a ground Faith." Next comes the king. Good men owe "loyalty and due subjection to their soveraigne, in their affection towards the safety of their Country." Country is defined as the laws made by the king and the House of Lords "with the free consent of his great Councell of State, assembled in Parliament." All three are interrelated. If God and king are disturbed, there is discord in the country. The principal obligation of Parliament is the service of God, King, and Country to redress grievances in church and state and to punish those who attempt to disaffect the king from his people and make innovations in religion. As commanded by Scripture, the goal of Parliament should be peace.[11]

The good member of Parliament protects king and country, defends the dignity of the crown, and maintains religion. Denial of these duties is "one signe of an evill and bad Subject." Another sign is to obey the king against the dictates of religion and the law. Since duty to God comes first, the good subject must refuse to obey a king who commands against religion. But because rebellion is as the sin of witchcraft, he must endure the consequences of the prince's "displeasure" while "submitting willingly, cheerefully himselfe and his cause to Almighty God." Subjects must offer passive resistance. In fact, this resistance confirms the subject's loyalty and Christianity.

11. From *Master Hollis His Speech . . . March*, sig. A2v; *A Discreet and Learned Speech*, sigs. A2v, A3; *Right Honourable the Lord Kimbolton His Speech in Parliament*, sig. A4; *Master Hollis His Speech . . . January*, sigs. A2v–A3.

Since Parliament defends religion and the law, those who wish to subvert it are the malignant party. They urge the king to surpass his "lawfull" power so that they may ingratiate themselves with him. By so doing, they turn the king against his country. This intent suggests treason.[12] John Glynn, recorder and member for Westminster, uses this line of reasoning in his attack on the attorney general. Glynn accuses Herbert and his party of devoting their lives to "the workes of darknesse and impurity, their desires altogether sensuall, carnall, and divelish, forgetting God, kicking and spurring with maliciousness." To save themselves from the just investigations and punishments of Parliament, Herbert and his faction commit a breach of parliamentary privilege and thereby an offense against the whole state by prejudicing the king against the Commons. Another writer argues that the malignant party intensifies the alienation of the king by refusing to go along with the majority.[13]

By carefully defining God, King, and Country, the opposition writers attempt rhetorically to put God on their side and justify particular actions. Although by law Charles is the head of the Church of England, opposition rhetoric makes the church a separate entity. Charles is also separated from the law, which becomes equated with Parliament. Both religion and law take precedence over the king, since he must himself obey God and confine his actions to his lawful powers. Violation of religion by the king or other persons threatens to unglue society, hence the significance of identifying Herbert and the supporters of the king with deviltry, immorality, and servility. Law becomes associated with Parliament and its privileges so Herbert and his associates may thus be attacked on both religious and legal grounds. Yet these writers do not urge rebellion. By arguing that malicious men turn the king against them they retain the assumption that the king himself wishes them well. Moreover, they take pains to define true loyalty so that all that they speak is a result of their desire to save religion and the country. But, by putting God and country before king, the opposition begins to drop Charles from the equation.

The king and his supporters acknowledge the power of Parliament by declaring his good intentions and his desire to preserve parliamentary privilege. They attempt to conciliate the opposition by stressing both the

12. *A Discreet and Learned Speech*, sig. A3–A3v; *Master Hollis His Speech . . . March*, sigs. A2–A2v; *A Discreet and Learned Speech*, sigs. A3v–A4; *Master Hollis His Speech . . . January*, sig. A2.

13. *A Speech Made in Parliament by Mr. Glyn*, sigs. A2v, A3; *Mr. Glyn, His Speech in Parliament*, sigs. A3, A3v; *A Discreet and Learned Speech*, sigs. A4–A4v.

king's prerogatives and his goodwill. Hales argues that Charles's declarations show his care for his country: "These Propositions . . . concerning the liberties and Priviledges of the Subject, the establishing of Religion and the indifferent use of such Ceremonies in the exercise thereof as may bee received, and used without offence, are gracious expressions of his Princely care and tender affection towards his good and loyall Subjects." In doing his duty to his people, Charles shows that he listens and responds to their concerns. A writer identified as "Sir William Wroth" also praises the king's motives. He points to a letter sent by Charles to the House of Commons and suggests that it and his other actions confirm his good intentions and demand "peace and unity among our selves." According to these writers, Charles seeks only conciliation, and the Commons ought to express "thankefulnesse" to His Majesty for his concern.[14]

The king himself chooses his language carefully while speaking to Parliament, declaring his respect for the privileges of the House of Commons and expressing his wish to conduct himself legally and fairly while asserting his own rights: "Whatsoever I have done in favour, and to the good of my Subjects, I do mean to maintain it." But Charles also asserts his own power. He insists that in the case of treason there can be no privilege. He has come "to apprehend some that by my command were accused of high Treason, whereunto I did expect Obedience, and not a Message." Therefore, as long as the Commons does not do as Charles orders, it must not be "in the right way."[15]

Already, crucial distinctions are emerging in the otherwise shared language of the king and his parliamentary opponents. Charles assumes that he possesses ultimate authority—*he* defines treason and must be obeyed. Opposition writers perceive a relationship approaching equality, in which they have the right to govern themselves without royal interference. In such a relationship, the king must bear the responsibility for the current discord. A pamphlet attributed to William Strode likens the king to the sun. As the sun's beneficence allows all living things to grow, the king's beneficence allows his kingdom to flourish. But, "by withdrawing his light being over shadowed with clouds keeps back the growing and flourishing of the creature, yea and by continuance in that his hidden

14. Hales, in his speech annexed to *To the Kings Most Excellent Majestie: The Humble Petition of . . . Glocester,* sig. A3v; *Two Speeches Spoken in Parliament,* sig. A2 (Hales), and sigs. A3–A3v (Wroth).

15. *His Majesties Speech, in the House of Commons,* sigs. A3–A4.

motion procureth at last the utter withering and perishing thereof."[16] Charles creates friction between himself and his people when he attacks their representatives in Parliament. His actions suggest "discontent and disfavour towards his People" and, as a result, they "wander in obscurity and darknesse." Although "evil counsellors" create the "discontent," Charles himself is responsible for its effects. As this writer believes, only Charles can resolve the present conflict. The king is thus the root of the problem.

While it isolates the king, opposition rhetoric identifies the Five Members with Parliament itself. This is the chief strategy the pamphleteers employ to defend the Five Members. In the speech attributed to him, "Master [John] Pym" defends himself by arguing that he always acted in and through Parliament: "Mr. Speaker, if to Vote with the *Parliament,* as a member of the House, wherin all our Votes ought to be free, it being one of the greatest priviledges thereof to have our debates, disputes, and arguments, in the same unquestionable, bee to endeavour to subvert the Fundamentall Lawes, then am I guilty of the first Article." The speeches assigned to the other four members follow the same line of reasoning. "Sir Arthur Haslerigg" argues, "In all Disputes and Conclusions of any matter by Vote of the House my Vote hath commonly agreed with the Major part then I hope my Vote in *Parliament* being free cannot be Treason." "Master Hollis" and "Master Strowd" also point out that each man has voted with the majority as loyal members of the House of Commons.[17]

The defensive strategy attempts to force the immediate audience—the other members—to consider the articles of impeachment as a collective attack on Parliament as a whole by demonstrating that the actions of the Five Members are identical to those of the body. As a consequence, it appears that "disaffected" persons are attempting to subvert an institution. "Master Hollis" underlines the seriousness of the accusation: "It is a strange thing . . . that any member elected and admitted in a free Parliament, and in the same altogether agreeing, both in debates and votes with the whole Councels of State should be accused, not onely as an ill-affected person to his King and Countrey, but as a Traitor to the same."[18] As an elected official, the member of Parliament represents not only himself but also his constituents. This point extends the argument to include the

16. *Master Strowd His Speech in Parliament,* sigs. A2, A2v.

17. *Master Pym His Speech in Parliament,* sig. A2v; *Sir Arthur Haslerigg His Speech in Parliament,* sig. A2v; *Master Hollis His Speech . . . January,* sigs. A2–A2v; *Master Strowd His Speech in Parliament,* sigs. A3–A4.

18. *Master Hollis His Speech . . . January,* sig. A2v.

general audience of readers. The articles attack individual liberties since they challenge the free votes of one's chosen representative. Defense of the Five Members by the House of Commons becomes real self-defense since by protecting itself the Commons protects the rights of all Englishmen.

Conversely, the true acts of treason must be those committed against Parliament. Real treason includes subverting the laws of the land and urging arbitrary government; treason fails to obey the decisions of Parliament, which constitute the laws. Traitors plot against Parliament, stir up resistance to it, deny its privileges, and "cast aspersions upon the same and proceedings; thereby inducing the King to think ill of the same, and to be incensed against the same, to procure the untimely dissolution and breaking off of a Parliament." In short, a traitor does not respect the integrity of Parliament.[19]

Several pamphlets list the particular instances of "breach of the priviledges of Parliament," that is, challenges to its integrity. The actions include informing the king of parliamentary proceedings before they are ready to be presented and misinforming the king of actions so that he is angered. Both breaches impair free debate and voting. Further, it is wrong to bring accusations against members or to seize them or their property without the knowledge or consent of Parliament. One must not attempt to prejudice people against members, to come into Parliament to arrest them or bring officers to arrest them, or to proclaim in the king's name that members be arrested without the knowledge or consent of Parliament. Anything less would deny the independent functioning of that body. For these reasons, "Pym" concludes, the king's accusations are "of great consequence, and much danger to the state."[20] As they appear in opposition rhetoric, the king and the state are separate entities.

Both defenders and opponents of the king strive for the power to define the issues at stake in the crisis. The side that succeeds in convincing readers to accept its definitions controls the readers' perception of the truth. Who are the "disaffected spirits"? What is treason? What is the source of the trouble between the king and Parliament? The king's party takes a traditional stance, supporting royal prerogative above parliamentary privilege and characterizing treason as disobedience to the sovereign. Opposition pamphleteers take a decisive step toward the radical discourse of the

19. *Master Stroud His Speech in Parliament*, sigs. A3–A4.
20. *A Discreet and Learned Speech*, sigs. A4–A4v; *A Speech Made in Parliament by Mr. Glyn*, sigs. A3–A4; *Master Pym His Speech in Parliament*, sigs. A4–A4v, A2.

Commonwealth, arguing that loyal countrymen support God, king, and the laws duly affirmed by Parliament. The king himself owes obedience to God and the law; therefore, the king himself may commit treason. Further, a subject may betray his country by following the king rather than God and the law. The language of the separates shows how far the common discourse of the political nation had diverged even as early as 1642. The two mutually exclusive definitions of treason deny any middle ground. There can be no compromise between groups that regard and depict each other as traitors.

The differences in language are more evident in the petitions and declarations. As collective, popular protests, the petitions frequently fuse both parliamentary discourse and the rhetoric of the Puritan opposition. Religious questions figure more prominently in these tracts than in the separates. All of these tracts are brief, often no longer than one page, and broken into sections with distinct headings. Much more formulaic than the speeches, the petitions rely on declaration and flat, undeveloped statements of purpose and, of course, contain a request. Most are directed at the king and attempt to praise while criticizing and to reaffirming the petitioners' loyalty and concern. The principal themes of the petitions—threats to religion, evil counselors, and devotion to the kingdom—reflect the speech-writers' theme of God, King, and Country. Even outside London, readers were beginning to adopt the rhetoric of the parliamentary opposition.

For their form, the petitions borrow principally from the epideictic and forensic genres. Writers and signatories must praise the individual or groups addressed and, in this case, defend themselves against charges of disloyalty or treason. The audience must be convinced of the petitioners' sincerity. Yet these petitions differ widely from the "petitory" epistles and other requests analyzed by Renaissance rhetoricians. The petitions are public documents rather than private, with three distinct audiences rather than one: the first is the one actually addressed in the petition; the second consists of those called upon to sign it; the third is the great number of potential readers of the printed version. The first and third audiences demand forensic techniques, since the petitioners hope to convince them of the honesty of their request. As in the speeches, we find pains being taken to define the enemy and clear the petitioners of suspicion. Again, the writers appropriate the power to determine what constitutes treason, disobedience, and public-spiritedness. For the second audience, however, the petitioners' task is deliberative. They must persuade this group to join with them in adopting a particular stance toward the first audience. To sign such a petition is to identify oneself with that cause. These petitions combine word and act since they are simultaneously requests and statements of protest.

Even more than the speeches, the petitions reflect their authors' fears of Roman Catholicism and resentment of the church hierarchy. One complaint maintains that the king's "poore Petitioners, and most Loyall Subjects" have been "oppressed" in their "spiritual estates" by "extreame, and unlimited power of Eclesiasticall government." In language echoing the rhetoric of Bastwick, Burton, and Prynne, the petitioners charge that the prelates have destroyed "liberty of consciences" by their actions and powers, causing the petitioners to fear for all their other liberties. Another tract recalls the Grand Remonstrance as it accuses "a malignant faction of Popish Lords, Bishops, and others" of plotting "to take from us all that little hope was left of a future Reformation." It demands that "popish Lords and Bishops may be forthwith outed the House of Peeres."[21] Readers are left to infer the specific nature of the plots and the powers of the prelates.

The open nature of these statements—their lack of definition—serves two purposes. The use of the undefined term as a strategy unifies the audience into a discourse community that possesses special understandings of particular phrases while encouraging readers to identify with the petitioners. *Religion,* for example, could mean Puritanism, any one of a number of sects, or simply anti-Laudian elements within the Church of England. In the context of the petition, the word could mean any and all of these. Similarly, the lack of specificity prevents the alienation of any group. Harsh though they may appear, the words are vague enough to forestall disagreement. On the subject of religion, then, the petition is intentionally unspecific, needing as it does to attract signatures. This purpose sets it apart from the speech and explains its hesitancy to define the issue.

On the subject of evil counselors, however, the petitions read as flamboyantly as the speeches. A common lament in the petitions decries the character of those closest to the king: "So long as whisperers and flatterers, whose sole Aimes, reach onely to their owne Benifit, are in places of Power and dignity, we conceive very small possibility of a flourishing Kingdome." This picture of the "malignant" party suggests secrecy and perhaps

---

21. *To the Kings Most Excellent Majestie: The Humble Petition of . . . Glocester,* sigs. A2, A3; *Two Petitions of the County of Buckingham,* sigs. A2v–A3.

even treason, since that party puts its own gain ahead of the welfare of the country. Also, as in the speeches, these words impugn the king's own conduct. They imply that he listens to these flatterers and must take responsibility for the crisis. As the same petition says, "We do conceive the Generall affaires of this Kingdome to be procrastinated and delayed, the Subject to be unrelieved, and your Majesty to be deluded."[22] Already, the rhetoric of the opposition separates king from people since it assumes that Charles can indeed harm his people through inaction or indifference.

Again too comes the declaration that the Five Members have been singled out because they have successfully opposed the enemies of the country. One of the petitions from Buckinghamshire states, "We believe it is the malice which (their Zeale to your Majesties service, and the State, hath contracted in the enemies to your Majesty the Church and Commonwealth) hath occasioned this foule Accusation rather than any desert of theirs, who doe through their sides wound the judgement and care of us your Petitioners and others, by whose choice they were presented to the House."[23] The king's displeasure with the Five Members directly affects the petitioners since it is through the members that their voices are heard. The petitioners tell Charles that he is influenced by "some evill instruments too neere your Royall Person" to violate the liberties of the subject as upheld by Parliament. More than the speeches, the petitions insist on the association of king and "malignant faction"—an association that makes Charles either a fool or a knave, a tool of selfish men or a tyrant. More strongly worded than the speeches, the petitions reveal a sense of collective popular outrage among writers and signatories.

Perhaps because of the strong words against the king's advisers, the petitioners typically protest their loyalty to the country. The men of Gloucester "doe here before God and the world make our Protestation, that we are not moved unto this our desire by any sinister [*sic*] or by respect, or that neither malice, nor envy unto any particular person, or more then ordinary affection unto any cause or person hath stirred us unto this desire, but onely our deepe aggrievances, the decay of this Kingdomes felicity in Trade." Parliament itself adopts a similar tone when addressing the king. It assures him that it seriously considers "the wayes and meanes of securing

---

22. *To the Kings Most Excellent Majestie: The Humble Petition of . . . Glocester,* sig. A2v.

23. *To the Kings Most Excellent Majestie: The Petition of . . . Buckingham,* sig. A2. See also *Six Great Matters of Note,* sig. A4v; and *Two Petitions of the County of Buckingham,* sig. A4v.

the safety of your royall person, preserving the Honour and Authority of your Crowne."[24]

Because of the attacks on the evil counselors, it is crucial to demonstrate devotion to the king, both office and man. The stance becomes even more pronounced when the members of the House of Commons plead for Pym. They "doe most obsequiously submit themselves unto your Majesty, as your loyall subjects, and liege People." Their words deny any suggestion that they wish to usurp the king's prerogatives. They become servants answering an order, implicitly answering the argument that accuses them of rebellion.[25] Cautious in the extreme, these words function as a disclaimer for the defense that follows since the petitioners return to their aggressive challenge to the impeachment.

In defense of their accused member, the petitioners make Pym the symbol of Parliament as a whole, identifying his cause as their own and seizing the opportunity to restate their grievances against the king's actions. Pointing to Pym's own speeches, votes, and loyalty, the petitioners affirm his innocence and his devotion to law. He "hath laboured rather to ratifie and confirme the fundamentall lawes, then either subvert or confound the same." The proof appears especially in his activities as a member of the House of Commons: "In his Diurnall Speeches in the *Parliament* was always specified his reall intent, in the institution, and not diminution or subversion of any law: which was not detrimentall to the safety, and prosperity of this Kingdome." Pym is forthright in his conduct in contrast to the subterfuge attributed to his opponents. Further, he speaks in Parliament, a place in which all his activities lie open to public scrutiny. His votes reinforce his loyalty since he votes against any move to limit the powers of the king "appertaining to your royall Selfe." Pym has firm principles. And since it is a free assembly, "no man in the *Parliament* can by coertion be compelled by any man to joyne with him in his assertion." These statements establish Pym as a leader who is truly representative of the Commons. His beliefs are shared by the majority of the members (sigs. A2v–A4).[26]

In defending Pym, the members also defend themselves. Since he is one of their leaders, any charge brought against him reflects upon them. When

24. *To the Kings Most Excellent Majestie: The Humble Petition of . . . Glocester,* sig. A3; *Six Great Matters,* sig. A2.

25. *The Commons Petition to the King,* sig. A2.

26. For the charges against the Members, see *Articles of High Treason,* sigs. A2–A3.

they praise Pym as an upholder of parliamentary privilege, they declare him to embody what they themselves support, and they show that they are united behind him. Their refutation, emphasizing "antient Rights, and Liberties," challenges the king and his party, juxtaposing it against their reassurances about obedience. The petitioners demand a balance between king and Parliament. In so doing, they define the terms to which their constituents rally. In asserting their integrity they invite allegiance.

The language of Parliament had immediate impact. The petition of the Trained Bands of London reveals the extent to which parliamentary writers succeeded in establishing the terms of public debate. Recalling the language of the separates, the Trained Bands swear they are obedient to the Commons and will "expose . . . their persons . . . for defense of the rights and priviledges of Parliament, wherein your petitioners humbly conceive doe consist the security of Religion, the safety of His Majesties Royall person, and the due execution of our lawes." These petitioners accept the idea that Parliament best defends God, King, and Country—even against Charles Stuart and his party. One of the Buckinghamshire petitions takes a step further. It offers the signatories' services to command as the Commons sees fit and promises that "wee shall with all alacrity addresse our selves, ready to live by you, or to dye at your feet, against whomsoever shall in any sort illegally attempt upon you."[27] In presenting this petition, the men of Buckinghamshire have chosen sides. By accepting Parliament's definitions, they also adopt its interpretation of events and commit themselves to action.

Nowhere is the success of the parliamentary writers more conspicuous than in the language chosen for the king's own declarations issued after January 12. On that date the king promised to waive all proceedings that the Commons considered illegal. In a message of the House of Commons, Charles expresses his hope that "all doubts by this meanes being setled, when the minds of men are composed, His Majestie will proceed thereupon in an unquestionable way: And assures His Parliament, that upon all occasions He will be as carefull of their Priviledges, as of his Life or Crown." In this phrase, Charles concedes that he has no power to force Parliament to take any other course.[28]

Two days later, his speech is even more conciliatory. He states that he

---

27. *To the Kings Most Excellent Majestie: The Petition of . . . Buckingham*, sigs. A4–A4v; *Two Petitions of the County of Buckingham*, sig. A2v.

28. *The Questions Propounded to Mr. Herbert*, sig. A4.

never intended to infringe upon the privileges of Parliament and promises to take whatever steps are necessary to insure those privileges. He also reminds his audience of their need to protect true religion, settle the problems in Ireland, and insure "mutuall defence of each other" (sigs. A4–A4v). Here is the God, King, and Country formula again, with Charles himself redefining *king* to include Parliament. In trying to reestablish his own position, he loses it by ceasing to insist on his own interpretation of the meaning of recent events. His declaration—especially as printed and distributed to the public—seems to assent to the entire position of the Commons and its Five Members. Now Charles protests his loyalty and insists on the importance of Parliament.

The rhetoric of a broadside declaration of Parliament issued on January 17 reveals what a serious concession Charles had made. Gone is any suggestion of request or humility. The broadside describes dramatically and in great detail the entry of the king into the Commons, accompanied by "soldiers & Papists." It then announces that the proclamations against the Five Members are false, that publishing articles against them is a breach of parliamentary privilege and a "seditious Act," and that there can be no redress of that breach unless the king reveals the identities of the agents responsible for the persecution. Finally, the declaration issues a demand that puts Parliament unquestionably at the head of the government. Any persons who have

> endeavoured to set or maintain division or dislike, between the King and Parliament, . . . or otherwise entred into any combination or agreement, to be ayding, or assisting, to any such councell or endeavour, or have perswaded any other so to do, . . . And shall not forthwith discover the same to either house of Parliament: . . . and disclaim it, are declared publike enemies of the State and Peace of this Kingdome, and shall be inquired of, and proceeded against accordingly.

Future loyalty or treason shall thus be measured by support of Parliament against the king, and Parliament itself shall be the final arbiter.[29]

By declaring opponents to be public enemies, Parliament establishes its claims to speak for the entire country, for public safety and concerns. Moreover, Parliamentary rhetoric proclaims the historic importance of the actions against the king. After the beginning of the first civil war, a declaration of Parliament issued on September 10 warns that there can be no peace until the king stops protecting those declared to be "delinquents"

29. *A Declaration of the House of Commons*, broadside.

and allows them to be punished "to the end that both this, and succeeding Generations may take warning with what danger they incurre the like hainous crimes."[30] Their rhetoric allowing no middle ground, the parliamentarians force a choice between two sides. The king having assented to their definitions and interpretations of events, they gain a psychological victory just as the war begins. Even Charles's declarations suggest that they are right.

The parliamentarians are clearly the winners of the pamphlet wars of January 1642. They succeed in making the conflict between themselves and the king a matter of public concern and a struggle they define on their own terms. The fact that the Trained Bands carried copies of the Protestation Oath as they accompanied the Five Members to Westminster shows that Parliament's argument about its privileges was convincing and presented in such a way that people agreed to take up arms against the king to defend Parliament. The pamphleteers of 1642 addressed several audiences simultaneously. No matter to whom the speech or petition was ostensibly directed, it always included the political reading public, and it actively encouraged this audience to follow and participate in events as they developed. While the pamphleteers did not create the two parties or the dispute, they gave both shape and character, made them public, and popularized them. Above all, the pamphlets defined issues that themselves turned readers into debaters, protesters, and finally soldiers.

The tracts of 1642 reveal the limits of political discourse at the beginning of the first civil war. Both royalists and parliamentarians adopt forms of discourse—the genres of traditional English debate—that endorse some version of the status quo, the existing political structure. What variations exist in partisan rhetoric occur within the structure of established parliamentary discourse. Parliamentary speeches, petitions, and declarations all assume a political situation in which those forms have meaning—they assume, that is, that listeners will receive and understand the communication. In using that discourse, both sides reveal that they intend to alter the current situation, but not fundamentally to change it. In that sense, historian Kevin Sharpe is correct in seeing the impending conflict as an "unwanted civil war."[31]

Nevertheless, the language of the tracts of 1642 makes crucial distinctions in ways of perceiving the structure of politics and society. Royalist

30. *Mr. Pym His Vindication in Parliament,* sigs. A4–A4v.
31. "An Unwanted Civil War?"

writers and Charles himself identify the commonweal with the king. From this perspective, disagreement with the king is actually disobedience. Any questioning of the king suggests disloyalty. In its most refined form, this is the language of sixteenth- and seventeenth-century absolutism, from James I's *Basilikon Doron* to Sir Robert Filmer's *Patriarcha*. In contrast, parliamentary writers separate king from commonweal. As early as 1642, Charles's opposition is suggesting that kings can and may commit offenses against their own countries. Further, parliamentary writers argue that true supporters of God, King, and Country may need to oppose a particular king to defend kingship and England itself. The extension of this argument—that kingship may become a threat to England—will appear in the legal arguments of John Cook and the radical rhetoric of John Milton. Articulation of a political stance makes that stance possible as action.

At the outbreak of hostilities, then, there were two general forms of political discourse already present in the minds of the reading public—the personal discourse of the religious opposition, as articulated by Laud's victims in 1637, and the public discourse of the governmental opposition, as seen in the parliamentary speeches and petitions of 1642. Both accommodate themselves to the existing political and social structures of the day. As such, they represent "traditional" political language—that is, the language later pamphleteers will remember when they structure their own arguments. Just as Foxe's *Book of Martyrs* provided an additional context for the discourse of Bastwick, Burton, and Prynne, so the rhetoric of the parliamentary pamphleteers will form the context for later political rhetoric, both monarchist and radical. For all their contentiousness, the pamphlets of 1642 represent debate carried on within a common political language. By 1649, that commonality of language had all but disappeared.

II.

The Rhetoric of Regicide: 1649

FOUR

Prologue: War, Law, and the Reading Public 1642–1649

The pamphleteer of 1642 wrote in a world in which conflict had known boundaries. At the time of the attempt on the Five Members, the king was still head of state. Factions in Parliament and their interests were comprehensible, if not simple. The separate and petition as forms immediately recalled a definite frame of reference. The parliamentary speech—real or fictive—was the orderly discourse of an elected representative addressing his peers and constituents. The petition was the orderly protest of identifiable groups within a political community. Both forms assumed an underlying political system in which individuals took on appropriate public roles. A polemicist on either side of Parliament's struggle with Charles could feel free to invoke in defense of his faction the equation of God, King, and Country. The genres of discourse reflected these shared assumptions. With minor variations, the pamphleteers of 1642 chose similar rhetorical strategies to debate their positions.

The events of 1648 and 1649 swept away any possibility of a common public language. The execution of Charles on January 30, 1649, marked both a political and a psychological crisis in the nation as a whole and in public discourse. Historically and socially, other methods of removing a troublesome king—deposition and assassination—left the foundations of the monarchical system and the language that supported it intact: one sovereign replaced another. The trial and execution of Charles, however, explicitly denied assumptions about the divine right of kings and obedience of subjects. The regicides effectively destroyed even the pretense of maintaining traditional order. To preclude the claims of Charles II to the English throne, they declared the Commonwealth. If pamphleteers had ever seen themselves as affirmers of community values, they could not do so after January 30. The execution fragmented their audience more than a lesser act could have. To support the regicides was to accept a fundamentally altered perspective on political institutions. To oppose them required more than reliance on the language of the Caroline court and personal belief in the rightness of one's cause.

With the collapse of traditional institutions and the subsequent, if temporary, freedom of the press, the arena for public debate shifted from speech to print. By writing, members of the "third culture"—sectarians, social outsiders, and the disenfranchised—could offer proposals to the commonwealth.[1] Excluded from Parliament by Col. Thomas Pride's Purge of opponents of the army on December 6, 1648, Presbyterians joined with their former enemies to write in support of monarchy. Pamphleteers of all convictions attempted to reconstruct the political nation in their respective images by means of their language. The structure they gave their discourse—the genres they chose—suggested the kind of audience they desired. The language that attracted and unified the largest audience would ultimately determine general public perception of the course of events. At stake for the pamphleteers of 1649, then, was the opportunity to create a new political community out of language. This chapter examines the contexts within which that creation took place.

Wars and Factional Realignment, 1642–1649

Despite several famous battles, the greatest part of the actual combat in the civil wars involved local fighting, town by town, village by village, estate by estate. Everyone from soldiers to children saw the direct effects of war. One of the most memorable features of Lucy Hutchinson's biography of her husband, the future regicide, is her vivid description of royalist attacks on cities and their aftermath. Her account focuses on civilian suffering, the burning of houses, and the incidental deaths of noncombatants. In any contended region, the civil wars were total wars, disrupting every aspect of village and city life and loyalties. The sorrowful petitions to Parliament decrying "decay of trade" pitifully understated the devastation and fear of those war zones.[2]

The economic and social upheaval caused by the wars themselves was merely the most visible manifestation of deeper changes brought about by the struggle between the king and Parliament. That political contest per-

---

1. The "third culture" is Christopher Hill's term for all those pamphleteers, thinkers, and sectarians outside both the Anglican/Church of England and Puritan/Presbyterian spheres of influence. Thus, William Prynne is not a member of the "third culture," while John Lilburne, Gerrard Winstanley, and John Milton are. See Hill, *Milton and the English Revolution*, 78, 95–97.

2. *Memoirs of the Life of Colonel Hutchinson*, 113–14.

meated to every county, whether or not the opposing armies clashed on its soil. Recently, several historians have convincingly argued that underlying the many local conflicts was the deep resistance of traditional society to the essentially modernizing pressures of both sides' national war aims. Military victory went hand in hand with efficient central administration and the attendant subordination of the localities. This process directly defied the structures of country life, which focused on loyalty to one's neighbors and community above all else and which had assumed great political importance during the years of the Personal Rule.[3]

In his study of staunchly royalist Kent, Alan Everitt contends that the great majority of county leaders were not Cavaliers but moderate opponents of Parliament with strong roots in their county rather than in the court. As revealed in their petition of 1642, these leaders' requests were "local in outlook," desiring religious reforms while preserving the structure of the Church of England. Both active royalists and active parliamentarians, in contrast, were relative newcomers to Kent, distinguished by long family traditions of either service or opposition to the crown. Invaded in August 1643 by Colonel Edwyn Sandys and London troops, Kent was forcibly kept under parliamentary control until 1648, the year of the great Kentish Rebellion. Even under this pressure, however, loyalties remained intensely local. Periodic royalist revolts tended to oppose Parliament rather than support the king, and at no time did moderate leaders, whom Everitt terms "county royalists," actively support the Cavaliers, the court royalists.[4]

The new leaders in both the army and the counties represented to many localities a lengthening series of parliamentary disruptions of traditional life. Parliament, in its wartime transformation from a legislative to an executive body, issued orders that totally upset the familiar functioning of local government. As J. S. Morrill notes, "In the course of 1643 almost every clause of the Petition of Right was ignored: imprisonment without trial or appeal, the suspension of courts of law, the imposition of arbitrary taxes and the subordination of property rights were all endorsed by parliamentary ordinance."[5] By 1645, Westminster forbade assizes and the council of war invoked martial law against rebels. Such a state of affairs

3. David Underdown, *Revel, Riot and Rebellion: Popular Politics and Culture in England, 1603–1660*, 146–82.

4. *The Community of Kent and the Great Rebellion, 1640–1660*, 95–107, 116–24, 231–70.

5. *The Revolt of the Provinces: Conservatives and Radicals in the English Civil War, 1630–1650*, 52, 98–111.

provoked the formation and activities of the Clubmen, neutrals strenuously committed to sparing their areas the catastrophes of war. Characterized by Morrill as "radical conservatives" defending "traditional values
and rights," the Clubmen formed in many counties, principally in 1645.
Finding strength in their numbers, they made tactical alliances with other
groups to fend off armies, joining moderate royalists in Kent to repel the
parliamentary invaders from London, combining with parliamentarians
in Devon to purge the region of the royalist commander Goring and his
ruthless troops.

According to Morrill, the Clubmen movement briefly created influential and historically significant opposition to the war and the two contest-
ing sides. In almost every area where they appeared, the Clubmen came
together in reaction to national events, whether the quartering of troops,
heavy taxation, or impressment. Above all, individuals joined the movement in 1645 when Parliament abolished the Book of Common Prayer. In
a manner reminiscent of the Levellers, the Clubmen invoked the doctrine
of popular sovereignty in refusing to endorse the Presbyterian Directory of
Worship. In adhering to local democracy, however, they clung as well to
familiar forms of life. As Morrill indicates, many ministers stayed quietly
neutral throughout the first civil war until they received the order to burn
the Prayer Book. To do so would have been openly to accept official
changes in their place and function in society. To the Clubmen also, the
local parliamentary associations, the Solemn League and Covenant, and
the Directory of Worship signified fundamental challenges to their entire
worldview—their individual relationships to their communities, country,
and God.

Traditional forms reinforced the traditional structures that defined the
individual within society. Far more than a simple wish to be left alone or a
reactionary resistance to change, the Clubmen's revolt was an attempt by
local people to define themselves in ways they understood. Clubmen movements only arose in war zones or areas near war zones where the combat
fractured even the smallest details of civilian life. In county after county,
the inhabitants cooperated with the forces in power, provided that familiar
forms and symbols were left intact. This phenomenon explains the greater
strength of Parliament in most counties. While parliamentary commanders denounced the Clubmen's activities and obstructionist local governments, their troops were well disciplined and largely kept to themselves.
Meanwhile, the king's efforts to fortify the Clubmen and his adoption of
their slogans failed terribly when the Cavalier spirit invaded a locality.

The "active neutrality" of the Clubmen and others ultimately crumbled, not through outside force but through its own inherent weaknesses as a political stance. As events unfolded after the battles of Marston Moor, Naseby, and the second civil war, it became an untenable position. First, the capture at Naseby and subsequent publication of Charles's private papers struck a hard blow at the king's image as protector of his people's religion and rights—these papers revealed scheming and plotting with foreign, Catholic powers.[6]

Second, Charles's actions effectively killed the Presbyterian peace movement in London and Westminster by providing a threat sufficient to mobilize Independents and the army against compromise.[7] While Presbyterian leaders attempted to rally citizens already suffering from the effects of war, the king, after May 5, 1646, in the safekeeping of the Scots, schemed with his new protectors for ways to revive hostilities and apparently discussed the possibility of establishing Presbyterianism in England. A Scottish "fifth column" clustered around the envoy Robert Baillie even began operating in London, helping to solidify ties between the peace party and Presbyterians. This was enough provocation for militant Independents, and in part prompted Cornet Joyce's seizure of Charles on June 3, 1647. After that date, it was impossible to disband the New Model Army, and the Presbyterians failed utterly in their attempts to raise a second army.

Last, Charles's leaguing with the Scots, which led to the second civil war, ruined his function as a positive rallying point for opponents of the Independents. Charles himself could only regain popularity with his death. After 1647, the English Presbyterians largely became passive neutrals, and the Clubmen gradually disappeared in all but intensely royalist areas. By their own actions, Charles and his party destroyed the chances for a via media. The army emerged as their only effective opponent.

As a result, the pamphleteers of the late 1640s faced an eminently "persuadable" public, in that large numbers of people were anxiously searching for a sense of social and political cohesion. The Clubmen movement in fact suggests not so much a disagreement with the course of political struggle as a legitimate fear of social collapse. After 1647, this fear gave the public two principal options: either support the army as a force

6. C. V. Wedgwood, *The King's War, 1641–1647,* vol. 2 of *The Great Rebellion,* 520–28, 543–44.

7. Valerie Pearl, "London's Counter-Revolution."

for order and the lesser of two evils, or lapse into passive neutrality and hope for the best. Thus, the parliamentarian writer could at minimum merely argue for tacit consent to a system, while the royalist had to urge active support for a person. The royalist's task was made easier by the execution, which shifted symbolic leadership of his cause to a more attractive and less problematic figure.

On both sides also, there remained people with strong ideological commitments. A small core of stalwart royalists continued plotting and sometimes carrying out guerrilla activities such as those practiced by Montrose, which the government pamphleteers could easily and with some legitimacy portray as a continuing threat to the security of England. The Kentish Rebellion of 1648 illustrated the continuance of localist feelings, however isolated and limited. Above all, there was the army which, as even the most antipolitical revisionists will admit, attracted men firmly attached to Independent and radical ideologies. On the eve of the king's execution, then, there existed those committed to action and those committed to neutrality. The members of the first group were already persuaded, with the self-contained worldview their ideologies provided. As the Parliament and then the Independent faction gained power, the new rulers needed the neutrals at least to stay neutral and accommodate themselves to new social and political structures.

Whatever may be argued about the relative popularity of the Rump, we must remember that it was not seriously resisted and that opponents failed to rally effective opposition. "War-weariness" is a historian's excuse, but not an effective explanation of the neutrals' acquiescence to the Rump, especially when we consider that the previously all-pervasive belief in kingship and hierarchy collapsed so quickly in 1649 and stayed collapsed for ten years.

The Divine Right of Kings and the Law

Whatever his political persuasion, any pamphleteer of the 1640s wrote within the context of several generations of official belief in the divine right of kings, refined and brought to a high pitch by the early Stuarts. The doctrine helped create and permeated the elaborate court culture of masques and the social poetry of the Cavaliers, sermons, and fine arts. Through emblems, allegorical paintings, and appropriate biblical texts, the creators of culture reinforced the otherworldly, mysterious, and symbolic nature of the king's person and function. Any opponent of king or monarchy therefore confronted a public consciousness deeply embedded with a self-confirming vision of divine, political, and cultural order, complete with special images and languages, and a history which provided ready-made attacks on criticism and critics.[8]

Fundamentally, the English version of the divine right of kings was a patriotic, nationalistic doctrine existing symbiotically with Anglicanism. Its traditional enemies drew from many quarters: common lawyers, some Puritans, and—most significantly—Jesuits. Since the Jesuits were the bêtes noires of English society, critics of either king or doctrine could expect swift, violent, and often irrational assaults on their arguments and sometimes themselves. Milton and fellow defenders of regicide advanced arguments that their audience—the vast sea of neutrals—had been raised to regard as subversive, treasonous, and heretical. Rhetorically and practically, the pamphleteers had recourse to the common law, and through the law Charles was tried and executed. Two conflicting commonalities of belief met head-on during and after the regicide, and the languages of that debate derived much of their resonance from their historical context.

As it appeared in England in the sixteenth and seventeenth centuries, the divine right of kings was both a theory of sovereignty and a method of controversy.[9] The theory held that in any state there was one sovereign—the king—who possessed supreme and independent authority from the grace of God. As James I expressed it, God "made [the king] a little GOD to sit on his Throne, and rule ouer other men."[10] Significantly, the theory gave the monarch absolute authority over every aspect of his subjects' lives—political, legal, and religious. As a result, the subjects owed absolute obedience in all things to the monarch, who was placed by God over them. A wicked king was God's punishment for the sins of the nation. Any challenge to the king's authority in any matter was a challenge to his sovereignty. The theory exalted the entire supremacy of the state as embodied in the king. Hence, it also became a method of controversy, a means of attacking rival interpretations of sovereignty. The nature of the opposition

8. See especially Jonathan Goldberg, *James I and the Politics of Literature: Jonson, Shakespeare, Donne, and Their Contemporaries;* Graham Parry, *The Golden Age Restor'd: The Culture of the Stuart Court, 1603–1642;* and R. Malcolm Smuts, *Court Culture and the Origins of the Royalist Tradition in Early Stuart England.*

9. G. R. Elton, Introduction to *The Divine Right of Kings,* xvi–xxiv; John Neville Figgis, *The Divine Right of Kings,* 81–106; and Charles Howard McIlwain, Introduction to James I, *The Political Works,* xxxvii–xliii, xlv–xlviii.

10. "Basilikon Doron," *Political Works,* 12.

changed over time, but it always maintained both a religious and a political character, reflecting the origins of divine-right monarchy.

The theory of divine right was perceived as a necessary by-product of the Reformation and the establishment of the Church of England. In the late Middle Ages, kings ruled the secular world, the pope the spiritual. The Reformation challenged the absolute authority of the pope in religious matters and yet maintained the idea of one true faith. Thus, anyone outside a particular sect was regarded as a heretic by members of that sect. This fact created serious political problems, as such beliefs led to questioning the need to obey possibly heretical secular authority. The creation of the Church of England, which made the monarch the head of the church, consolidated all power, political and spiritual, under a single authority. The justification, offered with plenty of scriptural evidence, was that the king, not the pope, was the earthly representative of God, and that the king was responsible solely to God. Therefore, religious obedience became a political and legal duty. Although acute problems with the doctrine arose in Mary's reign, it became politically necessary for the state upon the accession of Elizabeth.

For English Catholics, Elizabeth's succession produced a major crisis of faith, a dilemma exploited by the papal controversialists hoping to bring England back to the fold. Briefly stated, the problem was this: If Henry's divorce from Katherine was invalid, as the pope declared it to be, then Elizabeth was illegitimate and the crown should descend to the next legitimate heir, the Catholic Mary, Queen of Scots. To counter this argument, Anglican theorists elaborated on Elizabeth's claim to be queen by divine right. Under this doctrine, the true sovereign by divine right was the one generally recognized and habitually obeyed as sovereign, so the monarch de facto also became so de jure.

This argument, while practical and politically expedient, established the grounds of its own counterargument, eagerly pounced upon by the Jesuits, the leading defenders of papal supremacy. Starting from the need for popular acclaim, the Jesuits Robert Parsons, Robert Bellarmine, and Francisco Suárez advanced the principle of popular sovereignty, specifically the idea that a monarch's authority came from God through the consent of the people. Therefore, a king possessed no divine right to his office. The people granted authority to the king but owed primary obedience to God, whose earthly representative was the pope. King and pope coexisted as separate authorities. Anticipating the possibility of conflict between the two, Bellarmine further articulated the doctrine of the pope's indirect power. From this idea especially emanated English anti-Catholicism.

As Bellarmine expressed it, the church exercised an indirect power over the state, which enforced the church's doctrine. While the church itself did not govern, it would not tolerate heretics as kings. The pope held one weapon only against secular authority: the ability to absolve subjects of obedience to their king in the name of a higher law—God's. There were three means of enforcing this decree. First, the pope could urge a foreign power to invade the country in the name of another heir—on these grounds the Spanish Armada attacked England in 1588. Second, the pope could call upon subjects to resist and rebel against their ruler—this was the aim of the bull of 1570 excommunicating Elizabeth. From that moment, English Catholics were bidden to become traitors (as Anglicans saw it) in the name of religion. Last, the pope could encourage tyrannicide— throughout her reign, Elizabeth lived in danger of assassination. As these events show, then, the Jesuits' version of popular sovereignty indeed encouraged subversion and treason, and it called into question the political loyalty of recusants and, by extension, all critics of the Church of England.[11]

In this context, a refinement of the argument for the divine right of kings became the only effective political response. This response was provided by James VI of Scotland in *The Trew Law of Free Monarchies* (1598). There would be no real additions to James's expression of the theory, and he derived his reasoning from Scripture and Scottish-Roman law. From the Old Testament he took the notion of the king as God's representative. Thus, the king swore his coronation oath to God alone. The realm was God's grant to the king, so it became in fact the king's property.

This line of reasoning connected religious doctrine to Roman property law. James treats the realm and crown as inheritable property that the king owns absolutely. As such, they are both inalienable and indefeasible. To this notion James adds the principle of legitimism—the only true king is the legitimate heir of the previous monarch, and he is the only person the people are bound to obey:

> The duty and alleageance, which the people sweareth to their prince, is not only bound to themselues, but likewise to their lawfull heires and posterity. . . . So as no obiection either of heresie, or whatsoeuer priuate statute or law may free the people from their oath-giuing to their king, and his succession, established by the old fundamentall lawes of the kingdome: For, as hee is

11. Figgis, *Divine Right of Kings,* 100–104.

their heritable ouer-lord, and so by birth, not by any right in the coronation, commeth to his crowne; it is a like vnlawful (the crowne euer standing full) to displace him that succedeth thereto, as to eiect the former: For at the very moment of the expiring of the king reigning, the nearest and lawful heire entreth in his place: And so to refuse him, or intrude another, is not to holde out vncomming in, but to expell and put out their righteous King.[12]

The fundamental law is *jus Regis,* since the realm is his property and law presupposes a lawgiver.

As James clearly states, the people forever owe absolute obedience to their sovereign. They have no rights of their own, and every liberty they possess is a gift from the king that he may revoke. Only God may judge a king. If the king is wicked, the people may have recourse to prayer alone, "eschewing and flying his fury in his vnlawfull [commands], without resistance, but by sobbes and teares to God."[13] For the sake of harmony and peace, however, the king should strive to behave toward his people as a loving father toward his children, cooperate with their representatives in Parliament, and treat them justly. Only God may punish a king, but God will also reward a good king.

Like Elizabeth, James faced a vocal and articulate opposition, although during his reign the antagonists came increasingly not from the Continent but from Puritans and lawyers at home. Both groups challenged the idea of absolute single authority and appealed to higher principles. In this, their arguments frequently resembled and indeed often derived from those of the papal controversialists. Both Jesuits and English lawyers explicitly upheld the notions of distributive authority and mixed sovereignty, having recourse to what Ernst H. Kantorowicz terms a political version of "monophysitism," seeing kingship and the principles governing it as independent of any particular king. Hence, the individual monarch must be subject to the same laws as everyone else.[14]

Puritans in general relied on the doctrine of divine sovereignty, while Scottish Presbyterians maintained the ultimate supremacy of the Kirk and regarded civil authority as its enforcing arm. For all Puritans, obedience to God was the foremost duty of the individual, a duty that commanded resistance to any authority that injured the conscience. Presbyterians and Catholics alike urged popular sovereignty in the political sphere in the

12. "Trew Law," *Political Works,* 69.
13. "Trew Law," *Political Works,* 61.
14. *The King's Two Bodies: A Study in Mediaeval Political Theology,* 18, 21–23; John Dykstra Eusden, *Puritans, Lawyers, and Politics in Early Seventeenth-Century England,* 114–26.

name of obedience to the spiritual. More radical Puritans and republicans began to dispense with both institutional authorities, arguing solely for popular sovereignty and social contract.

The common lawyers also acknowledged a higher principle than the king, and their argument as well was to be adopted by republicans and regicides. That principle was the supremacy and primacy of fundamental law. In response to James's assertions that the king was the first lawgiver, the lawyers pointed out the antiquity of English common law, practiced in the land well before the advent of the "Norman yoke."[15] As the lawyers saw it, the fundamental law was "pure reason" and therefore a proper code to obey. The law was omnipresent, applicable everywhere at any time, and often corresponded to the Bible, so that it had the additional backing of God's law. The lawyers also possessed an advantage over the Puritans— they were a united profession integrated into the mainstream of public life. Their voices carried the message of institutional power.

Under James and Charles the law reflected the growing rift between two modes of political thought, both of which were expressed in legal rhetoric.[16] Royalist theory, garbed in the language of the divine right of kings and Roman law, was an unwelcome newcomer to England, especially when James tried to introduce it into English courts. Yet in the eyes of James, Charles, and their supporters, the English people appeared merely old-fashioned and hidebound in their adherence to native traditions in law and government. On the Continent, modern states, notably France and Spain, increasingly favored absolute monarchy and highly centralized administration, while their representative assemblies—the States General and *cortes*—lost their historic powers. Absolutism seemed the way of the future. In contrast, parliamentary conservatism, manifested as legalism, reflected belief in distributive authority vested in separate but interdependent institutions—the king, his council, Parliament, the church, the courts, the universities, and the Inns of Court—each of which held power by the authority of God and the fundamental law. To James and Charles, the king existed before the law. To opposition thinkers, the law existed before kings, or indeed, any society.

These were, of course, diametrically opposed theories of sovereignty,

15. J. G. A. Pocock, *The Ancient Constitution and the Feudal Law: A Study of English Historical Thought in the Seventeenth Century*, 31–47.

16. J. L. Duncan, "The End and Aim of Law: Legal Theories in England in the Sixteenth and Seventeenth Centuries."

and throughout the early seventeenth century and up to Charles's trial, major legal struggles clustered around questions of jurisdiction and the status of the royal prerogative. Since they were appointed by the crown, the chief legal officers of the first two Stuarts reflected James's tenets concerning the prerogative. In traditional practice, common lawyers and judges like Sir Edward Coke followed the concept of the king's two bodies. To his natural body, the aspect that never died, they assigned absolute power that governed a limited number of areas—personal, ecclesiastical, and international. To his politic body, which included his subjects, they ascribed ordinary power that he shared with the other institutions of the country. This sharing of ordinary power was known as mixed sovereignty.[17]

James's jurists, however, consolidated both capacities into the idea of a single, natural body. Lord Chancellor Ellesmere regarded this as the source of all prerogatives, of which there were two varieties: "the absolute prerogative which is in Kings according to their private will and judgement"; and "that absolute prerogative which according to the King's pleasure [is] revealed by his laws." The king alone could wield the first, and could delegate the second to judges, councillors, and other officers of the law who therefore always acted as his representatives. All laws thereby originated with the king and became positive law. As Louis A. Knafla describes it, Ellesmere "thus stated that the judges held their offices in place of the sovereign; that the judges were empowered by the King to execute his legal privileges in the courts of law" and rule according to the letter of the positive law. Yet in Ellesmere's theory, the monarch was accountable to the laws he had made and bound by obligation to his realm.[18]

Although in their writings and public utterances James and Charles made much of their duties to country and people, in practice they expanded and exerted powers of independent, individual rule. The pressure they applied to judges and juries procured favorable decisions. Under James, some acts of Parliament conferred additional powers on the king, and both monarchs often circumvented traditional practices by invoking their duty to defend public safety and order. Both stopped criticism and proclamations, Charles by dissolving Parliament and ruling alone for eleven years. In the name of national security he exacted ship-money, using

17. Stephen D. White, *Sir Edward Coke and the "Grievances of Commonwealth," 1621– 1628;* Charles Gray, "Reason, Authority, and Imagination: The Jurisprudence of Sir Edward Coke." I am indebted to my colleague Diane Parkin-Speer for these references.

18. *Law and Politics in Jacobean England: The Tracts of Lord Chancellor Ellesmere,* 66–68.

this pretense to defy the right of Parliament to direct taxation. Especially under Charles, public law frequently became the will of a king who claimed unilateral power to decide the best means of governing the country and the true definition of justice.

To the Stuarts as to the absolute monarchs of the Continent, the king was the "sovereign embodiment of the state," and under English law was also "a corporation sole, immortal, omnipresent, infallible."[19] Law and theory thus joined together to defend the rights of kings in language that emphasized mystical attributes of kingship, focused on one man as an entity both individual and symbolic, and assumed as an ideal that man's independent, powerful action. Challenging that ideal, parliamentarians and common lawyers alike responded by stressing history and precedent, the collective practice of the English nation. The two interpretations of law inevitably clashed in Charles's trial, when the regicides insisted upon the king's accountability to law while the king equally emphatically declared that only he could truly judge his actions.

As the regicides saw it, trying Charles as a tyrant, traitor, and murderer was a political necessity. Since the close of the first civil war, Charles repeatedly proved to be willing to plunge the country into chaos to regain the throne for himself, steadfastly refusing to give serious consideration to several attempts at compromise, including the Presbyterians' last grasp at peace, the Treaty of Newport, signed in November 1648. To Cromwell and the army, Charles's actions proved that God had judged against him. This belief became the driving force for many of the members of the High Court of Justice. The trial thus became the means for disposing what God proposed. As a result, the principal arguments in the trial, as articulated by the president of the High Court, John Bradshaw, echoed those of the opponents of the divine right of kings.

To justify acts against the king, Bradshaw and the other regicides had to defend their ultimate authority over him. Bradshaw drew his argument from feudal practice, stating that the king's sovereignty resulted from a "bargain" between him and his subjects. This was "the bond of protection that is due from the sovereign; the other is the bond of subjection that is due from the subject. Sir, if this bond be once broken, farewell sovereignty!"[20]

19. Sir William Searle Holdsworth, *A History of English Law,* 9:5.
20. Quoted in C. V. Wedgwood, *The Trial of Charles I,* 164, 161; cf. G. E. Aylmer, *The Struggle for the Constitution, 1603–1689: England in the Seventeenth Century,* 137–39; Adele Hast, "State Treason Trials during the Puritan Revolution, 1640–1660"; Conrad Russell, "The Theory of Treason in the Trial of Strafford." For the last reference, I am

Charles clearly had waged war on his people, so, Bradshaw charged him, "Whether you have been, as by your office you ought to be, a protector of England, or the destroyer of England, let all England judge, or all the world that hath look'd upon it." In breaking the bond, Charles *as king* ceded sovereignty to the people, in whom it originated.

The basic principles of the argument agree with the traditions of common law in England by appealing to past practices, however distant, and with the Puritan and Catholic conviction that the people are not bound to obey a king who breaks faith with them. According to the court's reasoning, then, Charles's actions negated any claims he had to sovereignty, but they in and of themselves did not depose him. He retained the title, but sovereign authority passed to the people, as represented by Parliament. This was the justification for the court's claim to authority and for its procedure of simultaneously trying Charles as both a king and a man.

Charles's dual character is reflected in the threefold charge against him. The charge of *Tyrant* could only apply to a king and explicitly concerned the ruler's bond to his people. In becoming a tyrant, the ruler ceased to be a king and, according to classical, Catholic, and Puritan theory, could justly be deposed. The charge of *traitor* harked back to the medieval notion of the king's two bodies. The individual king, regarded both as a special person and as a man among men, could betray the king's politic body. This idea naturally put the collectivity above the individual and provided the basis for the dictum *salus populi suprema lex*—let the welfare of the people be the supreme law. At the most fundamental level, the charge of *murderer* declared that Charles was a man like any other, subject to and appropriately tried under the same laws.

The court stressed this last point in its procedure and in its presentation of the case against Charles. A long procession of witnesses appeared to prove that the defendant actually had committed the acts of which he had been accused. He was given the opportunity to respond to the charges and to speak in his own defense. Legally, Charles was convicted on a technicality. He refused to plead—an act which until the Commonwealth period was taken as an admission of guilt. Throughout the trial, as contemporary accounts noted, Charles repeatedly insisted that, as he was a king, he was above the law, while Bradshaw repeatedly answered that, as he was

grateful to Howard Nenner for allowing me to read his manuscript "The Trial of Charles I and the Failed Search for a Bounded Monarchy."

a man, he was accountable for his actions to the people and the body politic that he had injured.

However legally suspect, the trial even as it happened marked a major shift in public debate. For the first time in generations an official body advanced a theory in direct contradiction to what had been the dominant form of English political thought. Emanating from the High Court of Justice, the theory and language of popular sovereignty partook of the court's quasi-institutional character. Although the divine right of kings had a long, patriotic tradition, its rival theory had power that gave legitimacy and weight to antimonarchical arguments that now could not be dismissed by calling names. Practically overnight, mainstream Anglican opinion became risky to voice. It still retained the vision of the king as the single source of sovereignty and of law, order, prosperity, and peace, but it lost the corresponding and necessary confirmation in the daily operation of the world. In fact, Charles himself had effectively undermined that vision with his own plotting and hard line against compromise. Moreover, with the establishment of the Commonwealth, the ranks of royalists were swelled by Presbyterians and others who, though supporting kingship, did not share the complete Anglican ideology of the divine right of kings.

The new opposition to the new government thus confronted the need to alter the presentation of its arguments in order to gain allies. The new government, however, was politically and practically unable to use familiar models. It suddenly required a language of institutional power from spokesmen trained in and oriented toward the language of outsiders. The polemical tasks set before all groups of writers were immense, and yet those of the new opposition were more congenial. Required of them was an act of adaptation. Demanded of the new government was a full-fledged act of creation.

FIVE

Icons of the King

The two civil wars and the regicide profoundly disrupted both English society and the ideology that held it together. At national and local levels, new leaders—at least temporarily—replaced old, while the theory of divine right would never fully recover from the fact that a king had been tried and executed by some of his own people. The divine-right theory and the court culture that supported it so profoundly influenced public life that, until Charles's actual condemnation and execution, few men active in Parliament or even in the army believed that his trial was anything more than a final effort to force him to compromise. On November 20, 1648, Fairfax himself endorsed a remonstrance demanding that Charles "be speedily brought to justice," although the king's execution later prompted Fairfax's withdrawal from public life.[1]

In Parliament, opposition was strong enough among the Presbyterians to block any discussion of the trial, even while the king was at large after his escape from Hampton Court. Despite pressure from the army, Parliament continued to negotiate the proposed Treaty of Newport until the morning of December 6, when Colonel Pride prevented Presbyterian members from entering the Parliament house.[2] After Pride's Purge, which was in itself the result of a compromise between army radicals and parliamentary Independents, the remaining Rump assumed the responsibility of trying Charles for treason.

The available evidence shows that the trial was a matter of expediency rather than an act of coherent policy. Too many of Charles's opponents hoped for some kind of ultimate compromise, while a small but active faction desired nothing less than revolution. Cromwell and those close to him knew that Charles would never accept any diminution of his own

---

1. C. V. Wedgwood, *The Trial of Charles I*, 18–53, 129–65.
2. David Underdown, *Pride's Purge: Politics in the Puritan Revolution*, 88–90, 123–43; Derek Hirst, *Authority and Conflict: England, 1603–1658*, 284–87.

power and, therefore, that a political settlement with Charles still on the throne would be impossible. To Cromwell's party, the regicide—as opposed to the trial—was the surest way to bind together the remaining opposition. After Charles's execution there could be no retreat. Further, many zealous revolutionaries saw the parliamentary victories as a sure sign that God had turned against Charles and approved of the new course of action.[3]

But all supporters of the regicide acted alone, without any indication or consideration of popular sentiment. Although the trial was public knowledge and its proceedings widely reported, no "tumults" occurred, as they had in 1642, and no open protest met the proclamation of Charles's sentence.[4] With few exceptions, the huge crowds who witnessed the trial maintained order. No one attempted to stop it. No one demonstrated support. There was simply nothing in people's experience to prepare them to understand and act upon what they saw. London crowds groaned at the actual execution; the silence of the preceding weeks was the silence of incomprehension.

As of January 30, 1649, the future was an open question. In the absence of clearly organized parties, the shape that future would assume depended upon whose rhetoric would best integrate readers into a new political nation. In turn, the forms the rhetoric assumed depended upon each writer's perception of the situation at hand. For a modern reader, the circumstances of the king's execution would seem to have lent themselves almost exclusively to forensic rhetoric—there was the trial itself, and there was an act to be defended or attacked. But for a seventeenth-century writer, the choice of genre resulted not merely from the circumstances, but from his interpretation of the execution, derived from his ideology, his understanding of political order.

The members of the High Court of Justice, together with Milton and other radical pamphleteers, saw the trial and execution from the perspective of English common law and contract theory. Assuming that the people did indeed have the power to depose a king and choose the form of government they desired, the regicides viewed the institutions of king and monarchy as things of the past. Their task was to defend their past act of regicide. Hence, their rhetorical invention proceeded from their choice of

3. Christopher Hill, *God's Englishman: Oliver Cromwell and the English Revolution*, 95–99.

4. Christoper Hill, *Milton and the English Revolution*, 167.

the forensic genre. Consequently, these writers depended upon logical exposition and intellectually independent readers capable of evaluating arguments.

In contrast, monarchists generally interpreted the death of Charles in accordance with divine-right theory. From this perspective, human action and desires were irrelevant to the existence of the monarchy. The crown was never vacant; upon the death of a particular king, it passed instantly to the lawful successor. The king continued to exist, independent of the death of Charles Stuart. Monarchy and royalist values existed and needed to be supported *in the present*. Consequently, monarchist pamphleteers began their invention with the choice of the epideictic genre. Appropriately, their arguments depend upon emotional narration and intellectually dependent readers bound by duty to obey the orders and act in the interest of the sovereign.

The monarchists' choice of genre suited their task. Suddenly finding themselves on the outside of the new political center of the nation, they—like the Puritans and radicals before them—needed to integrate as many people as possible into an effective opposition. Potential supporters ranged from Roman Catholic ex-courtiers to Presbyterian ex-parliamentarians, drawn together by outrage at the king's execution but kept apart by conflicting philosophies. To pamphleteers, this situation could potentially result in disaster for any particular rhetorical strategy. To argue strictly from divine right would alienate Presbyterians, while to depend upon explications of the law could insult the sensibilities of royalists.

Regarded by ancient authors as the genre most easily accommodated to others, the epideictic genre allowed monarchists the opportunity to combine argumentative strategies and hence to adapt to their diverse audience. In monarchist tracts, the epideictic genre frequently combines with the forensic and sometimes with the martyrology popularized by the old Puritan opposition. The flexibility of the epideictic genre also accounts for the peculiar success of the *Eikon Basilike,* arguably the most popular tract of the seventeenth century. Its unique combination of epideictic and Puritan rhetoric with the deliberative genre and its corresponding vision of the future created a rhetoric of unusually integrative power—one that would dominate monarchist discourse in years to come.

Appearing ten days after Charles's execution, the *Basilike* provided the monarchists with the greatest rhetorical victory of the revolution. In 1649 alone, the book went through thirty-five English editions, twenty-five En-

glish-language editions printed in Ireland and abroad, and several translations, including Latin, Dutch, French, German, and Danish. Ghostwritten
by the Presbyterian divine John Gauden—a secret carefully guarded until
1690—the *Basilike* declared itself "The Povrtraictvre of His Sacred Maiestie in His Solitvdes and Sufferings." Broken into twenty-seven chapters
beginning with "His Majesties calling this last Parliament" and ending
with "Meditations upon Death," it recounts recent history, giving what an
anonymous attacker described as the "late King's *ipse dixit*" to a royalist
interpretation of Charles's conflicts with Parliament and the civil wars.[5]

As the epideictic genre demands, the *Basilike* concentrates not on the
facts of Charles's legal defense but on narration. As recommended by the
ancients, this narration occupies the bulk of the text. Each chapter presents
the king's view of a particular event and closes with a prayer to God asking
for protection, aid, and advice. Its famous frontispiece prepares the reader
for a proper response to the contents: on his knees, clutching a crown of
thorns, Charles gazes toward a vision of a martyr's crown in the sky while
before him on a table lie a paper labeled "Christi Tracto" and an open
book bearing the legend "In verbo tuo spes mea," in your word is my hope.
Identified with Christ and hope, the words of Charles—in the open book
facing the reader—are offered as consolation and encouragement to the
disorganized and despairing monarchists. Throughout the book, readers
are encouraged to sympathize with their king's suffering as they overhear
his private meditations. They become his companions and confessors and,
in the last chapter, parties to Charles's political advice for the future. His
cause becomes theirs.

In epideictic oratory, when praising a person, the speaker attempts to
unify his audience by evoking the values of their community and showing
how those values are represented by his subject, who is to then become
their hero. Identification with Charles the man and heroic sufferer—not
Charles the king—is the primary goal of the *Basilike*, a goal shared by most
monarchist tracts that decry the trial and execution. Paradoxically for
supporters of a king famous for his promotion of royal iconography,
monarchist pamphleteers promoted their ideology and political stance by
stripping their depiction of Charles of most of the residue of the culture
nurtured by his court. Like John Bradshaw and his fellow members of the
High Court of Justice, monarchists portrayed Charles Stuart as a man—a

5. Francis F. Madan, *A New Bibliography of the Eikon Basilike*, 2, 50–69, 126–33.
The quotation comes from the anonymous *Eikon Alethine*, sig. Av.

heroic man, surely, but not a divine-right monarch. In these presentations he became a human being, reduced to a scale most readers could easily grasp and placed within a sequence of events arranged in familiar terms. By removing the court iconography that had separated Charles from the people, monarchist writers popularized him at just the time when the army and the Rump needed that support for their own programs. Through rhetoric, the man whose agents had persecuted Bastwick, Burton, and Prynne joined those three men as a popular hero and martyr.

As a generation of persecuted Englishmen had done before, monarchists appealed principally to their readers by presenting Charles as an innocent victim or, in the words of pamphleteer Fabian Philipps, "No Man of Blood, but a Martyr for his People." Charles himself seems to have initiated the effort. In *His Majesties Declaration Concerning the Charge of the Army,* issued on January 1, Charles is reported to have said that

> if any . . . Charge of Impeachment should be exhibited against him, . . . he would not give any answer thereto, but declare against it, to be both Arbytrary and unlawfull; and that if they sought to depose and degrade him of his Titles and Honours, or to spill his Royall bloud, by separating his Soule and Body, he was resolved to sacrifice his life with patience, and to cast himself in the Armes and Bosome of his sweet Lord and Saviour, and only Redeemer; to the end, He may dye like a Martyr, in prosecution and defence of Religion and Country. (sigs. A2v, A3v–A4)

Further, Charles claims that, since he has endured so much on Earth, he will "receive an everlasting Crown of glory" in Heaven. The king's own words suggest the eventual design of the *Basilike*'s frontispiece as he casts himself in the role of martyr.

Charles's ability to appeal to the emotions appears again in *A Message from the Royall Prisoner at Windsor,* dated January 3. The reporter of this "message" cooperates in the production of the heroic image. He describes the king speaking "with a sad and melancholy heart, and tears trickling down his sacred cheekes." The theme of this tract is the king's tender conscience, which he refuses to bend to save himself from adversity. The tract deals with controversial details of Charles's life and his conduct of the wars by omitting them to focus strictly on his present hardships. Readers see the king at prayer for two hours, asking God to help him answer the charges to be leveled against him, and again during a walk, "fixing his eyes towards *London,* . . . uttering many sad and mournfull expressions" (sigs. A2–A2v). In this tract, Charles's emotions are all that matter. The specific nature of his troubles, and indeed what he is thinking, is left for readers to infer. The choice of the epideictic genre governs these presentations. While forensic rhetoric demands facts, the epideictic depends upon character and its emotional impact, often to the exclusion of specifics.

In neither tract is there any reference to immediate past history nor any effort to present the king's version of events from 1642 to 1648. Both tracts instead evoke readers' sympathy by depicting a man in distress because of his beliefs. In the context of the times, which included a generation raised on Foxe's *Book of Martyrs,* such a figure was decidedly heroic. The language suggests Bastwick's and Burton's characterizations of themselves as lonely victims crying out against injustice despite personal danger and suffering gladly in defense of their own consciences. Charles's role had been written by others years ago.[6]

Charles's most triumphant claim to heroic suffering is also his last. The scaffold gave much more validity to his sincerity than any depiction of tears and sighs. Addressing the crowd assembled for his execution, Charles explains that he does not wish to appear to "submit to the guilt." Instead, he declares, "I think it is my duty to God first, and to my countrey, for to clear my self both as an honest man, and a good King, and a good Christian."[7] Speaking in his own voice, not as a king but as "an honest man," Charles echoes the parliamentary rhetoric of 1642 by blaming the wars and his own trial on unnamed, disaffected persons. Confessing his conscience, Charles accepts responsibility and punishment for the "unjust Sentence" and execution of Strafford in 1640. Finally, asserting that if he had truly used his full powers he would not be standing on the scaffold, the king announces, "I am the Martyr of the People."

Aside from providing a title for Fabian Philipps's pamphlet, Charles accomplishes two major goals in the scaffold speech—goals that are supported by the earlier pamphlets issued in his name. First, he himself discards most of the iconography of kingship by speaking in the first person, declaring his private griefs, and presenting himself as a humbled man. Ironically echoing the charges against him at his trial, he allows himself to become simply Charles Stuart, a man like any other. Second, in

6. On the rhetorical connection between the Puritan pamphleteers of 1637 and the *Eikon Basilike,* see my article "Rhetorical Genres and the *Eikon Basilike.*"

7. *King Charls His Speech Made upon the Scaffold,* sigs. A3, A3v–A4, Bv, B2. See also Nancy Klein Maguire, "The Theatrical Mask/Masque of Politics: The Case of Charles I," 10–11; and Lois Potter, *Secret Rites and Secret Writing: Royalist Literature, 1641–1660,* 156–93.

his insistence on his prayers, pained conscience, and private agony over current events, he places himself firmly in the company of English Protestant martyrs, from those in Foxe's *Book of Martyrs* to Bastwick, Burton, and Prynne on the pillory. In effect, he revives their method of "apology" and self-defense. And significantly for the reception of the *Basilike*, Charles's words and reported behavior establish a standard for monarchist works. Any tract echoing Charles's principal themes and tones would immediately possess an aura of credibility. The ideas of the *Basilike* were not new—a month's worth of pamphleteering had already laid the groundwork for its rapid welcome.

The martyrology of the *Basilike* appears principally in the "prayers" following the "meditations" on the events of the civil wars. The meditations and prayers serve as confirmation by amplification, appropriate to the epideictic genre and no other. Each meditation confirms by adapting historical events to suit the present character of the king. Like all martyrs before him, Charles justifies all his actions by appealing to his own conscience, most prominently in his discussion of the Nineteen Propositions, points of possible negotiation offered him by Parliament in June 1642. While the Parliament's terms were harsh, the king flatly refused to discuss any of them, thus destroying a chance to compromise and end the hostilities.[8] The Charles of the *Basilike* justifies his response by arguing with analogy and emotion, rather than logical—and forensic—refutation. He is, of course, the king, and any believer in monarchy by divine right would accept this as reason enough for his refusal. But the *Basilike* does not use that doctrine as part of Charles's primary answer. The theory remains an unspoken assumption.

Instead, Charles centers his response on his conscience and an attack on his opponents. Historically, Charles refused all the propositions as an insult to kingship. But this king says, "Some things here propounded to Me have been offered by Me; Others are easily granted; the rest (I think) ought not to be obstruded upon Me, with the point of the Sword; nor urged with the injuries of a War; when I have already declared that I cannot yeild to them, without violating My Conscience: 'tis strange, there can be no method of peace, but by making warre upon My soule" (sig. F6). After preserving "the Incommunicable Jewell of my Conscience" (sig. F6v), this king is willing to grant almost anything that would benefit his subjects.

8. Perez Zagorin, *The Court and the Country: The Beginnings of the English Revolution*, 318–19.

Emotionally, he wants compromise and peace. In this context, political considerations do not exist.

The intensely personal, private tone of the *Basilike* turns Charles's political failures into moral victories. Against obstacles that would prove overwhelming to the average person, Charles actually grows in fortitude. The *Basilike* attempts, through martyrology, to turn the king into a Protestant everyman, a familiar companion to frightened readers. Further, this use of martyrology enables the *Basilike* to combine forensic emphasis on the ethos of the speaker with epideictic emphasis on community values and emotional unification of the audience. These techniques explain the enormous success of the *Basilike* as opposed to such works of overt king-worship as Philipps's *King Charles the First, No Man of Blood* (June 25) and the anonymous *New-Yeeres Gift for the Kings Most Excellent Majesty* (January) and *A Hand-Kirchife for Loyall Mourners* (January 30). While all three use the martyr image and often similar words, the very fact that they come from "reporters" and not from the king's own hand severely undercuts their overall effect. In these tracts, the reader is invited to identify with the emotions of the writer, not the king. Hence, the reader indeed becomes a fellow king-worshiper instead of a companion in suffering. These tracts invite public action, not private meditation or reflection, as they urge readers to become royalist partisans.

Probably written in early January, *New-Yeeres Gift* exhorts readers to envision a portentous future under Charles:

> He whom we for a long time sought, and for whom we have sighed, sobbed, wept, prayed, fasted, I and fought too, to gain, that is, our most gracious and truly dread Soveraigne Gods anointed King *Charles,* is now by divine motion, with peace and joy, with serenity and affection, after so long absence, coming to capitulate with his great Councell the Parliament, concerning our malady and cure; to express this generall exultation in it's true dimensions, let us forme in our fantasie the Idea of the Tribes of Israel when they came to Hebron . . . to choose *David* for their King, after the death of *Saul* and *Ishbosheth* his son, we are, said they, thy bones and thy flesh, ah sweet expressions: so near a connexion is there between all good Kings and their Loyall Subjects. (sigs. A2–A2v)

Despite his misapprehension of the reasons behind Charles's arrival in London, the writer attempts to rally popular opinion in favor of the king by urging readers to see their times in terms of providential history. He addresses readers as one nation, sharing common beliefs and goals. "We" sobbed, prayed, and fought for the king, who is now going to yield to "his"

Parliament. In the language of *New-Yeeres Gift,* no wars ever really happened. Parliament still belongs to Charles and the whole country fights for him. Charles's opponents simply disappear. Refusing to offer explicitly political arguments, the author offers a purely fictive vision of the future.

Philipps's *No Man of Blood* characterizes Charles as a frustrated peacemaker, an attribute derived from the court culture of the early years of his reign. Charles, readers are told, "was the only desirer of *Peace,* and laboured and *tugged* harder for it then ever Prince or King, Heathen or Christian, since Almighty-God did his first days work" (sig. G3). His only fault was perhaps being too generous: "The King was willing for the good of his People to give away almost everything of his owne; but the Parliament would never yeild to part with any thing was not their owne" (sig. H). According to Philipps, Charles worked harder for peace than King David, and ultimately acted like the true mother in the case before Solomon. But Charles most clearly shows himself a *"pater patriae"* (sig. Hv), "a weeping father defending himselfe against the strokes and violence of disobedient Children" (sig. G3v). Philipps, like the *Basilike,* presents Charles as a martyr, ennobled by his suffering.

To the author of *A Hand-Kirchife,* the king's fate proves his similarity to Jesus: "Christ suffered for the good of his people, so did he: Christ for the freedome of his people, so doth he for the freedome of his. . . . Christ he suffered for the whole world, he but for his three Kingdoms: Christ to free his people from an eternall captivity and the Tyranny of *Sathan:* He to free his Kingdoms from a temporall captivity and the Tyranny of wicked men. . . . Christ was a King and so was he, Christ the supreame and *Charles* his substitute" (sig. A3v). This is true king-worship. More extreme even than divine-right theory, it comes dangerously close to idolatry. Both this author and Philipps idealize Charles prodigiously, going much further than the *Basilike* itself in attributing to him not simply honorable but saintly motives. This king never committed any offense against his people, although the *Basilike* admits that some things turned out badly. Discarding the theory of divine right, these two writers present Charles not as a king favored by God, but almost as a god himself. In contrast, the Charles of the *Basilike* is a man.

The figure of Charles the martyr functioned as a rallying point, turning readers into a community of mourners. Of all monarchist pamphlets that characterize Charles, the *Basilike* emerges as the most effective precisely because it is not simply king-worship. Purporting to be the king's own thoughts, it can excuse, rationalize, and gloss over events without really doing violence to the facts. It provides a ready-made motive for casting circumstances in a favorable light. Moreover, its "I," its speaker, is the martyr himself. This claim carries far more power than the testimonies of the most grief-prostrated followers, and it is the most powerful weapon the monarchists have.[9] They use it time and again as a self-justifying answer to any opponent's charge.

The *Basilike* and other monarchist tracts also involve their readers by presenting an interpretation of recent history. In so doing, the authors transform forensic facts into epideictic narration, thus fixing their readers' attention on the present. The tracts collapse past into present as they give the king's and the monarchists' current interpretation of the past, thereby integrating diverse opinions and disagreements with official policy into a coherent, concrete, and unified perspective. In this vision of history, the king, like the Puritan writers before him, becomes the spokesman for an entire group, an impression reinforced by Charles's own scaffold speech, as well as the posthumously published *His Majesties Reasons Against the Pretended Iurisdiction of the High Court of Iustice,* Philipps's *No Man of Blood,* and George Bate's *Elenchus Motuum Nuperorum in Anglia.*[10] With the very minor exception of Bate, the *Basilike* makes a unique contribution to monarchist narration by offering a clear program for the future, giving readers a collective and practical goal. It reaches into the deliberative genre to produce a peroration by means of further examples—examples of benefits to be derived from the program it advocates. Defined by the manipulation of history, this approach was the ultimate source of the *Basilike*'s popularity. It made readers look forward rather than back, to a potentially achievable future instead of an irretrievably lost past. Herein lay its power.

This positive program appears as the climax of the *Basilike* in its last section, "To the Prince of Wales." In this, the only section not followed by a prayer and thereby not directed to God, Charles speaks to his son, giving him advice to govern his actions once his father is dead. This "meditation" becomes an essay on public policy, reviving and reaffirming the formula of

9. Generically, the *Eikon Basilike* is allied to radical puritan discourse despite numerous superficial similarities to Roman Catholic martyrology. For the latter, see for example Richard Helgerson, "Milton Reads the King's Book: Print, Performance, and the Making of a Bourgeois Idol," 8–12.

10. According to Francis F. Madan, "Milton, Salmasius, and Dugard," the *Elenchus* was printed by William Dugard, author of the Ramist rhetoric text *Rhetorices elementa* and printer of the *Eikon Basilike:* a literal example of the interconnectedness between rhetorical theory and political pamphleteering.

God, King, and Country—an idea terribly important in the debates of 1642 but vanished by 1649. Presenting this formula, Charles explains that the prince is potentially the source of all good in his country, provided he remembers one fundamental tenet: "The true glory of Princes consists in advancing Gods Glory in the maintenance of true religion, and the Churches good; Also in the dispensation of civill Power, with Justice and Honour to the publick Peace" (sig. Q5v). An English king must always be conscious of the public impact of his actions—a lesson that, as all the preceding meditations show, Charles has learned painfully over the last decade.

Above all, the king must save his own soul. Charles's own beliefs, he explains, have drawn him closer to God during his imprisonment, and those beliefs correspond exactly to those of the Church of England. Thus, Charles's son will be true to his father's memory by defending and preserving that church, the only true religion of the English people. The best way to preserve the church is to be steadfast in one's own faith so that one will not be tempted. Since "the Devill of Rebellion, doth commonly turn himself into an Angell of Reformation" (sig. Q6), one must be wary of people who profess piety and zeal. They do this to impress the "vulgar" and win others to their true cause—"Sedition and Faction." Charles cites his dealings with the Presbyterians as an example. The king believes that his own faith will preserve him from the doubts they try to provoke.

Charles's words on religion address three separate contexts. First, they advise "you," his son, as future ruler of England. In this context, the words become suggested policy for governing the affairs of the Church. But clearly, since these words are mass-produced and designed to be read by thousands of Englishmen, they address "you" the readers as well in two additional contexts. Immediately, the advice locates readers in the present. Governed by the army and the Rump, which are composed mainly of Independents and other "factions," readers are warned against their current leaders, whose own devotion to the inner light and professed zeal may now appear sinister and dangerous. By implication, the only hope for real stability lies in leadership loyal to the principles Charles has just enunciated. Since the primary recipient of Charles's counsel is his son, the son becomes the logical future leader. Hence, these words also project readers into the future and urge their loyalty to Charles II. In describing his own misfortunes and the heinous behavior of his enemies, Charles I establishes an implicit contrast to the figure of Charles II, who is formed by his father's sage advice rather than by rash example.

Continuing his exploration of the king's proper role, Charles turns to the desirable relationship of king and Parliament, anticipating as he does so the fears nonroyalist readers may have about a Stuart restoration. As explained by the *Basilike,* the laws establish certain obligations for the king. No longer is he above the law. Further, the laws "reserve enough to the Majesty and prerogative of any King, who ownes his People as Subjects, not as Slaves; whose subjection, as it preserves their property, peace, and safety, so it will never diminish your Rights, nor their ingenuous Liberties; which consists in the enjoyment of the fruits of their industry, and the benefit of those Lawes to which themselves have consented" (sig. Q7v). According to the *Basilike,* the people have innate ("ingenuous") rights. This position contrasts sharply with the view of James I that all rights are gifts from the king. Moreover, the *Basilike* recognizes at least partial popular sovereignty. The people give their consent to certain laws. Therefore, the consent is theirs to withhold as well. They have some degree of inalienable power.

This advice assures readers that a restored house of Stuart will not share the characteristics of its first two kings. The *Basilike* echoes the language of the parliamentarians of 1642, not Charles I, in its insistence on a balance between king and Parliament and special rights for both sides. In its closing remarks, the *Basilike* presents a picture of future reconciliation, peace, and harmony as Charles warns his son against "meditating any revenge, or executing Your anger upon the many" (sigs. R2v–R3). Rather than a meditation on the past, the final chapter of the *Basilike* presents an integrative vision of the future. Readers may forget their differences over the past because everything they fought for will be realized upon the return of Charles II.

Of the companion monarchist tracts, only Bate's *Elenchus,* written very late in 1649, makes any plea for the future. The remaining pamphlets, from the scaffold speech to *No Man of Blood,* retain their forensic and epideictic mixture, dwelling on the past, trying to reclaim history for the monarchists. From the scaffold, Charles pleads his good intentions. Ignoring the raising of his own standard at Nottingham, he insists that the Parliament began the wars. His sole message to sympathizers is that things will never be right until the people give his successors and God their due (sigs. A3v, A4v). *His Majesties Reasons,* appearing on February 5, gives a formal defense of the charges against Charles and an interpretation of the events preceding the trial. In this broadside, Charles claims that he always wanted to preserve the laws and had offered to make concessions, his goodwill being preempted by his arrest. It offers a congenial view of

Charles and confirms the suspicions of readers alarmed by Pride's Purge, as it suggests that the army prevented reconciliation.

Another broadside, *A True Relation of the Kings Speech to the Lady Elizabeth,* dated March 24, resorts to pathos to preclude one possible outcome of the execution. Instead of politics, the writer offers sentiment:

> Then the KING taking the Duke of *Gloucester* upon His Knee, said Sweet heart, now they will cut off thy Fathers head; . . . . Mark child what I say, they will cut off my head, and perhaps make thee a King; But marke what I say, you must not be a King, so long as your Brother CHARLES and JAMES do live; For they will cut off your Brothers heads . . . and cut off thy head too at the last. And therefore, I charge you, do not be made a King by them: At which the Child, sighing, said, I will be torn in peeces first: which falling so unexpectedly, from one so young, it made the KING rejoyce exceedingly.

Here, the author makes compassion for the child speak in place of political considerations. Instead of addressing arguments advanced by the army and the Rump, the writer uses a pathetic appeal to turn his opponents into monsters—faceless "they" who chop off heads. Retaining its predominately epideictic character, the tract thus relies on invective rather than logic or factual evidence to confute its opponents.

Fabian Philipps adapts strong invective to the forensic genre in *No Man of Blood* as he interprets recent history by means of questions. As does the *Basilike,* he examines specific moments in the course of the past decade, asking in chapter headings, "Who first of all Raised the Feares and Jealousies?" (sig. Av), "Whether a Prince or other Magistrate, labouring to suppresse, or punish a Rebellion of the People, bee tyed to those rules are necessary for the justifying of a Warre; if it were made betweene equalls?" (sig. C4), and "Whether the Parliament, in their pretended Magistracy, have not taken lesser occasions to punish or provide against Insurrections, Treasons, and Rebellions, as they are pleased to call them?" (sig. Gv). Bolstering his arguments with numerous examples, Philipps turns law, precedent, and the whole of Western history against his targets.

He reserves his worst invective for the present. The results of parliamentary rule are "unchristian usages of old and sick people, Women and Children, beaten, wounded, or killed upon no provocation; Women and Maids ravished; and their fingers cut off for their rings, old *Best* of *Canterbury* hanged up by the privities, . . . their sheep, cattel and provisions devoured, houses ruined or burnt" (sigs. D2v–D3). Whatever the full truth of his accusations, Philipps's charges are likely to have been believed by an audience that had recently witnessed the execution of the king. Associating wartime atrocities with the triumph of Parliament—and Parliament alone—may be an extreme example of a post hoc fallacy, but political history is not Philipps's goal. Polemical "history" is.

Compared to its contemporaries, the *Basilike* is a masterpiece of mixed genre, cleverly using an epideictic base and corresponding readers' expectations in new ways to produce what proved to be an impregnable monument to the house of Stuart. Like the scaffold speech and *His Majesties Reasons,* the *Basilike* borrows from the forensic genre in presenting a refutation of charges against the king. Yet, instead of answering those charges point-by-point, as do the two shorter pamphlets, the *Basilike* incorporates its answer into a first-person narrative covering the same ground but in a manner more likely to engage the readers' emotions than his intellect. Like *A Hand-Kirchife, New-Yeeres Gift,* and *No Man of Blood,* the *Basilike* also employs martyrology, which shares with epideictic oratory the end of unifying the audience around a set of community values exemplified in a hero. Again, the *Basilike* stands apart from other attempts to arouse pity for Charles precisely because it alone uses the form of heroism made familiar to English readers through Foxe's *Book of Martyrs* and the Puritan pamphleteering.

Finally, the *Basilike* alone engages in a particular kind of deliberative oratory in portraying a positive, alternative vision of the future. In surveying the past through the king's meditations, the *Basilike* implicitly criticizes parliamentary behavior and policy, so that when Charles's advice appears at the end it emerges as a model of sanity and coherence amid the chaos of contemporary politics. Its closest competitor, *No Man of Blood,* attempts a similar analysis of past events, yet leaves the alternatives only implicit. Also, it is quite obviously a partisan piece aimed more at vituperation of the enemy than praise of a hero. It decidedly preaches to the converted, indulging in common criticism of the current regime and assuming that the audience already knows what should take its place.

By focusing attention solely on the king and making him the only character in the narrative, the *Basilike* assumes no specific political persuasion among its readers. It is essentially apolitical, as the king himself belongs to no faction. It re-creates not only history but also Charles's whole personality, recasting him as a Protestant martyr, moderate ruler, staunch Anglican, and forgiving father of his rebellious children/subjects. And since the real Charles is dead, he can do nothing to tarnish the image of the hero created by the *Basilike.* Like Bastwick, Burton, and Prynne on the pillory, the image of Charles tearfully kneeling at his devotions in prison entered the popular consciousness, remaining impervious to the most determined blows of the most vigorous icon-breaker.

Even before Charles actually stood trial, the army, the Rump, and the supporters of both attempted to insure that their actions and charges against the king should not be distorted. Their concern extended not only to presentations of current events but also to the imagery employed in describing them. Their apprehensions were totally justified. The *Basilike* and its fellow tracts built a powerful image that captured readers' hearts and made them invulnerable to assaults of reason. Both Milton and the anonymous author of the *Eikon Alethine* found Charles's image in the *Basilike* so popularly attractive that they believed it necessary to attack its authenticity as well as its content. Out of historical contexts, imagery, rhetoric, individual words, and traditional genres, the author of *Basilike* had indeed created a formidable idol—one that derived its power from the multiplicity of its roots. Such a work by its very nature defied the techniques of traditional refutation, or indeed, any single genre of response.

In defending the regicide, radical pamphleteers were handicapped by their choice of rhetorical genre. Forensic rhetoric kept them and their discourse focused relentlessly on the past. As a result, these writers were generically restricted from presenting an integrative vision of the future. Further, forensic rhetoric assumes that the audience shares the assumptions of the writer. Agreement on initial premises is the necessary beginning of any logical argument. In a forensic argument, reorientation of the audience (its determination of innocence or guilt) occurs within accepted limits—those of the legal system. The limits themselves are rarely questioned. Yet the execution of Charles and the declaration of the Commonwealth did just that. For radical pamphleteers, this meant that in the absence of a full defense of the new political system, their arguments could reach only those who already shared their convictions.

Moreover, the success of the monarchist tracts—in particular, the *Basilike*—led radicals to an attack on rhetoric itself. Like Plato, when radical pamphleteers spoke of "rhetoric," they singled out epideictic rhetoric, the favorite of the sophists. While monarchists used epideictic rhetoric to construct a positive vision of monarchy, radicals distrusted the genre to the extent that they often neglected the ethical proof of self-praise in their own arguments. This concentration on the language of the law ironically made regicide rhetoric essentially conservative at a time when its practitioners sorely needed to change their readers' attitudes toward the country's institutions.

Of the radical pamphleteers, only Milton makes a serious attempt to transform his readers. Characteristically, he does so by reeducating them, teaching them not how to feel but how to read. His method deliberately precludes rhetoric as it attacks not only the ideas of the *Basilike* but also its language. This approach has led many scholars to regard *Eikonoklastes* as a retreat from polemics, agreeing with Keith W. Stavely that "when such density of matter is unfolded with little support from emotional emphasis or imaginative coloring, we have a rhetorical persona disavowing rhetoric and politics, speaking in a tone of cold rational contempt for a nation that has neither eyes to see nor ears to hear the obvious truth."[11] Whatever its degree of success, however, Milton's antirhetoric does reflect the practice of his radical contemporaries. Parting company with them, Milton adopts a genuinely revolutionary stance as he attempts to re-create his readers as the proper citizens of the new Commonwealth.

Eikonoklastes appeared on October 6, 1649, roughly eight months after the execution of the king and the first printing of the *Basilike*. By that date, there had also appeared several other works designed to halt the propagation of the story of Charles the martyr. As early as January 1, in *His Majesties Declaration Concerning the Charge of the Army*, government pamphleteers refuted Charles's contentions about the legality of his trial. On January 12, already aware of the elaborate rhetoric generated by the proceedings of the trial, John Redingstone published *Plain English to the Parliament and Army*, which fully supported Charles's prosecution. On the same day the *Basilike* was published, February 9, the king's chief prosecutor, John Cook, presented *King Charls* [sic] *his Case*. Finally, on August 16, came the first response to the *Basilike*—*Eikon Alethine: The Povrtraitvre of Truths Most Sacred Majesty Truly Suffering, though Not Solely*—an attempt to discredit the "king's book" primarily by challenging its authorship and language. This work was almost immediately answered by *Eikon Episte: Or, the Faithfull Portraicture of a Loyall Subject,* on September 11. All these works, but especially the last two, provided the immediate context for Milton's task and also defined the limits of the formal assaults on Charles's cult of personality.

11. *The Politics of Milton's Prose Style,* 85–86. Recent criticism tends to view the *Eikonoklastes* favorably as a piece of philosophical and religious iconoclasm. See Thomas N. Corns, *The Development of Milton's Prose Style,* 87–91, 101–2; David Loewenstein, " 'Casting Down Imaginations': Milton as Iconoclast"; and Lana Cable, "Milton's Iconoclastic Truth."

As demanded by the forensic genre, radical writers typically concentrate on confuting the royalists by challenging their logic and presenting responses to each major point. Milton and fellow regicide polemicists primarily try to expose the distortions in the king's words, showing how he alters events for his own polemical ends. All aim at reestablishing the context that Charles strips from history. At the most basic level, this means direct refutation of his statements. The compiler of *His Majesties Declaration Concerning the Charge of the Army* presents a complete set of Charles's "Queries" to the High Court of Justice, queries that contain a highly optimistic vision of the state of affairs in England, only to answer each one with devastating references to what the judges of the court perceive as facts. To Charles's comment that his son can raise an army in France and Holland, for example, the judges respond that the French have "troubles enough at home" (sig. A4), while Charles possesses far too little money to raise an army in Holland.

This is a classic point-by-point refutation, countering one accusation with another. For it to succeed, the author or speaker depends upon his audience's general agreement with his point of view and his interpretation of events. This writer and the men whose answers he reports base their responses on their assumptions about the nature of Charles's actions: first, that he acted contrary to his trust in "departing from Parliament"; second, that he violated his trust by making war against his people; third, that he caused the second civil war by giving commissions to "Incendiaries and Malignants"; and finally, "That the said *Charles Steward* hath acted contrary to the Liberties of the Subject, and tending to the destruction of the fundamentall Laws and Liberties of this *Kingdome;* all which, amounts to a forfeiture of the said trust reposed in him by the People at his Coronation" (sigs. A3v–A4v). All of these points derive from the assumptions of the common lawyers and other challengers of divine-right theory. Further, these assumptions influence the writer's presentation of his facts. Each point is actually an interpretation that derives from the initial premise. They can only influence readers who have already rejected the idea of a perpetual monarchy. *His Majesties Declaration Concerning the Charge of the Army* begins with its conclusion, assuming a favorable reception.

Redingstone's *Plain English* and Cook's *King Charls his Case* both take greater pains to answer the chief arguments of the monarchists. Their authors, addressing simply "the reader," are much less sure than the members of the High Court of Justice of the overall sympathies of their audience. They take fewer chances in trusting what their audience already believes. As a result, following the constraints of their interpretation of the common law, they depend further on explications of history, scriptural justifications, and lists of legal precedents to justify actions against the king. Of the two tracts, *Plain English* leans far more heavily on scriptural precedents, placing current events within a providential context, while *King Charls his Case* relies more extensively on recent history, judging Charles's motives by examining his actions.

Plain English asks readers to challenge their own views of kingship by evaluating it according to Scripture. Like Jesuit and Puritan controversialists before him, Redingstone finds divine approval for popular sovereignty. When rulers "pervert Justice, and become a terrour to good workes: and justify the wicked in their evil: such tyrants are not only *abomination to the Lord,* but by the testimony of the Gospel, they doe forfeit their authority also" (sig. A2). The king's own actions ultimately may absolve the people of their obedience and permit their active seeking of redress. The point to argue, then, is whether Charles in fact committed the kind of deeds that would invoke God's judgment against him.

Redingstone argues by evaluating the king's actions from the perspective of popular sovereignty. First, he argues that the king raised arms "to subvert *Salus populi*" (sig. A2v) by making war on Parliament, the representative of the people. This was a clear violation of the coronation oath and, as such, a breach of promise to God. This action must have angered God since his blessing on the opposition may be seen in its success. Moreover, Charles himself turned away from God by ignoring the advice of the faithful, listening instead to "perverse, foolish, slanderous, wicked, proud, haughty, deceitfull, murtherous mens councels" (sig. A3). Last, all the king's vows and promises reveal the strongest charges against him, since he used them to deceive the people. This deed in particular should earn him God's punishment.

As Redingstone argues, Parliament should be instructed by God. Drawing a parallel between Charles's actions and the Old Testament story of Naboth's vineyard, he says that Charles should be handled like King Ahab, and since "God hath delivered the King into their hands" (sig. A3v), the Parliament and army should execute God's judgment. To Redingstone, then, the whole argument comes down to the conflict between Charles's word and God's. Whatever Charles claims, his actions and the whole outcome of his struggles with Parliament—as interpreted through their correspondence to events in Scripture—reveal him to be in the wrong. His own words are therefore either irrelevant or lies. Since his audience knows God's words to be true, Redingstone merely presents them as refutation, ignoring altogether Charles's own arguments.

In *King Charls his Case,* John Cook pursues his argument in the other direction, bolstering his words with a few choice quotations from Scripture but focusing principally upon the events of Charles's reign. Beginning with the king's activities after the death of his father, Cook surveys the fruits of Charles's kingship, placing them in historical and legal contexts. Concentrating on the coronation oath, Cook demonstrates how Charles had always acted contrary to the traditions of England. According to Cook, the oath was always temperate. It did not mean "that any man should sweare to give any one leave to cut his throat" (sig. A3v). Rather, it meant that the people acknowledged their king to be supreme in England, as opposed to the pope or any other prince.

As English law and forensic rhetoric demand, Cook concentrates his confirmation on intentionality. He therefore interprets recent history to trace Charles's motives. Readers may judge Charles's intentions by the "wicked design" exhibited from the beginning of his reign, leaving the phrase *"which the people shall chuse"* out of the coronation oath so that he need not assent to the laws passed by Parliament. Cook finds further evidence of perfidy in another of Charles's actions at the coronation— telling knights that they need not appear and then fining them for nonattendance. Worse, the king linked the tenure of judges to good behavior. This meant, Cook charges, that judges were required to do as bidden by the crown. Heading the list of abuses, however, is Cook's accusation that Charles consistently exhibited "his restlesse desire to destroy Parliaments, or to make them uselesse," only calling them when he needed money (sigs. A4–B2v).

All of these incidents confute the monarchists' claims that Charles meant well, since they all cast doubt upon his sincerity. In monarchist tracts, Charles's conscience is the principal explanation of all his questionable acts. Cook attempts to undermine the reliability of Charles as witness, and he does so by repeatedly asking a classic legal question—who benefits? In answering, he revives memories of the Personal Rule, during which Englishmen suffered "incroachments and usurpations upon their liberties and properties." Brushing aside the possible objection that it was Charles's evil counselors who caused abuses of the judiciary, Cook indicates that the king could remove judges if he chose, that he benefited from the fines they assessed, and—"Mark a Machiavel-policy"—that the king refused to call parliaments, conveniently remembering that the people's representatives cannot question judges when the Parliament is not sitting (sigs. A3–B3v).

Cook's techniques attempt to prevent readers from being misled by Charles's and the monarchists' sympathetic retelling of history. He reminds readers of the events leading to the wars, the events that gave the grounds for the charges at Charles's trial. Against what he perceives as fiction, Cook marshals what he considers facts, presenting a coherent picture of Charles's abuses in such a way that readers may doubt the king's goodwill. Yet Cook's focus on the first fifteen years of the reign creates its own problems. In 1649, many members of the audience had no direct recollection of actions occurring twenty-four years before, and still others were unlikely to allow distant memories to affect their reactions to Charles's apparently noble suffering, especially when the alternative was to support the army.

Cook's rhetoric reveals the limits of the forensic genre. As a court case, his presentation may have been effective, but readers outside the strictures of the legal system react to far more than direct presentations of issues and outcomes. The forensic genre itself makes no provisions for examining the social and political contexts of the case at hand, while the deliberative and epideictic genres may make free reference to the situation outside the immediate subject.[12] Cook's attacks are essentially vague, concerning questions of motive that cannot truly be resolved simply by looking at results, nor does it respond to the image of the king present in most readers' minds. The allusion to Machiavelli may have been accurate to Cook's way of thinking, yet it hardly corresponds to the figure on trial and on the scaffold.

Such attempts to discredit the king, whether in *King Charls his Case* or *Plain English,* finally did not touch the questions of his sincerity or repentance. The *Basilike* more than any other work answered those questions with a well-integrated portrait of anguish built up carefully through a narrative concerning the events of the wars. This monarchists' vision of history had to be challenged on its own grounds.

Milton and the author of the *Eikon Alethine* mount such a challenge in their attack on the *Basilike.* Both focus on its method of presenting its case, undermining its versions of events by questioning the logic of those ver-

12. In both Aristotle and Cicero, persuasion in the forensic speech must develop from logic and its topics rather than external social and political circumstances. See Cicero, *De Oratore,* 2.10.43.

sions—both internal and external. Of the two attacks, however, the *Alethine* remains superficial, relying principally on the charge of forgery. Milton's goes far deeper, examining the very means by which the *Basilike*'s case is constructed—its words and phrases as well as its facts. In so doing, Milton instructs his readers how to read actively and independently, thus teaching them to be politically astute citizens.

The contrast between the methods of Milton and the *Alethine* appears distinctly in the two authors' responses to the *Basilike*'s version of the attempt on the Five Members. In both the *Basilike* and his own declarations and speeches, Charles insisted that he had legitimate reasons for appearing in the House of Commons and did not have as many men in his retinue as his enemies claimed. The *Alethine* responds to the logic of the king's claims, first by questioning the manner of Charles's arrival in the Commons. The author points out that the king could hardly have been ignorant of parliamentary procedures or the fact that members could not be legally tried while sitting. Therefore, he declares, "the late King would have taken his place in the House of Lords, not have thrust into the Chaire among the Commons, had he no intent to invade their priviledges." So, he continues, the reader must consider other possible motives: either the king wanted to test members' reactions, the better to insult them in the future; or he wished to stop their defense of the Commonwealth; or maybe he planned to do something even worse, since the queen was very angry when he failed to make the arrest (sigs. C4–D2).

Continuing his attack, the author shifts to a quasi-legal interrogation of the *Basilike*'s description, maintaining that the "forger . . . wrongs" the king with contradictory statements. To the claim that the king could produce evidence that would convict the members, the author responds by asking: Did the king see it? Did others tell him about it? And why did he not have it after the search of the members' property? Finally, he asks, would not the king have made specific charges in order to clear himself if such charges could be made? Similarly, why should the king apologize for his retinue if, as he claims, there were so few (sigs. I2v–I4)?

The *Alethine* continues in this fashion to question the entirety of the *Basilike*—not by bringing in scriptural or historical examples but by relentlessly scrutinizing the logic of the king's claims. In so doing, the author also attempts to undermine the ethical proofs of his opponent's text. By claiming that the *Basilike* is forged and internally inconsistent, the author of the *Alethine* challenges the principal source of power of the "king's book." He aims at nothing less than impeachment of its principal witness. In an analysis of the meditation on the Nineteen Propositions, the author destroys Charles's claim to sincerity simply by indicating that he contradicts himself. On the one hand, the author shows, Charles maintains that his opponents are making war upon his soul, while on the other hand he calls for a Synod of Divines to resolve the religious questions and then declares himself to be willing to concede much more than the propositions demand (sig. O3). Throughout his analysis, the author reminds his readers of other events occurring outside the scope of the *Basilike*'s discourse, including the outcome of the king's various actions. The author reveals how the *Basilike* distorts history: it isolates particular moments, lifts them out of their immediate context, then presents only one side of the argument, and even that not completely logically. Yet nowhere does the author of the *Alethine* offer any alternative to the vision presented in the tract he attacks.

Milton adopts a similar stance in *Eikonoklastes*. Instead of examining the political program of the *Basilike*, he focuses on its logical inconsistency. But, consistent with his own plan to reeducate his readers, he demonstrates as well how the words themselves—the very fabric of the text—belie the king's arguments. By way of method, Milton quotes extensively from the *Basilike*, turning its own words against it.[13] Discussing the attempt on the Five Members, he explains:

> Concerning his unexcusable, and hostile march from the Court to the House of Commons, there needs not much be said. For he confesses it to be an act which most men, whom he calls *his enemies* cry'd shame upon; *indifferent men grew jealous of and fearfull, and many of his Friends resented as a motion rising rather from passion then reason:* He himself, in one of his Answers to both Houses, made profession to be convinc'd that it was a plaine breach of thir Privilege: Yet heer like a rott'n building newly trimm'd over he represents it speciously and fraudulently to impose upon the simple Reader.[14]

A "simple Reader," as Milton will demonstrate, is not only one who is unaware of Charles's other words in other places but also one who is not sufficiently alert to catch the shifts in meaning conveyed in the *Basilike* itself.

Quoting further, Milton shows that the king claimed to have "*just motives and pregnant grounds . . . against the five Members, whom hee came to dragg out of the House*" (377). Like the author of the *Alethine*, he speculates on why

13. Cf. Cable, "Milton's Iconoclastic Truth," 138–42.
14. *Complete Prose Works*, 3:376–77. All references to Milton in this chapter are to vol. 3, and will hereafter be cited in the text by page numbers.

the king did not produce his evidence, and then deflates Charles's allegations: "*He mist but little to have produc'd Writings under some mens own hands. But yet he mist, though thir Chambers, Trunks, and Studies were seal'd up and search'd; yet not found guilty. Providence would not have it so.* Good Providence, that curbs the raging of proud Monarchs, as well as of madd multitudes" (379). By highlighting the significant words in the king's sentences, Milton shows how those sentences are constructed to hide their true meanings. The point is not that Charles almost found evidence, but that he failed to find it. The following mention of the search only reinforces the point that Charles is manipulating his words to hide the truth. Whenever possible, Milton makes only short references to contexts outside the *Basilike*. Instead, he guides readers through the text itself, presenting Charles's words often one by one or phrase by phrase so that readers may see for themselves the falsity those words conceal when read together and inattentively.

In the presentation of words, Milton differs dramatically from his contemporaries. Redingstone and Cook provide external commentaries on Charles's actions. The author of the *Alethine* places Charles's allegations in context by revealing what facts were left out of the *Basilike*. Milton, by focusing his attention on the king's words and phrases, forbids any section of the *Basilike* to stand as a whole. By destroying its wording, development of ideas, and use of euphemisms, Milton attempts to undermine not simply the logic but the entire vision of the *Basilike*.

In a departure from the standards of forensic rhetoric, Milton and the author of the *Alethine* go beyond merely challenging the integrity of the text of the king's book. They attack it as an image as well. As his own title proclaims, Milton sees image-breaking as his primary task—not only to destroy the text of the book but also to thwart readers' desire to worship any thing or any person instead of truth, hence debasing themselves.[15] Noting the "op'nness" of the author in giving his book the title "The Kings Image," Milton argues that the book creates a "Shrine" for the king so that "the people [might] come and worship him" (343). Milton intends to break the image to restore civic faith in the public and community. Only with this faith can people truly be free, as God intended.

To Milton, Englishmen's natural freedom and civic faith had been systematically destroyed by kings and especially by the hierarchy of the church. Only under the rule of the prelates and "men divided from the public" could people be taught to "fall flatt and give adoration to the Image

15. Cf. Loewenstein, " 'Casting Down Imaginations,' " 255–56.

and Memory of this Man" (344). Such idolatry kills public-spiritedness—that is, the upholding of "all our laws and Native liberties" and the traditions that insure individual and collective rights (347). Milton regards the *Basilike* as a false scripture blasphemously setting up a new god—Charles—who equally blasphemously compares himself to Christian martyrs and even to Jesus. This idolatry is encouraged by prelates who urge false religion. Such a mentality turns people away from both God and the Commonwealth.

This state of affairs goes beyond the logical and ethical confutations of forensic rhetoric. To meet these circumstances, Milton charges the *Basilike* not simply with logical inconsistency but with impiety. He strongly condemns the *Basilike*'s exalting of Charles's deeds and words, especially the depictions of him comparing himself to Christ on the pinnacle of the temple (405) and claiming to *"wear a Crown of Thorns with our Saviour"* (417). The most stringent censure Milton saves for the thesis of the whole work—that Charles is a martyr. Milton declares:

> He who writes himself *Martyr* by his own inscription, is like an ill Painter, who, by writing on the shapeless Picture which he hath drawn, is fain to tell passengers what shape it is; which else no man could imagin: no more then how a Martyrdom can belong to him, who therfore dyes for his Religion because it is *establisht*. . . . And if to die for an establishment of Religion be Martyrdom, then Romish Priests executed for that, which had so many hundred yeares bin establisht in this Land, are no wors Martyrs then he. . . . if to die for the *testimony of his own conscience,* be anough to make him Martyr, what Heretic dying for direct blasphemie, . . . may not boast a Martyrdom? (574–76)

The *Basilike* itself is the label on Charles's shapeless conduct, forming an otherwise unpopular king into the contours of a martyr. More than that, however, Milton cautions against allowing individuals to establish the criteria for martyrdom. The public itself must approve these criteria before they may be applied to single persons. Milton's audience would not perceive heroism or martyrdom in a person they believe to be in the wrong. Hence, why would they allow Charles Stuart to dictate to them the standards for a martyr, regardless of how much he suffered, since he is as wrong as a "Romish Priest" or blasphemer?

Fellow radicals also condemn the sanctification of Charles. The author of the *Alethine* asks, "Can the counterfeit be more reall then the substance? . . . and shall experimentall knowledge bee confuted by this forgers bare assertions?" (sig. A3). In *Plain English,* Redingstone attacks the metaphors of Stuart kingship, defining Charles as a "corrupt fountaine, poisoning

every streame and rivolet he hath had accesse unto," an adulterous husband and a murderous father (sig. A3v). All three authors see that by
allowing the king or his spokesmen to characterize him—whether through
the *Basilike* or through Stuart mythology—the people lose their dignity and
become servile, worshiping false gods and false values.

The radicals' ultimate concern, then, is not so much the defense of a
specific act or political stance but the character of their potential audience—and whether that audience can be persuaded. Forensic rhetoric
demands logical proofs and an audience prepared to listen to them. Milton
and his fellow radicals fear that prelacy and monarchy have already dimin-
ished the capacity of readers for critical thought and cool judgment, so that
those readers will be overwhelmed by emotional appeal. Hence, the author
of the *Alethine* suspects that "multitudes byassed by affection to the late
King would readily and very credulously take for currant any thing stamped
with his effegies" (sig. Av) and exhorts readers not to be geese or asses
gulled by the book (sig. A3v). This fear also prompts Milton's indictment
of the "image-doting rabble; that like a credulous and hapless herd, be-
gott'n to servility, and inchanted with these popular institued of Tyranny,
subscrib'd with a new device of the Kings Picture at his praiers, hold out
both thir eares with such delight and ravishment to be stigmatiz'd and
board through in witness of thir own voluntary and beloved baseness"
(601). The rhetoric of the *Basilike* is thus dangerous because corrupting.
Worse, such a misuse of words can cause readers to doubt the sincerity of
all words and to rely instead solely on their emotions and the words that
pander to them.

The fear that this will occur leads the radical writers to their attack on
rhetoric itself, especially the rhetoric of the epideictic genre—the genre
designed for public show. Like Plato and the early seventeenth-century
Ramists, radical pamphleteers distrust any language that they believe to be
more concerned with effect than truth.[16] The *Alethine* warns against "the
allurements of effeminate Rhetorick" and "this painted Cherubin armed
with a seeming Sword of Sophistry flashing with Rhetoricke" (sig. A3v),
urging readers not to let "the Sunne of your reason . . . bee darkened by a
Cloud of wordes" (sig. A4v). Similarly, Milton calls the author of the
Basilike the king's *"Houshold Rhetorician"* (383), its reasoning "the artifi-

16. This distrust places Milton firmly with both the Ramists and other individualistic English radicals. See Thomas O. Sloane, *Donne, Milton, and the End of Humanist
Rhetoric,* 211–25; and Diane Parkin-Speer, "Robert Browne: Rhetorical Iconoclast."

cialest peece of fineness" (392). Further, he condemns a "sentence faire in seeming" (418), "petty glosses and conceits" (430), "flashes" (478), "flourishes and colours" (552), all "using the plausibility of large and indefinite words, to defend [Charles] at such a distance as may hinder the eye of common judgement from all distinct view & examination of his reasoning" (456–57). The words deliberately become a barrier to understanding, designed to obfuscate the truth behind a fancy front. They create a fiction rather than communicate reality.

Ultimately, the radicals fear, misuse of words will corrupt the reader's ability to read. In *King Charls his Case,* John Cook makes exactly that charge against the king himself, commenting that "he was no more affected with a List that was brought in to *Oxford* of Five or six thousand slain at *Edgehill,* then to read one of *Ben: Johnsons* Tragedies" (sig. A3v). Moreover, Cook suggests that both kingdom and king would have been better served "had he but studied Scripture half so much as *Ben: Johnson* or *Shakespear*" (sig. B3). As Cook understands him, Charles prefers pleasant-sounding words to the truth of Scripture to the extent that he can no longer distinguish fact from fiction. Real dead and fictitious dead are all one. Such a reader and such a king inevitably fail to govern properly.

Milton also concerns himself with Charles's ability to read, but he makes no heavy distinction between "fact" and "fiction." Instead, he considers the process of discernment—the exercise of reason and right judgment in reading, no matter what the text. Milton's Charles is simply not a careful, reasonable reader, but instead is highly selective, choosing only what he wishes and ignoring the remainder. Art itself, Milton warns, contains sufficient examples of good words perverted for evil ends. Many poets have put "pious words" in the mouths of tyrants: "I shall not instance an abstruse Author, wherein the King might be less conversant, but one whom wee well know was the Closest Companion of these his solitudes, *William Shakespeare;* who introduces the Person of *Richard* the third, speaking in as high a strain of pietie, and mortification, as is utterd in any passage of this Book" (361). The example of Shakespeare should have warned Charles's supporters and should now warn readers, if they retain sufficient judgment to read critically.

Throughout *Eikonoklastes,* Milton reveals a strong concern for the readers, and in this concern he departs significantly from his contemporaries. While they are content to point out errors and trust that this act alone will suffice to alert readers to the falsity of the *Basilike,* Milton concentrates most of his attack on the words themselves, recognizing that it is on that most basic level of discourse that most readers will be led astray. He perceives a duty to expose those words and reveal what ideas lie behind them. As he explains in his preface, "In words which admitt of various sense, the libertie is ours to choose that interpretation which may best minde us of what our restless enemies endeavor, and what wee are timely to prevent" (342). We may be free individuals and exert our power over words or else we may be servile, as the king's followers wish, and allow his words to control us by letting them form our thoughts. Whether in examination of contexts, images, or rhetoric, Milton stands alone in understanding that the arguments of the *Basilike* function best when they work as a unit. The *Basilike* presents readers with a complete vision that, if accepted, colors perceptions of individual arguments. Once the vision supplants individual reason, it controls how that reader interprets words. Milton does not merely "answer" the *Basilike*—he presents the whole book piecemeal so that readers may evaluate the words first, before they consider the vision.

Only by examining each word carefully, Milton believes, can readers "choose that interpretation" that will maintain their freedom and civil liberties and, ultimately, the Commonwealth itself. Assenting to the vision of the *Basilike* means assenting to its political vision and hence to the restoration of the house of Stuart. To Milton, the words of the *Basilike* are the seeds of oppression.

The culture of the Stuart court and Charles himself made a political issue of the representation of the image of the king. Whether in court masques, Charles's own speeches, or the *Basilike,* the monarchical system depended upon that representation. Hence, Charles's own personality played a key role in the arguments for and against the regicide. To his defenders, Charles was not merely the king but also a hero—one who, in the best tradition of the Stuart masque, embodied the values of the political nation. To the regicides, Charles's actions made him a bad man and thus a tyrant rather than a true king. That the political system could encourage such conduct was the strongest argument against monarchy.

Epideictic rhetoric proved to be readily adaptable to Charles's personality as well as to the chief arguments of the monarchists. Through that genre, Charles easily became not only a king but a cultural hero, embodying noble, selfless devotion to God and Country. Further, the genre effectively appropriated the language of the Puritan opposition. Decades before the execution of the king, the autobiographical martyrology of Bastwick,

Burton, Prynne, and numerous others prepared a generation of readers to sympathize with the persona of the suffering, patriotic Protestant speaking truth to power. By employing the language of the old opposition and abandoning court iconography, monarchist pamphleteers could unite both the old royalists and their new Presbyterian allies with a shared political discourse.

In contrast, the predominantly forensic attacks on Charles by Milton and other radicals put their writers on the defensive. Concentrating on the past and being narrowly focused, this discourse by its very nature precluded the integrative language that identifies and unifies a political community. It addressed only those that already shared the assumptions of the writer. Moreover, the regicides' own proclaimed suspicion of rhetoric prohibited them from offering new heroes to take the place of the dead king or his surviving sons. Rhetorically as well as politically, when they discussed the character of the king, the regicides committed themselves to fighting a rearguard action. Meanwhile, through Charles I, the monarchists reconstructed the future.

SIX

Icons of Government

The struggle to gain primacy in the reconstruction of public discourse necessarily extended beyond the issue of Charles I and his trial. In the months surrounding the execution, writers of all political convictions presented their visions of the public weal. Rhetorically, pamphleteers faced the deliberative occasion par excellence: the opportunity to advise both a governing body—the new Commonwealth—and the political nation as a whole. The titles of their tracts—bearing such words as *declaration, protestation, vindication, advice,* and *queries*—testify to the deliberative orientation of the discourse. Almost without exception, the writers of 1649 present themselves as individual public actors, not spokesmen, either supporting or attacking the group in power but not identifying with any party. Their tracts reflect attempts to redefine both the writers' and the readers' perceptions of kingship, government, public life, and political participation.

Decidedly more radicals than monarchists contributed to the debate surrounding the examination of kingship that followed Charles's death. The principal reason for this imbalance was, of course, that to dedicated royalists—the original supporters of the king—the nature of kingship was self-evident and had been for generations.[1] But the execution added others to their cause, most notably the Presbyterians, who presented a political and rhetorical problem. While dedicated supporters of kingship, the Presbyterians could not accept divine-right theory and had not accepted Charles's conduct before and during the first civil war. Therefore, opponents of the Rump Parliament and army had to alter their arguments to become more inclusively monarchist, and to do so they could not simply revive the works of James I and memories of the Personal Rule in defense of their position. Although some monarchist investigations of kingship echoed the *Eikon Basilike* by presenting a Christ-like Charles and an appeal

1. Known as "swordsmen," such hard-line royalists alienated moderate supporters of monarchy, such as Hyde. See David Underdown, *Royalist Conspiracy in England, 1649–1660,* 1–17.

to the reader's conscience, most writers steered their arguments away from specific personalities. Instead, they shifted their attention to broader issues of principle, addressing questions of law, tradition, and especially religion.[2]

The language of religion and custom became the chief vehicle by which monarchists constructed a broad-based integrative discourse. Religion and custom provided the copious examples and analogies that allowed royalists and Presbyterians alike to make epideictic modifications of their fundamentally deliberative rhetoric. As did the author of the *Basilike,* writers could both urge a particular course of action and draw together an audience fragmented and distressed by current events. By adopting the methods of the epideictic genre, monarchist discourse emphasized collective identity and values over substantive argument. With particular matters of doctrine and politics minimized, individual writers could address a wide audience, including all but committed regicides, in a reconstructed worldview of authority, hierarchy, security, and harmony that defied the supporters of the Commonwealth.

Rhetorically as well as politically, the Independents had the most at stake in the public debate preceding and immediately following the regicide. Although the two groups shared the need to reconstruct a vision of society within the minds of the political public, the monarchists covered familiar territory in their tracts while the Independents faced a clean slate in theirs. They had no true English precedent to evoke and few contemporary or historical examples of successful republics. As a result, they often actively reinterpreted history and English law to give their arguments the ancient foundation they believed their arguments must have. Moreover, as the monarchists well understood, most familiar religious arguments were firmly on the side of the king and kingship. Some Independent pamphleteers thus restructured and reevaluated Scripture to support their arguments. Many, however, adopted another strategy. As Margaret A. Judson has shown, the Independent pamphleteers of 1649 were some of the first modern writers to take a secular approach to political theory. As a group, Independent writers seem to have understood that the political discourse they had inherited was inadequate to the task of building a new society.[3]

2. See William L. Sachse, "English Pamphlet Support for Charles I, November 1648–January 1649."

3. See especially J. G. A. Pocock, Retrospect from 1986 to *Ancient Constitution and the Feudal Law: A Study of English Historical Thought in the Seventeenth Century,* 306–34; Judson, *From Tradition to Political Reality: A Study of the Ideas Set Forth in Support of the Commonwealth Government in England, 1649–1653,* 81–83.

Above all, Independent writers knew that, for their rhetoric to succeed, they needed a different kind of reader. Only a reconstructed reader could listen to radical arguments with the kind of logic and detachment demanded by a political vision that contradicted the familiar past, or what Milton calls the "tyrannie, of Custom."[4] This reader would be unafraid to confront both the present and future, ready to assume the public role required of him by a republic. Ultimately, the reader should be willing to realize his own human dignity rather than deliver it to a king or anyone else. Of all the Independent pamphleteers, Milton understood the need for this quality most fully.

Like the monarchists, the Independents faced a fundamentally deliberative occasion. They needed to advise readers of a course of action. Also like the monarchists, the Independents employed mixed genres to create their new political discourse. But the two groups' choices of genre to mix with their deliberative rhetoric reveal fundamentally different rhetorical strategies. With an integrative, if static, worldview, and their corresponding use of the epideictic genre, the monarchists kept their ideology alive by bringing the past (their idea of monarchy) to the present, thereby making it a possibility for the future. Desiring a logical, rational reader as their ideal member of the new Commonwealth, and recognizing the need to have proofs for their arguments, the Independents adopted the forensic genre. Unfortunately for them, however, that genre is inadequate to the task of articulating values. As a genre for integrative rhetoric it is useless. The reader must share the writer's basic assumptions before the argument begins. Moreover, and most important, the forensic genre keeps the reader's and writer's focus in the past and asks that they debate the significance of past actions. Thus, as Independent writers needed to make their readers look forward, their rhetoric moved their readers' attention to the past. The mixture of deliberative and forensic genres they chose could not reconstruct their readers as they needed to do. As a result, regardless of their intentions, the Independents limited the audience for their arguments.

The tracts of 1649 indicate that monarchist writers immediately understood that the argument they engaged was a struggle of two competing visions of the world. Therefore, they carefully present coherent statements of basic principles to justify their position. These statements typically

---

4. *Complete Prose Works,* 3:190. All references to Milton in this chapter are to vol. 3, and will hereafter be documented in the text by page numbers.

appear in tracts as early as the exordia and underlie all further development of monarchist discourse. Royalists have perhaps the easiest task. To
these writers, there can be no gradation of opinion, no options in determining the best course of action for the future. Since monarchy is divinely
ordained, there can be no quarter with its opponents. There is also no
point in investigating individual arguments or specific charges against a
particular king. As Thomas Bayley succinctly explains in *The Royal Charter
Granted unto Kings by God Himself,* "If Kings held their Crowns by Indentures
from the People, then were the People disobliged to their obedience unto
him, upon his failing . . . but if they receive their Crownes immediately
from God, and that by him alone Kings Reigne . . . then all the failings that
can be in a King, can but make him a bad King; but still he must remain a
King" (sig. F5).[5] These are Bayley's alternatives. If his opponents are right,
then the people truly rule. But if he is right, then God ultimately rules and
events unfold according to his will. Bayley appears to offer his reader a
deliberative choice, but in fact he presents only one. Ignoring the tradition
of *vox populi vox Dei*—the voice of the people is the voice of God—Bayley
assigns God's approval only to the monarchist argument. This strategy
calls not for debate but for assent, in epideictic fashion.

Bayley's approach also exemplifies another basic technique of royalist
rhetorical strategy. By identifying God with monarchy, these writers dismiss as irrelevant any argument about a particular king's personality or
actions. The anonymous author of *God and the King: Or the Divine Constitution of the Supreme Magistrate* defines kingship totally in terms of role and
function. An individual king's success or failure has no bearing on the
ultimate rightness of the role. The author of *An Apologetick for the Sequestred
Clergie of the Church of England* affirms the "absolute, independent, and
Supreme Dominon [*sic*] of God's Vicegerent, the Sacred Majestie of His
Anointed" (sig. A3v). In the best tradition of divine-right theory, these
authors imply that popular objection to a particular king is defiance of
God's will. Readers must thus shift their attention from the public sphere
to the spiritual, from the deeds of Charles I to the word of God.

The royalists' chief task is then not to defend Charles I but to establish
God's word and purpose. Hence, their confirmations rely upon examples
of the revelation of God's will. In a pamphlet addressed *To the Right*

---

5. Published after the revolution, Sir Robert Filmer's *Patriarcha* was the first royalist tract to argue exclusively from natural rather than divine order. See James Daly, *Sir
Robert Filmer and English Political Thought,* 151–71.

Honourable The Lord Fairfax and His Councell of Warre, Henry Hammond declares that there was never at any time full equality among persons—"even in state of innocence, God designed superiority, not equality." Men are superior to women because they have greater power, and power comes from God. Moreover, there is subordination even among angels. Hence, God wishes hierarchical order (sigs. Bv–B3). Similarly, Bayley devotes an entire chapter to the exposition, "Of the necessity and excellency of Monarchy," arguing first that hierarchy is natural, as shown in the great chain of being, and second that it is God's will—"The further off any government is to Monarchy, the worse it is." As proof of God's preference, Bayley uses the fact that Christ was born under an earthly emperor and spoke of the "kingdom" of heaven (sigs. H2–H4). The author of *God and the King* argues that "Gods Dominion" is both "Naturall and Vniversal," and that God sets up a supreme magistrate in every kingdom. Therefore, to do God's will, every country must properly have a king (sigs. A3v, B).

The reliance on examples and the prompting of assent and acceptance of a group of values indicate the mixed genre of these confirmations. Examples appropriately belong to the deliberative genre—the only one of the three in which it is permissible to develop an argument almost exclusively by example. The emphasis on values, however, belongs to the epideictic genre—the one designed for reinforcing the collective identity of the listeners. The writers of these tracts encourage a political stance in readers by validating their religious beliefs. Drawing their proofs from Scripture, all these authors appeal to both divine and natural order to place the king in a firm position of authority over the people.[6] God's word holds primacy of place. Any perceived difference in the order of nature is either a violation of God's law or simply a misreading of the Book of Creatures—nature as "read" for signs of the mind of God. According to this line of reasoning, there is only one choice the audience can make: the king must receive his crown from God. To be religious is therefore to be a royalist.

From this premise, the readers may derive only one conclusion—their duty is obedience, no matter what transpires in the kingdom. To the author of the *Apologetick,* humble suffering and loyalty to God's order are the true marks of the good Christian and a proof of faith (sigs. A3–A3v). In *The Royal Charter,* Bayley explains obedience at length, extending the meta-

---

6. See for example *A Declaration and Protestation of Will. Prynne;* John Gauden, *The Religious and Loyal Protestation of John Gauden, Dr. In Divinity,* sigs. B2–B3; *Humble Advice,* sig. B; and Henry Hammond, *To the Right Honourable Lord Fairfax,* sigs. B3v–C2.

phor of the king's subjects as God's children. As a mother forbids her children to touch a mirror, knowing that they may break it, "so God is very chary of his King, wherein he beholds the representation of himselfe, and knowing him to be but brittle, and though the most refined Earth, yet but glasse: he commands his people that they should not touch his Anointed; knowing that if they were permitted but to tamper with him in the least degree, their rude hands may break it in peeces, when they do but thinke to set it right" (sig. E4v). One touches the anointed not only by doing violence against him but also by defending oneself against him, failing to protect him, touching "his Crowne and dignity," killing his soldiers, taking away his revenues, speaking against him, or cursing him in one's heart. Since the king is the reflection of God, whatever the king wishes ought to be. Because everyone else is but God's child, no one is competent to interfere with God's design. To do so would be to presume to be wiser than God (sig. E5–Fv).

The issue of obedience also gives the monarchists the opportunity to address Presbyterians and other sectarians, since it raises a question of paramount importance to them—that of Christian liberty. This question forms a crucial part of many monarchist confutations, as it allows the writers another opportunity to articulate their own convictions. In his pamphlet to Fairfax, Hammond explains that true Christian liberty means liberty "not from obedience to Superiours, but from slavery to lusts and passions, which Christ came to bestow upon us" (sig. B). Pointing to "the vile sect" of Gnostics, Hammond contends that only heretics and heathens have urged freedom from legal constraints (sig. Bv). Thus, Christian liberty cannot mean complete political liberty.

It cannot mean complete liberty of conscience either. As Bayley argues,

> If by Liberty of Conscience, [one means] that it shall be lawfull for everyone to chuse his own Religion, or to be of his own opinion, those are things which we ought not to have, much lesse to Fight for; for then let us not blame every Panim that bakes his cake to the Queen of heaven, or every ignorant votary, who creepes to his own Image, or makes his owne Idoll, for in this kind of Liberty, we do but sacrifice unto the net wherein we see our selves caught, and burne incense to the drag that hales us to destruction. (sigs. A6v–A7)

Behind the direct attack on religious radicals is reassurance of the readers. Bayley's statement insists on the basic truths of the Christian religion and the existence of transcendent principles that must not be subject to debate. Bayley implies that any questioning of established doctrine undermines faith—admitting any private divergence ultimately admits all, thus denying the universality of the Christian revelation.

To these pamphleteers, Christian liberty can only mean the liberty to serve Christ as he is defined by an established church. Hammond's argument suggests that any challenges to his position come from heretics or rebels. Bayley's argument sets up a dichotomy of "we" versus the "Panim" or the "ignorant votary." As is the case throughout his tract, his method admits no third position. Here, it pits an individual pagan against "us"— writer, reader, and community. A threat to "our" values threatens "us" completely. Both writers wish to define Christian liberty in such a way that it does not disturb what they perceive as the community, their own group of shared values. Their rhetoric, by drawing such a heavy line between "us" and "them" and exaggerating the character of "them" to the point of absurdity, portrays "us" as the more reasonable alternative. The readers are led to dissociate themselves from "them" so that they may better ally themselves with the writer and his values. Such an argument legitimizes any doubts the readers may have about the plans of the new Commonwealth and its sectarian adherents.

With this bifurcated view of current events, monarchists in general prefer to eschew theory, debate, or any direct kind of deliberation in favor of praise or blame—pure martyrology, as in the *Basilike,* or vituperation of opponents. Their confutations may thus be solidly devoted to questions of their opponents' character and designs for the future. Since their method of attack polarizes the argument, the monarchists indirectly advocate their own position as they challenge the Independents. The most common theme in monarchist pamphlets—rebellion and its consequences—touches by inference on most of the values of the conservative wing of the old ruling class. Readers are to be moved through horror at and rejection of "rebels" to desire that which the rebels challenge. And what they challenge is the prewar past, the memory of which, after nine years of war and civil disturbance, is already obscured by the hardships of the present.

Most frequently, the monarchists uphold a vision of a harmonious, religious community under assault by vicious and often evil men. Bayley closes his tract by charging bluntly that "all the specious pretences of popular Government, Free-State, Liberty of the Subject, are but figments and delusions of the people, obtruded by vaine-glorious and haughty men, who knowing that they could not by that one Governour of all the rest, yet they hope to be one of many" (sig. H5). Those who rebel, therefore, are self-serving and wicked. As proof, Bayley offers a list of comparisons—"the works of the flesh" to "the fruit of the Spirit" (sig. A8). While they read his list of opposites, Bayley asks his readers to consider "by which of these two was CHARLS *the First's* Head cut off?" Since the tract has already allied kingship with God and true religion, the implications of the list are obvious. The regicides must be the party of "Adultery, Fornication, Uncleannes, Laciviousnes, Idolatry, Witchcraft, Hatred, Variance, Emulations, Wrath, Strife, Seditions, Heresies, Envyings, Murders, Drunkennesse, Revellings" (sigs. E2v–E3). To be on the side of the spirit, readers must dissociate themselves from both the works of the flesh and the Independents.

This approach is echoed by many monarchists. The *Apologetick* asks, "What wise and honest man could rationally imagin, that such unnatural, unheard of thoughts could probably possess the hearts of anie, who had not first cast off Humanitie and Reason, not to speak of Concience [*sic*] and Religion?" (sig. B4). "Lodowick Frederick Giffeheyl" argues that "the Devill hath . . . wholly possessed" the regicides (sig. A2). Henry Hammond calls them "evill Spirits" (sig. A2v). Given the absoluteness of the argument, any opponent of the regicide must be good. But further, such characterizations of one's enemies also serve to cancel any thought of negotiation or serious argument. One does not negotiate with the Devil since to do so would be to admit some common ground or interest. This rhetoric denies any community with its enemies.

The Independents thus appear as a fundamental threat to religion. The monarchist but not royalist Banbury clergy explicitly makes this charge in an eleventh-hour (January 25) attempt to avert the regicide, *The Humble Advice and Earnest Desires of Certain Well-Affected Ministers,* pleading that "it will hazard Religion, by rendring the Professors of it odious to the Common Enemy without" (sig. A3), and maintaining that a "Jesuitical party has been striving from the beginning of the wars to destroy the Protestant faith through toleration" (sig. A4v). In *A Briefe Memento to the Present Vnparliamentary Iunto,* William Prynne repeats this last charge, warning the readers that the Rump is riding in "*Ignatius Loyola* his fiery Chariot, like so many young *Phaetons*" (sig. B4). The anonymous broadside *The Last Damnable Designe of Cromwell and Ireton* accuses the Rump of caballing with every "Popish" king and rebel on the face of the earth to destroy England's religion, government, and prosperity. In these tracts, the regicides embody the powers of darkness. Anyone who wishes to preserve English Protestantism must fight them. And since these pamphlets name toleration and the Jesuits as the chief threats to religion, readers are led to understand that the true protector of religion against Catholicism, sects, and heresies is the established church.

After the Church of England, these pamphleteers defend the old form of government, which they characterize as the only possible kind of government. As Bayley argues, "The worst Governour is always better then the best Rebell" (sig. E2v). Most pamphleteers support their arguments by evoking images of political chaos. John Gauden envisions a "deluge of miseries" following the execution of Charles (sig. B2). *The Humble Advice* predicts "perpetual engagement of the three Kingdoms . . . in blood" (sig. A3v). The broadside *A Declaration and Protestation of the Peers* fears the establishment of "the most transcendent *Tyranny and usurpation* over the King, Kingdome, Parliament, Peers, *Commons,* and Freeemen [*sic*] of *England* ever practiced or attempted in any age, tending only to dishonor, enslave, and destroy this ancient flourishing Kingdome, and set up *Anarchy* and confusion in all places."

Against "tyranny," all these pamphlets and many others uphold the familiar Parliament and political organization of the past. As *A Declaration and Protestation of the Peers* argues, this organization must be made up of king, lords, commons, and freemen—no servants, rabble, or others. The pamphlets all advocate a balance among traditional institutions, with proper restrictions on all, although some writers exempt the king. To these pamphleteers, their country is by nature a kingdom. Anything else is unnatural. By recalling the forms of the past and prophesying utter disaster in the future, the writers leave no doubt about the present. The only alternative they acknowledge is a return to the past. This alone, they believe, will save the country from anarchy and protect what the writers value.

Along with king, traditional parliaments, and some variety of established church, these pamphleteers value property. In the defense of property, monarchists appeal to the former "natural" leaders and anyone who fears changes in the economic and social structures of England. Gauden attacks the Independents as "Pyrats and Robbers," whose crime is taking by violence other people's property (sig. B). Bayley sneers at the suggestion that the Rump desires to protect property and suggests that, by their actions, they really seem to want "*all things in common*" (sig. A7v). Several broadsides discuss this theme even more specifically. Most notably, *A Declaration and Protestation of the Peers* pronounces that the acts of the Rump are "*Treasonable, Detestable, Tyrannicall, and destructive* to the . . . Lives, Liberties, Propertyes and Estates of the People." This tract defines "the people" as property owners and the Rump as dangerous because it threatens property owners.

Many writers argue that the Rump is beyond the control of the class of "the people" and not a part of it. The broadside *To the Present Visible Supreame Power Assembled at VVestminster* complains that we "shall expose our selves, and Estates, into the power of those, who . . . have no power over us, and to be tryed, and disposed of by unwritten, and uncertaine Dictates, Lawes and Rules, to which we never gave the least consent." "We" are property owners, and the writer argues that the government is illegitimate because it lacks the consent of this class. Also assumed in this passage are the convictions that this class *should* have the authority to veto a government and that the government rules by consent, not of all the governed, but of "men of substance."

The Last Damnable Designe of Cromwell, in contrast, addresses a larger and less affluent group, utilizing fear and anti-Semitism. According to this tract, the army ultimately plans to "Plunder, and Dis-arme the City of *London*" and sell the whole city to the Jews, who will become the army's bankers and

> merchants to buy off for ready money, (to maintain such wars as their violent proceedings will inevitably bring upon them) not only all Sequestred, and Plundred goods, but also the very bodies of Men, Women, and Children, whole Families taken Prisoners for sale, of whom these Jewish merchants shall keep a constant traffique with the *Turks, Moores,* and other *Mahometans;* . . . and this is the meaning of *Hugh Peters* threat to the *London* Ministers, That if another War followed, they will spare neither Man, Woman, nor Child.

The reference to the radical Peter lends credibility to the charges, which in any case prey easily upon the fears of the tradesmen and merchants of London, already suffering "decay of trade" because of the wars. The vision of slavery by itself answers the Independents' claims of "liberty," and both Jews and Muslims are convenient bogeymen, depicted as destroyers of Christian family life. The Independents thus become economic, political, and personal threats, extending their grasp to the most intimate areas of personal life.

Hence, the monarchists evoke God, property, and family in defense of their ideology, manipulating traditional values and borrowing their positive connotations. The question of values lends itself most appropriately to epideictic rhetoric, and, in turn, epideictic rhetoric mixes easily with the larger question of future action addressed by the deliberative genre. Even though the king's trial and execution logically could prompt discussion of legality, only Prynne—himself a lawyer—makes any attempt to employ forensic rhetoric, and even he does so within an epideictic attack on the Independents. The relative legality of the procedures against Charles was simply not an issue to most of these pamphleteers. After seven years of being targets of popular discontent, the court party and many members of the traditional ruling class saw an opportunity to regain the political and social power and influence they had previously possessed by rhetorically denying legitimacy to their opponents' political aims. Further, Presbyterians and other disaffected parliamentarians readily joined the attack. To advocate their own version of leadership, monarchists first had to establish themselves as the arbiters and defenders of community values. By adapting the epideictic genre, they rhetorically claimed those values as their own, providing in the process a coherent vision of stability and peace.

Only after creating this vision could the monarchist pamphleteers urge their particular course of action. Several tracts, such as Bayley's *Royal Charter,* explicitly call for an immediate restoration of the house of Stuart. Others propose such actions as restoring the excluded members of Parliament, holding new elections, convoking to reestablish the church, revising the laws, and praying for salvation. And, of course, those appearing before January 30 urge reconsidering the proceedings against the king. Given the vision they present, these writers do not need to give any particular examples of the benefits of a monarchy. Specific plans—beyond the mere proposals—are unnecessary to the arguments. By combining the epideictic genre with the deliberative, these pamphleteers can urge a course of action without giving the specific examples demanded by the deliberative confirmation. Rhetorically, even in 1649, monarchist pamphleteers held that their position needed no real defending. Its rightness was self-evident and the writers' surety gave it power.

Through these strategies, royalist and monarchist pamphleteers drew readers to their own political convictions. To a confused, fearful, and war-impoverished reader, mystified by the rapid changes in government, the monarchists' coherent vision could be comforting and appealing. It provided a sense of direction and purpose often absent from the public declarations of the regicides. The only effective resistance to this persuasion was the possession of a skeptical, critical mind; helping to produce such minds in the people became one of the principal goals of the Independent pamphleteers.

The Independents' break with the political structures of the past demanded not only a new system of government but also a discourse to support it. Their own ideology denied them the use of the old, conventional formulas of God, King, and Country. Yet they inherited a language of public debate that was bound by oratorical conventions and an audience that had been schooled to respond to those conventions. Unfortunately, the tropes governing English political language—drawn from history, common law, and religion—had always supported monarchy. The problem facing the Independents, then, was to reach their audience in a language that audience could understand but that did not predispose it to favor monarchy. Rhetorically as well as politically, the Independents needed to perform true acts of creation, defining their own terms and debating from new grounds.

The most prominent Independent writers of 1649—John Milton, John Goodwin, and others—attempt to do just that. Through their careful mixing of deliberative and forensic rhetoric they aim to re-create humanity as well as a political system. By means of extensive, logical exposition, they begin by instructing their readers how to read political arguments. The process and aims of reading explained, Milton and others reread history, including the ancient Jewish history presented in law and Scripture itself— the proofs upon which the monarchists traditionally based their arguments—to build a new vision of political and spiritual community. Through their rereading of evidence, the Independents question the monarchists' assumptions about the origins and uses of power, justice, accountability, and covenant. These general principles established, the Independents then turn to their specific defenses and attacks. Through the logical proofs demanded by their choice of forensic oratory, the Independents attempt to encourage in readers the kind of intellect demanded for free inquiry and full participation in their anticipated new society.[7]

The complexity of the aims of Independent rhetoric in 1649 is nowhere more evident than in Milton's *Tenure of Kings and Magistrates*. Numerous modern readers have noted its significance for the development of Milton's political ideas but tend to discount its rhetoric. Much of this response to the discourse is attributable to confusion over genre. W. E. Gilman long ago identified the *Tenure* as an example of deliberative oratory while criti-

---

7. The association of forensic oratory with inquiry had some classical precedent. Quintilian, *Institutio,* 3.4.9, and *Rhetorica ad Alexandrum,* 1421b18–1427b31, identify "investigational oratory" as a subgenre of forensic rhetoric.

cizing the apparently limited nature of its advice.[8] More common is the view that the *Tenure* is a formal defense, focusing on legal questions and Milton's view of his audience.[9] The resulting critical dismay over his logical proofs—demanded by the forensic genre—loses sight of Milton's particular use of those proofs. Milton is one of the very few Independents to present a full rereading of history, law, and religion in one tract. Further, Milton is unique in his extensive emphasis on public character. While instructions to the reader are common in the Independent tracts of 1649, Milton is the only author to make transformation of the reader his principal concern. Milton's is thus one of the most fully articulated examinations of the revolution to emerge in the months following the regicide. More than any other Independent writing in 1649, Milton based his hopes for the Commonwealth on the transformed reader.

Independent writers recognized that defining proper readers and reading was absolutely crucial to their arguments. As a result, their tracts begin with such definitions, in keeping with the forensic concern that presentation of ethos appear in the exordium. Traditionally, the ethos to establish is that of the speaker, so that the audience might appreciate his goodwill and be favorably disposed to him. Readers could thus anticipate such a statement. However, when a definition of the reader appears instead, the reader is identified with the writer, underscoring their commonality of purpose. Hence, Milton challenges readers to evaluate their own characters as he argues the affinity between tyrants and bad men:

> Tyrants are not oft offended, nor stand much in doubt of bad men, as being all naturally servile; but in whom vertue and true worth most is eminent, them they feare in earnest, as by right thir Maisters, against them lies all thir hatred and suspicion. Consequentlie neither doe bad men hate Tyrants, but have been always readiest with the falsifi'd names of *Loyalty,* and *Obedience,* to colour over thir base compliances. (190–91)

Just as bad men are naturally servile, so to be servile is to be a bad man. A truly free individual cannot and will not be a slave. If readers wish to be good and free, they must learn to distinguish true loyalty and obedience from servility. To be capable of true loyalty, Milton argues, one must be

8. *Milton's Rhetoric: Studies in His Defense of Liberty,* 101, 109.

9. The *Tenure* has not undergone the same revival of interest as *Eikonoklastes* and very recent analyses are lacking. See Christopher Hill, *Milton and the English Revolution,* 166–69; Andrew Milner, *John Milton and the English Revolution: A Study in the Sociology of Literature;* and John T. Shawcross, "The Higher Wisdom of *The Tenure of Kings and Magistrates.*"

able to give it freely—one must be able to consent. If readers wish to be virtuous, therefore, they must be able to give their consent. Milton immediately establishes the premises that the king rules by consent of virtuous people, that he is accountable to them, and that those people may depose him. Readers must understand this basic point—the linkage of virtue and true power—before they can continue with Milton's argument.

Other Independent writers not only define their readers but also include detailed instructions for reading their tracts. Milton's admirer and competitor John Goodwin acknowledges that many readers may be confused by recent events, since "the first apparitions of things new and strange, especially when the reasons and causes of them are unknown, . . . are usually disturbing, and offensive to their apprehensions" (sig. A3). Readers must realize that their fears come from uncertainty and that they are ripe for exploitation by politically ambitious, "turbulent, and most inveterate spirits" (sig. B). Readers, then, must educate and thereby protect themselves by reading Goodwin's tract. "Turbulent" people, readers learn, are those who oppose the Commonwealth. Peace-lovers should therefore recognize that the Commonwealth represents order and harmony. The author of *The Resolver Continued,* N. T., agrees with Goodwin in contending that many people resist the Independents out of ignorance, arguing further that readers should use their logic rather than emotion. Emotions may prevent readers from judging his arguments properly—that is, emotions predispose one to royalism. This writer, then, instructs his readers that only reason will lead to the "light" of the Commonwealth (sig. A3).

A similar stance leads the author of *Rectifying Principles* to characterize opponents as bad readers. Writing on January 4 in an attempt to warn people away from the Presbyterians and reconciliation with the king, the writer charges:

> There is a crew of crafty knaves and traytors lately returned into the Kingdome, who formerly pretended the King, but intended themselves onely; so politickly to deceive the people, they made use of the Kings name to draw the people on their side, who thought they fought for the King, but it was to raise the fortunes of these fellowes, by raising themselves. And thus those crafty knaves caused the poore ignorant sottish people to murther one another to make themselves great; for which the Fooles were jeered by these Knaves. (sig. A4)

Unguided by reason, "silly people" listen since they misread and therefore "idolatrize" the names of the king, prince, and duke. The author leaves nothing to chance in his tract. The entire text of *Rectifying Principles* bears elaborate marginalia, as the author glosses his own words, adding the particulars to his general argument and reminding his readers to observe them, "lest thou come short of our intention—thine instruction" (sig. A3v). The glosses insist on the readers' full attention as they work their way through the text. It leaves no room for the wicked operations of the will.

To these writers, then, support of the monarchy is a product of ignorance and a betrayal of humanity's higher principles. As "Eleutherius Philodemus" writes in *The Armies Vindication,* monarchists are "befool'd" by kings and have become *"tame asses . . . to be ridden and beaten by them"* (sig. A4v). To be adult—indeed, to be human—readers should exercise their reason and learn that they themselves are the true sovereigns of England, that they have the power to change their government to suit the dignity of a free people. In short, they must already believe that sovereignty resides in the people before they begin to read the pamphleteers' arguments, just as a jury must already accept the legal system in which it participates before it hears the arguments of a case. The pamphleteers thus define their audience and in so doing limit the number of readers who will accept the premises necessary to read the evidence the tracts present.

Readers must be inspired with a sense of their own dignity before they will accept the Independents' fundamental argument—the humanity of kings and the essential kingship or sovereignty of the people. According to this argument, political power naturally resides in the people, law is the expression of nature, and religion explains how wickedness is anything counter to that nature. Milton explicitly bases his version of this argument on natural law.[10] This law holds that humanity, in its perfect, unfallen state, was governed by "primary law"—no government of any kind was necessary. The Fall, however, impaired the perfection of God's image within and the full knowledge of God's will without; "secondary law" became all that fallen human beings could know of original perfection. By this law, human beings "agreed by common league" (199) to form political units to assure peace and "to bind each other from mutual injury" (199) caused by the evil in the world. Thus, civilization resulted from agreements of mutual respect. Since not all were trustworthy, people constituted authority in either one or a group of especially chosen individuals, "not to be thir Lords and Maisters . . . but, to be thir Deputies and Commissioners" (199). Government arose from human cooperation and consent.

10. Ernest Sirluck, "Milton's Political Thought: The First Cycle," 209, 210–11.

To support his argument, Milton presents general principles drawn from his survey of history, instructing his readers in the proper application of its lessons. As his opening suggests, he writes to reestablish the principles by which all people may aspire to and exercise their full human dignity. By insisting on natural law and the primacy of justice for the individual rather than, for example, protection of estates or property, Milton includes all people as public actors in the sense of the Greek *politikoi*. In this context, wickedness is any act against the public good. It manifests itself in slavishness—the desire to curry favor for oneself, which is the refusal of public-spiritedness—the desire to uphold the community. Kings and magistrates themselves become wicked when they begin to serve themselves rather than their communities (212). Since they receive their power from the community in order to protect it, they are accountable to it; the community has the right to depose them when they violate their trust. Milton thus rewrites political power to include the idea of accountability to the community.

To Milton, only mutual accountability can preserve essential human dignity. Kings are like other men and therefore must be bound by the same laws that govern the people. Special status for the king by implication degrades the people.[11] Any king who would claim special status reveals his contempt for his people and therefore his unfitness to govern:

> No Christian Prince, not drunk with high mind, . . . would arrogate so unreasonably above human condition, or derogate so basely from a whole Nation of men his Brethren, as if for him only subsisting, and to serve his glory; valuing them in comparison of his own brute will and pleasure, no more then so many beasts, or vermin under his Feet, not to be reasond with, but to be trod on; among whom there might be found so many thousand Men for wisdom, vertue, nobleness of mind, and all other respects, but the fortune of his dignity, farr above him. (204–5)

Anyone who sets himself above others reveals his own pride and brutish nature. "Dignity," or social station and wealth, is only an outer form, not substance. All men's substance is the same; they are "Brethren." Proud kings and, by extension, their supporters, degrade people by refusing to reason with them. Milton dignifies his readers and affirms their worth by presenting a reasonable argument rather than an exhortation, and readers

---

11. See also *The Resolver Continued: Or, a Satisfaction to Some Scruples about Putting of the Late King to Death,* sig. A3v: "And certainly, such a Covenant as this [*"Per fas & nefas"*], had it passed the hands of some *Minions* of *Monarchy:* could never have entered into the hearts of any that are *Lovers of equity.*"

should raise themselves by acting reasonably. Accountability of kings preserves, demands, and encourages "nobleness of mind" among the members of the Commonwealth.

Many Independent writers regard the argument from the laws of nature as so essential and so right that any challenge to it must be a logical or religious error, a challenge to God's will. In *The Resolver Continued,* N. T. explains that "*God made Power,* but *People made Princes*" (sig. A2v). To N. T., this argument is axiomatic—he makes little further justification. In *Ubristodikiai: The Obstructions of Justice,* John Goodwin agrees, declaring that "the Crown is but the Kingdoms, or peoples livery" (sig. C2v). The king is therefore the people's servant, so they may dismiss him. So basic is this idea and, in Goodwin's view, so logical, that only private, corrupt interests could have concealed it. N. T. charges suggestively that "the Popes infallibility, and the unquestionablenesse of Kings, are both of them Monsters of the same Litter. . . . And the downfall of Papal Bishops, and Tyrannous Kings, will not differ much in the time" (sig. A3).

For most of these writers, then, justification of their position depends simply upon confirming God's will in the matters of power and accountability. The anonymous tract *Eye Salve to Anoint the Eyes of the Ministers of the Province of London* flatly denies that the king is God's anointed, contending further that God desires justice "without *respect of Persons*" (sig. A2). The tract makes a special case for trying Charles because he has been "a notorious enemy to the Lord Jesus Christ, and sought (*quantum in se fuit,* as much as it was in his power) to lay violent hands on his Throne, and to make his heritage desolate, and to introduce an arbitrary and tyrannicall power into the civill State" (sigs. A3–A3v). The religious error results in political error, and God demands that both be corrected. *The Armies Vindication* makes a similar argument with scriptural evidence: the Israelites "might not only resist but also depose their kings for wickednes & idolatrie, yea; that al the people were justly punished by the Lord because they removed not their wicked Kings out of their places" (sig. H2). To these writers, Charles I deserved his fate because of his offenses against God. As the monarchists invoke God's order, so the Independents invoke God's justice. They argue that accountability of kings is itself inherently part of God's design for the world. As *Eye Salve* explains, only as long as any person, including a king, may be "called to an account" by those he has wronged can justice exist (sigs. A2–A2v).[12]

12. See also [Robert Bennet], *King Charle's Triall Iustified,* sigs. A2–A3, A4.

Their scriptural evidence reveals the principal effort the Independents make to rewrite the character of kings. To monarchists, kings are God's vicegerents who are above all human justice. To justify human proceedings against a particular king, the Independents argue that God himself does not distinguish among his children. In the most outstanding example of this line of scriptural proof, John Goodwin's *Obstructions of Justice* contends that God "*accepteth* not *the* persons of Princes" and arises, often through unlikely instruments, to defeat those who oppose him (sig. A2). Those ministers who claim that Charles is exempt from justice "were not ashamed to make God himself a Patron and Protectour of murtherers" (sig. A2v). Further, it is wrong to assume that God wishes only the poor to obey his laws, since "Were not this to represent God unto the world, *as an accepter of persons?* and so to *turn the glory* of his unpartial justice *into a* lie?" (sig. B). To Goodwin, as to most Independent pamphleteers, God's word makes all equal in the sight of divine justice. When they call Charles to account as one of themselves, the people of England are merely asserting the dignity that God gave them.

However, as is exemplified best by Milton, many Independent writers look not to Scripture but to secular arguments, maintaining that a king's or magistrate's accountability to human justice preserves the secular, political community. To Milton, political society itself exists so that fallen humanity may have justice. The role of the leader or leaders is to insure that justice be done. Law and justice predate the magistrates and are natural principles. Milton explains how, over time, other aspects of government—oaths, counselors, and parliaments—grew as checks and balances to the magistrate and how the people were bound to the magistrate by covenant to obey the laws they had made or agreed to, provided the magistrate continued to be just (200). To preserve justice, the people, acting politically, may resume the power that is inalienably theirs. Moreover, human history proves the truth and desirability of these assertions. Milton asks, "How then can any King in Europe maintain and write himself accountable to none but God, when Emperors in thir own imperial Statutes have writt'n and decreed themselves accountable to Law. And indeed where such an account is not fear'd, he that bids a man reigne over him above Law, may bid as well a savage Beast" (206). Without accountability, then, a ruler may be corrupted by the absolute power he wields, forget his basic kinship with the other members of his community, and finally reject both civilization and humanity itself.

Many Independent pamphlets agree with Milton in arguing that the people may reclaim power when the magistrate becomes unjust and threatens the community. From a perspective similar to Milton's, the anonymous *The Resolver, Or, a Short Word* contends that acts of injustice are signs of selfishness and a lack of public spirit. A ruler becomes a tyrant when he invades a commonwealth without having a legitimate claim to it, or, having a legal claim, when he abuses his power. He may do this by violating the laws, injuring the subjects, impeding the functions of Parliament, or attempting to "*overthrow the state of the Common-wealth*" (sig. A3v). Laws, parliaments, and people all exist independently of the king and retain the ultimate powers of self-preservation, even after creating the king and delegating power to him. Further, parliaments and laws are themselves of the people—part of their community and equal to them as upholders of justice. As "Eleutherius Philodemus" argues, if kings are not subject to justice, then justice can truly have no force for others. The king must be an example to the people of the principle that binds them all within the community (sigs. G3–G3v).

Laws are the chief expression of the will of the community. Hence, legal arguments and proofs—like those the Independents use in their arguments—assert the existence of that community. The community preserves itself by enforcing its laws. In a just community, all members are equal before the law. Goodwin asserts this point when he refutes the claim that kings are understood to be excluded from obedience to the laws of the land. Conceding that they may at one time have been understood to have been excluded, he asks whether such a possibility in the past should govern the actuality of the present. To include the king is to accord with "reason and equitie" and to promote the public "interest, peace, and safety" (sig. B4v). Contemptuously, Goodwin dismisses the lack of precedent in applying the law to the king: "Very possibly it was never (in such a sence) extended unto musitians, or moris-dancers, yet this, if it could be proved, would be no proof, that therefore it was never *understood,* or meant of them" (sig. B4). *The Resolver* offers similar logical arguments, maintaining that killing a king is a natural consequence of deposing him, an act that many agree was necessary for the justice and the security of the kingdom. As for scriptural prohibitions, *The Resolver* simply comments, "*Jus politicum* [political law] is enough in *Politicks*" (sig. A4).

Like Milton, the author of *The Resolver* refers to the classics and English history for examples of bad or proud kings being brought to justice. As he does so, he strives to show the will not simply of the English but also of the typical human community when its safety is threatened. "Eleutherius

Philodemus" offers an elaborate and comprehensive survey of European history, illustrating the principle, declared in the English statute 28 Henry VIII, chapter 7, which states that when a king becomes an enemy to his kingdom and subjects, he *"doth forfeit his very title to the Crown"* (sig. Hv). Beginning with the Romans, "Eleutherius Philodemus" chronicles the depositions of kings, touching on events in the Holy Roman Empire, France, Spain, Hungary, Bohemia, Poland, Denmark, and Scotland, and ending with English examples. These include "ancient *Brittish Kings,*" John, Edward II, Richard II, and Henry VI. History itself thus offers precedents enough of people asserting their rights over those kings who betrayed the public trust by serving themselves rather than God and their people (sigs. H2–H3). As the *Book of Martyrs* had done in the sixteenth century, these writers urge their readers to see themselves acting within the great scheme of history, carrying out the will of God in striking down their king.

The insistence on laws and precedents underscores the fundamentally forensic nature of these confirmations and confutations. Independent authors call upon readers to evaluate actions, engaging them as if they already belonged to the kind of community the Independents desire. In such a community, all members have rights, dignity, and power. To assert such power and such character and to assent to its exercise is to declare membership in the community. In this way the Independents attempt to create or, as they believe, re-create the political nation along the lines urged by the Commonwealth.

This goal of re-creation results in the general nature of the Independents' political discussion. The few specific issues they address are those that appear as challenges to the legitimacy of the new community. Their investigation of the nature of covenants results from the basic question of how a community can be founded on broken agreements, especially when that community claims to uphold the public trust. Similarly, the Independents must defend the legitimacy of the Rump to establish its authority to govern. Finally, the few explicit attacks appearing in Independent tracts address not monarchists but Presbyterians and other suspected defectors from the cause. Through their abandonment of the principles of the regicides, the Presbyterians raise the most serious challenges to the Independents' vision of community. Their objections cannot go unanswered if the Independents are to continue to argue that they defend the public good.

The discussions of covenant arise from the writers' anticipation of public distress at the breaking of the Solemn League and Covenant—the alliance with the Scots, dating from September 1643, that secured Scottish aid to the English Parliament in exchange for English adoption of the Scottish religious system. Regicide by the English of the monarch of both kingdoms was considered a violation of the Covenant. The majority of Independent tracts deal with the subject simply by ignoring it. Only three address it in detail. These are the ones that attempt to present an inclusive philosophical basis for regicide: Milton's *Tenure of Kings and Magistrates,* Goodwin's *Obstructions of Justice,* and N. T.'s *Resolver Continued.* All attempt to transcend specific arguments about breaking the Solemn League and Covenant by investigating the nature of covenants in general. By discussing the circumstances under which they may be broken, the writers indirectly define the conditions necessary for covenants to be valid—conditions that require the revaluation of all parties concerned.

Milton insists on the essential equality of both sides entering into a covenant. As Milton explains them, covenants require that both sides live up to their promise. Further, when contracted between human beings, they are temporal in nature, "ever made according to the present state of persons and of things" (232). It is foolish to insist that one must remain faithful to a covenant long after the other person has broken faith:

> If I make a voluntary Covnant as with a man to doe him good, and he prove afterward a monster to me, I should conceave a disobligement. If I covnant, not to hurt an enemie, in favour of him & forbearance, & hope of his amendment, & he, after that, shall doe me tenfould injury and mischief, to what he had don when I so Covnanted, and stil be plotting what may tend to my destruction, I question not but that his after actions release me; nor know I Covnant so sacred that withholds me from demanding justice on him. (232)

Putting the issue in personal, individual terms, Milton emphasizes the equality of persons under covenant to each other. Both must be bound by the same rules. Milton also stresses that this is a *voluntary* covenant. He assumes that both sides are able to give their consent freely. Otherwise, such an agreement cannot be truly binding. The inference is clear. The people are qualitatively the equals of their king. They entered into an agreement with the king to establish monarchy. It was a voluntary action and the people did not surrender their dignity in taking it. As the king broke his agreement, so the people may now demand justice for themselves.

N. T. and Goodwin extend the arguments concerning the equality of persons making a covenant. N. T. raises four points concerning the Solemn League and Covenant with the king: first, that it was conditional on the good behavior of both sides; second, that it was explicit, keeping the king within the pale of the *"Rights and Priviledges of Parliament, the true Religion and Liberties of the Kingdom"*; third, that it was not eternal but for wartime and only binding if mutual; and, finally, that it was only sworn to uphold just power. As for the sacred nature of covenants, N. T. turns to the marriage bond, a favorite metaphor of Bayley and other royalists.[13] As N. T. explains, sacred though that bond is, "When my *Wife* turneth *adultresse,* my *Covenant* with her is broken, And when my *King* turneth *Tyrant,* and continueth so, my *Covenant* with him also is broken." Such a covenant exists only as long as both parties agree to maintain it. Further, N. T. argues, readers must consider the nature of the Solemn League and Covenant to see whether it was indeed broken and, if so, by who. The end of this particular covenant, he says, was reformation of church and state. There-fore, the execution of the king who tried to impede that reformation "is no more a breach of *Covenant;* then the throwing of a Logge out of the way, is a deviation from that Journey, the Arrivall unto the end of which, the logge did hinder" (sigs. A3v–B). Through these analogies, N. T. systematically demystifies the idea of covenant. Instead of carrying sacred import, each covenant becomes a simple legal agreement, with each party agreeing to be governed by the rule of law. In N. T.'s arguments, the king becomes first a breaker of agreements, then an adulterous wife, and last an inanimate object, to be thrown out of the way. In each case, the writer deliberately inverts the traditional monarchist analogies. The king of *The Resolver Con-tinued* is, at best, an equal to his people; at worst, having broken faith, he is far beneath them.

Goodwin refuses to exaggerate, but joins with Milton in declaring to readers that they, equally with the king, have a right to have promises kept and grievances redressed. As N. T. does, Goodwin uses the analogy of marriage, noting that a legal and social inferior may compel a superior to make good on a broken bond. A king is to a tyrant as a husband is to an adulterer: God never said that an adulterer should be the head of a woman, and a woman may be legally separated from an adulterer (sigs. E4–E4v, Hv–I2v). Goodwin transforms the traditional metaphor, not by inverting it—as does N. T.—but by revaluing the subordinate partner, insisting upon her dignity. So, a king's subjects have a basic right to be treated well and to be separated from those leaders who injure them.

---

13. The marriage metaphor inevitably evoked political allegiance; hence, any dis-cussion of divorce inevitably had political overtones. See John M. Perlette, "Milton, Ascham, and the Rhetoric of the Divorce Controversy."

Goodwin also stresses the conditional nature of covenants, arguing that they are only enforceable under the conditions in which they were made: "Suppose a State of Prince, should swear a Covenant, or League of perpetual Amitie, with another Prince or State; in case this Prince or State shall at any time in an hostile manner invade the territory of the other, the State or Prince invaded are disobliged from all ingagements by such an Oath" (sig. I2). Oaths must be considered in themselves. Not all should be kept, as Herod should not have kept his oath to kill John the Baptist. He implies that it may be positively wicked to keep some oaths, especially when doing so would bring about greater evils than those entailed in breaking a promise. Rather than lowering the king to the level of the common individual, Goodwin raises the individual to the level of the king. He strongly implies that the readers have no less essential worth, no less integrity, than their rulers.

To Milton, such revalued people—out of a sincere desire to pursue virtue—have the right to choose their rulers. True, valid covenants must be founded on that right. Hence, the covenant exists to protect the people and guarantee their rights. When it ceases to protect—regardless of the degree of failure—the people have the right to demand a new one. Milton argues, "Since the King or Magistrate holds his autoritie of the people, both originally and naturally for their good in the first place, and not his own, then may the people as oft as they shall judge it for the best, either choose him or reject him, retaine him or depose him though no Tyrant, meerly by the liberty and right of free born Men, to be govern'd as seems to them best" (206). Ultimately, to Milton, debates about kings versus tyrants and about covenants and loyalty are totally irrelevant to the question of how a free people shall be governed. Their liberty and choice are all-important. Any civil official may be recalled if he no longer performs his function to the satisfaction of the people, his true masters. Milton leaves "the people" an undefined term, allowing all readers, in their aspiration to virtue, to count themselves as members.[14] Within his domestic audience, Milton repeatedly tries to exhort his readers to regeneration, never a state to be achieved passively or taken for granted. Believing regeneration possible for all, he cannot rhetorically close the door to any and still hope to persuade people to his cause.

Relentlessly logical and legalistic, all three writers engage their readers'

14. Milton's changing definition of and often negative attitude toward "the people" is frequently discussed by his critics. See for example Keith W. Stavely, *Politics of Milton's Prose Style,* 74–84.

minds, urging them to dignify themselves by listening to reason. All address the personal questions of conscience, obedience, and loyalty while assuming that such questions may be discussed calmly. If readers rise to the occasion and join the argument rationally, they confirm both to the writers and themselves their own worthiness to judge and govern. Assured of their own ability to judge, readers thus understand that it is up to them to determine when they ought to keep a covenant. There is no need of external rules that take the place of the people's power. To Milton above all, the essential dignity of the people gives them the power to govern themselves; their exercise of that power confirms their dignity.

Because they assert the reason and dignity of the regenerate English people, the Independent pamphleteers must answer the challenges of the Presbyterians. More than the monarchists, the Presbyterians' attacks on the king's trial and the legitimacy of the Rump seriously threatened to disrupt the Independents' vision of the regenerate, reconstructed community of the Commonwealth. Being excluded from the outset from membership in that community, the monarchists could easily be dismissed and their arguments ignored. The Presbyterians criticized from within, potentially calling into question the foundations of the Independents' arguments and values. Hence, when answering the Presbyterians, the Independents resorted to invective, thereby mixing their epideictic concern for group identity with their predominantly forensic confutations.

The typical invective addresses the Presbyterians' possible motives for their attacks on the Rump. *Eye Salve* argues extensively that Presbyterian divines criticize the mote in others' eyes while ignoring the beam in their own and suggests that their hatred of the army might result from their fear that this body is "about to pull the *Dagon* of the presbytery, viz. Tyths & offrings, &c. the which you so much strive to keep up" (sigs. A3, A4). In *King Charle's Triall Iustified*, Robert Bennet refutes his opponents simply by pointing out that from the beginning opponents argued that Parliament was not free—the characteristic Presbyterian argument against the King's trial—just as they do now and with the same lack of justification (sig. B2). The charge of greed—extreme self-interest—implies that the Presbyterians are unfit members of the new Commonwealth, that they set themselves apart from others in their desire for their own enrichment. Bennet accuses the Presbyterians of opportunism: the monarchists had originated the idea that Parliament was not free, which the Presbyterians initially rejected, taking it up only when events began to go against their own wishes. Bennet therefore asks the Presbyterians what they truly want.

Milton offers the most extensive refutation of the Presbyterians, condemning them from two directions. First, like his Independent counterparts, he questions their motives. Second, he quotes Protestant authorities against them. The two strategies are related. Together, they reveal and criticize the Presbyterians' apparent lack of logic concerning kingship, the consequences of their beliefs and, ultimately, their character. Through his attack, Milton shows the Presbyterians to be not merely wrong but also unsuitable as political actors or free people in any commonwealth.

In attacking their motives, Milton challenges the very notion that the Presbyterians are standing on principle. "The King," notes Milton, is an office, not a person, so when a king is deposed, his deposers have in fact killed the king. Any scruples after that point make no sense and call into question the sincerity of such deposers (232–33). Milton asks what the Presbyterians would have done with Charles in permitting him to live, and he wonders if keeping him a prisoner would have been more to their liking (234). The consequences of such a course of action are only too clear. Milton reminds readers that history is full of examples of massacres perpetrated after royal assurances of safety (240) and of kings violating oaths of reformation, including "Chrisiern the second, King of Denmark . . . driv'n out by his Subjects, and receav'd again upon new Oaths and conditions, broke through them all to his most bloody revenge" (239).

The Presbyterians must then be either fainthearted or treacherous—either not fully committed to true reformation or opposed to it. These new friends of the king give "the most opprobrious lye to all the acted zeale that for these many yeares hath filld thir bellies, and fed them fatt upon the foolish people" (236). They are "ministers of sedition," "mercenary noise-makers" who claim to be free but who refuse sovereign power and "please thir fancy with a ridiculous and painted freedom, fit to coz'n babies" (236). Their desire to cheat and deceive weak and foolish people reveals their hostility to any kind of truly free commonwealth, the good of which all political people must want more than their own. Any reader who does uphold the community must therefore strongly oppose these new "Priests of *Bel*" who would lead all England back into slavery.

Milton's exposition of Protestant authorities aims not at refuting the Presbyterians but at discrediting their character. The texts he marshals are meant to show readers "the difference between Protestant Divines and these Pulpit-firebrands" (243). These texts warn that a tyrant, by his very nature, compromises the dignity of freeborn people and therefore must be combated. Milton crowns his procession of authorities with citations from the Marian exiles, whose suffering preserved the purity of English religion until it was threatened by greedy divines renouncing episcopacy only to curry favor with the new civil powers (251–52). Readers, Milton argues, should recognize frauds and resist them before it is too late.

With his presentation of texts and arguments, Milton asks the readers to judge on the basis of the evidence they have received whether to reject the Presbyterian party or not. When he questions the Presbyterians' motives and sincerity he is ultimately questioning their character. The readers must decide not what they are but what they intend to do. If their true intention—revealed in their character—is to restore slavery, then any readers aspiring to freedom must resist them, no matter how appealing their words sound. Readers must exercise their own critical faculties in evaluating the case Milton presents. In giving readers this opportunity to decide freely, he also accords them respect and gives them a taste of the political freedom he envisions for England.

As a group, the Independent pamphlets represent widely diverging rhetorical stances and strategies. Most of the short works carry titles that indicate their authors' attempts to settle questions or solve problems. A few works, notably Goodwin's *Obstructions of Justice* and the anonymous *Resolver, Or, a Short Word,* present clear rhetorical personae explaining political matters to their readers. Two tracts—*The Armies Vindication* and N. T.'s *The Resolver Continued*—discuss the merits of forms of government, the first by simply criticizing monarchy, the second by suggesting an ideal form, which the writer feels is "*Aristocracy* . . . mixed with *Democracy*" (sig. Cv). Only four Independent pamphlets aim at presenting a comprehensive account of regicide philosophy—the two *Resolvers*, Goodwin's *Obstructions of Justice,* and Milton's *Tenure*—a reflection of the disorder in the country. No writer could be absolutely sure whom he was addressing—he knew only that his readers could not be committed royalists or Presbyterians, for their assumptions were so different from those of the Independents that there could exist no ground for real discussion.

Aiming at the confused and the neutral, the writers of these philosophical tracts attempt to establish credibility by proving the antiquity of their thought, even though their actions appeared new. Then, to win the readers' assent, they urge the best reasons they can for supporting the action—the readers' own inherent dignity as free individuals and Christians. To convert the readers is, then, the chief means the Independents seek to their end of social, political, and moral reformation.

Above all other writers, Milton focuses on conversion of his readers. By speaking impersonally, in general terms, and by offering scriptural, historical, and legal texts as supporting evidence and not arguments in themselves, Milton presents a case derived from ideal human nature, designed to encourage readers to realize their own worth. In following his arguments, reasonable readers should experience the active powers of their own natures as Milton exhorts them to noble aspirations. In essence, Milton's argument leads to both self-confirmation and self-discovery. If readers desire the good, desire to be free and independent individuals, they will find through reading the *Tenure* the strength to translate their faith into action. Any readers rejecting or demurring from Milton's argument, in contrast, reveal slavishness, sinfulness, and their own unworthiness to participate in the political process.

The focus on the individual and especially the regenerate individual determines Milton's and the others' selection and use of genres. Assuming that the cause they support follows naturally from the regenerate person's commitment to free political action, these pamphleteers design their tracts to help readers realize their own political nature. The writers gravitate to the forensic genre, piling proof upon proof, debating definitions of tyranny and tyrants, describing the nature of political crimes. Their techniques demand that readers engage their intellects. In employing the forensic genre, the pamphleteers declare their belief in the reader's ability to use his reason, his higher faculties, which most closely reflect the image of God.

Yet understanding and giving assent to the Independents' arguments are not the only goals the pamphleteers have in sight. They hope to inspire regeneration and confidence in the readers in order to urge them to *participate* not only in one political action but also in a complete political life. To this end, they combine the forensic genre with the deliberative. Facts, proofs, and authorities—sufficient for a forensic argument—are, finally, not enough to promote the desired adoption of political life. This is why Milton, Goodwin, and others commit their best efforts to their discussions of the nature of the human being and incorporate these discussions into their overall arguments. These writers hope that, in arriving at the forensic end, the readers will have also gained enough knowledge about themselves to arrive at the deliberative end and engage themselves in wise public life.

Given their aims—nothing less than the transformation of society—the Independents were handicapped both through their choice of genre and through their training in classical rhetoric. While the epideictic genre, which they employ briefly in their attacks on the Presbyterians, is well suited to the advancement of public values, no classical genre can truly be adapted to question the fundamental premises of a society. In effect, the genres are the linguistic embodiment of the premises of the society. Mid-seventeenth-century writers could assume readers' understanding of new structures, but they possessed no genre for explicitly urging a new structure. Their efforts at mixing genres show that they perhaps intuited the need for new structures of language to communicate the idea of a transformed society, yet their continued use of the genres shows that, as a group, they were unable to break completely from the political and social order that they challenged.

In 1649, the execution of Charles I provided a rallying point for the conflict of ideologies that extended far beyond the specific issue of the regicide. War and revolution undermined "moderate" arguments and conventional rhetorical structures. Yet the genres of rhetoric, imbedded in readers' minds, remained to define the writers' relationships with their audience. The execution demanded that people respond in some way to the results of the seven-year conflict and take sides for or against the new government. The pamphleteers strove to give order to the chaos of events and provide the structure that prompts assent. Both Independents and monarchists alike chose genres and forms that reflected their ideologies. Their choices corresponded to their fundamental beliefs about human nature and the end of politics: the Independents encouraged regeneration and participation, the monarchists identification and obedience.

The sheer number of pamphlets illustrates the fact that, as recent historical research has underscored, there were in each writer's audience a majority of uncommitted, confused, or otherwise neutral readers. Having many undecided people requires many attempts to persuade. Monarchist writers achieved their peak in the *Basilike* and similar tracts, works that could skirt direct discussions of policy, government, and ideology in favor of more subtle persuasion through symbols. Charles himself provided the best focus, permitting writers to apply to their arguments traditional imagery associated with what was the distant and clouded past by 1649. Such tracts also shrewdly manipulated traditional genres, notably martyrology, to prompt readers to identify emotionally with Charles. These and similar presentations both confirmed the readers' status as members of a community and reinforced their hostility to the Independents who, by their own declaration, were attempting to alter that community. Independents attacking such tracts bore the onus both of speaking ill of the dead and of attempting to destroy the semblance of stability readers sensed in the monarchists' vision. While the monarchists had the recent past to rely on, the Independents could only look into the uncertain future. Their allusions to the ancient constitution were perhaps too esoteric to attract a large following.

This contrast in strategy appears vividly in the discussions of government. While some monarchists, notably Bayley, allowed their rigid, hierarchical visions to come to the surface, most used the disarray in government and the shock of the execution to their advantage, making valid attacks on the Rump and army while advocating a return to the less troubled and imperfectly remembered past. Independent writers knew that they had to re-create the readers before they could truly achieve their political vision, which they knew had not yet arrived. At best, they could only defend the Rump and army as the means to that end. They acknowledged the failings of their government by declining to discuss or defend it extensively. In trying to educate their readers and suit them for the future Commonwealth, the Independents, Milton among them, neglected to present a coherent, concrete vision of the future. Even those few tracts that discuss forms of government do so in only the most general terms. To assent to such tracts was to leap into the dark.

Compared to those of 1642, the tracts of 1649 reflect wider, deeper cleavages in ideology and expression. There appear few shared formulas, even fewer shared assumptions. Between parliamentary factions in 1642 there still existed a common language, albeit with variations. Between monarchists and Independents in 1649 there was no common ground. The tracts of both groups were informed by diametrically opposed ideologies that transformed even the writers' basic assumptions about their own roles, audiences, and ends. To read these works is to enter into two different worlds that perhaps inevitably could not coexist. In 1649, the monarchists possessed at least the familiar outlines of a resolution to the political crisis; the Independents possessed only an assemblage of convictions and hesitancy about the future—conditions that prefigured the decade to come.

III.

The Rhetoric of Resolution: 1659–1660

SEVEN

Prologue: Politics and the Reading Public 1649–1660

The regicide of 1649 utterly destroyed the conventions and assumptions governing public discourse. Both defenders and opponents of Charles's trial and execution struggled to present a coherent, integrative vision of society that would appeal to their readers and provide a new structure for people searching for stability amid rapid, radical change. Royalists successfully combined the tradition of radical Protestant autobiography with epideictic oratory to make divine-right theory and outright king-worship palatable to a wide audience. They asked readers simply to endorse an attractive presentation, and, upon endorsing it, readers were integrated into that group. Regicides, defending a violent and shocking act, demanded the transformation of their readers. Combining forensic and deliberative oratory, they addressed their readers as they wanted them to be—logical and independent. In rejecting the ideology of the past, however, the regicides still found themselves confined by its forms, if they were to reach their audience at all. The diverse, mixed genres of pamphlets on both sides reflected the active battle for the audience, although there now existed two separate and exclusive conceptions of that audience.

If the political community was fragmented in 1649, it was shattered ten years later. While the pamphleteer of 1649 still retained some notion of identifiable groups of readers, his counterpart in 1659 faced true anarchy—a multiplicity of ideologies and a total lack of political direction. Although all factions competed for an audience, pamphleteers had only the vaguest idea of who that audience might be throughout 1659 and into 1660. Confronting the chaotic political scene, these writers took on two burdens: as before, they had to identify and persuade an audience, but they also had to create and present a resolution to the conflict. To take any position at all meant also to take a philosophical stance and to demonstrate that stance's rightness and practicality.

The course of intellectual events in the 1650s made this task extremely

157

difficult. The decade witnessed not only the continual alteration of government but also the growth and able articulation of widely divergent political theories. These theories frequently departed from the old foundations of established religion and reconstructed new ones on mathematical, economic, or individualistic principles. This new context of political debate altered still further the conventions of political language. The pamphleteers of 1659 and 1660 had to be rhetoricians, politicians, and philosophers. Their tracts represent the search for an audience and for the means to draw together enough fragments of the political community to redefine and set in motion a new public order.

The pamphleteers faced the same difficulties as the whole political nation. The eleven years from the execution of Charles I to the restoration of the Stuarts saw constant change in the form and substance of government. A return to monarchy under Charles II was at no point a serious possibility until March–April 1660. For over a decade, English people thus confronted the spectacle of perpetual instability in a central government increasingly detached from the localities, the traditional "natural leaders," and, ultimately, many of its earliest and potentially most vigorous supporters. Scattered throughout the country, disfranchised royalists remained implacably opposed to any settlement that excluded the Stuarts, and they repeatedly fortified their resolve with armed action. Former Parliament men, alienated by the course of events, retreated to local politics, thereby sabotaging efforts at building local support for any central government. Radicals—especially those belonging to the lower classes—found themselves closed out of the political process by the very people whom they had helped the most. Reflected in both pamphlets and current events was the conviction that there existed even less of a real center to political life than there had been in 1649. By 1659 and 1660, events were changing so rapidly that many contemporaries believed anything could happen.

In the localities, efforts from Westminster to centralize government, law, and society were met during the 1650s by equally vigorous local efforts to resist the process. Whatever their political sentiments, villagers tended to adhere to traditional practices and forms, consistently opting for the familiar instead of the alien. Superficially, the changes appeared radical. In 1650, the Engagement—the official pledge of loyalty to the new Commonwealth—altered the face of local politics by shutting out of government anyone who refused to take it. Die-hard royalists, of course, were the immediate targets. Their main strength was concentrated in the hands of the aristocracy and the gentry—many of the "traditional rulers" of local government. With these men removed, the old system of patronage collapsed, dissolving many familiar ties to local authorities and routes into public service. As a result, some traditionally powerful families found themselves, at least temporarily, outside the societies they had once controlled.

In conservative Kent, the coalition of the 1640s between moderate royalists and Cavaliers split from the bitterness and recriminations that followed the failure of the rebellion. A few Cavaliers, like the poet Richard Lovelace, were jailed, while others continued their ineffectual plotting in alehouses. Most royalists, however, were more concerned with composing—raising sufficient funds to pay Westminster-imposed fines and to regain their estates. Kentish moderates preferred order to the house of Stuart and willingly cooperated with efficient and effective local authorities.[1]

In Somerset, the Engagement initially had the opposite result. Many radicals, objecting to the conservatism of the Commonwealth, dropped out of local commissions. Radical activity continued, but it focused on the community rather than the political structure. In 1651, for example, Charles II surreptitiously entered Somerset and attempted to hide in Trent, only to find that "the minister at Trent, Thomas Elford, was a fervent Independent, and as Charles himself admitted, most of the villagers were 'fanatics.' On one occasion a rumour that the king had been killed threw the village into a frenzy of jubilant celebration."[2] During the course of the third civil war, most of Somerset united against the Scots while old families, disaffected or simply overburdened by the process of composition, disappeared from local government, to be replaced by "radicals and upstarts."

In both Kent and Somerset, the localities lacked a clear sense of either organization or direction under the Commonwealth. Familiar names and faces were out and new ones were in, but initially none presented any coherent plans for restructuring local political activity. With the advent of the Protectorate, and for the following five years, the localities passed through short-lived but sharp changes in law and administration. In effect from 1654 to 1657, the Instrument of Government extended to Cromwell the power to issue ordinances that had the force of the old royal proclamations. Bypassing the county committees, Cromwell's ordinances attempted to advance social and economic reform, encouraging fen-drainage projects

1. Alan Everitt, *The Community of Kent and the Great Rebellion, 1640–1660*, 271–81.
2. David Underdown, *Somerset in the Civil War and Interregnum*, 162.

and outlawing dueling, cock-fighting, and horse-racing—the track being a favorite meeting place for royalist plotters. Cromwell also attempted a religious settlement. In March 1654 he established in London a commission of "triers" to approve public ministers, and in August groups of "ejectors" in the counties to expel "immoral" ministers and schoolmasters. Typically, the severity of enforcement varied with the local community— harsh in heavily Puritan areas, lenient in others. Otherwise, Cromwell gave very little support to the local committees in the first year of the Protectorate, concentrating instead on national matters. Consequently, many structures of the old order continued to function, most notably the legal system.[3] With no support from above, many radicals remaining within the local governments failed to implement any coherent policies. Gradually, they were replaced by the "moderate gentry."

This process of transition back to "traditional" leadership was sharply interrupted by Penruddock's Rising and the ensuing rule of the major-generals (1655–1657). The mandate of these military administrators was explicit: "Riots and unlawful assemblies, horse-races, stage-plays were to be put down. Superfluous ale-houses, haunts of the disaffected and anti-social, were to be suppressed; laws against enclosures, depopulation and neglect of tillage enforced and the poor code implemented."[4] Further, they were charged with internal security in their districts and collection of penal taxes. Some major-generals interfered strenuously in local affairs. All carried out their commissions efficiently and effectively, leaving lasting scars on the localities, though not so deep as Restoration propagandists suggested.

Strong opposition to military rule, and to the military in general, sprang up among county voters. The elections of August 1656 for the second Protectorate Parliament significantly increased the number of civilians in Westminster, even with voters carefully scrutinized and with royalists and strong anti-Cromwellians completely excluded from the polls. For years to come, the rule of the major-generals exemplified for many the worst aspects of government. The reaction prompted by the major-generals increased the rate by which old county families made their way back into local government. Anxious for familiar forms and faces, the political public turned back to their formerly powerful neighbors while, excluded from

3. G. E. Aylmer, *The State's Servants: The Civil Service of the English Republic, 1649–1660*, 305–17.

4. Ivan Roots, *Commonwealth and Protectorate: The English Civil War and Its Aftermath*, 193–202.

the political process from the start, most radicals and social outsiders were powerless to impede the change.

In the last years of Oliver Cromwell's rule, county conservatism increased as did conservative pressure in Parliament. These changes were manifested in the Humble Petition and Advice, which officially succeeded the Instrument of Government on May 25, 1657. Under this new constitution, Cromwell became Protector for life and the title was made heritable. The Protector's council was reconstructed to have the same powers and function of the old Privy Council—it became an advisory body only, unlike the Council of State, which had been a check on the Protector. The new constitution also created a new "Other House," an upper house that, like the lower, could not overrule the Protector. While dedicated royalists despaired of ever restoring the Stuarts, this change in government reassured many conservatives in the counties, encouraging them to join forces again, while it fragmented the republicans and other radicals.[5]

In Somerset, for example, moderates and conservatives united in face of a common fear of radicals, while in Kent minor landed families generally supportive of Cromwell came to compose 72 percent of the county committee by 1659. As Alan Everitt cautions, this conservative tide in Kent represents not sentimentality for the king or even reviving royalism so much as a desire to "return to the older forms of society and government."[6] Many local leaders easily transferred their loyalties from Charles to Oliver Cromwell—a single ruler was what they wanted. Also, unorganized radicalism continued. Individual villages and cities staunchly resisted kings in any form, willingly opposed Cromwell, his son Richard, and Charles, and in the Restoration would rise for the Duke of Monmouth. In the localities, the political public did not reject an ideology so much as opt for a form. The traditional forms of government offered the semblance of continuity as a relief from rapid social change.

In the 1650s, England did pass through changes in the social and economic order—changes that to contemporaries must have seemed more dramatic than they do to modern scholars. G. E. Aylmer indicates that, under the Protectorate, different groups did enter the civil service: fewer aristocrats and greater numbers of gentry, many more ex-apprentices and medical men. However, "the change was not so much from one social class

5. G. E. Aylmer, *The Struggle for the Constitution, 1603–1689: England in the Seventeenth Century,* 150–56.

6. *Community of Kent,* 301–12.

to another as from one stratum to another within a single class."[7] In absolute terms, the society was less stratified than it was before, or would be after, the revolution.

As well as the civil service, more people entered the land-owning class. After 1649, church properties came onto the market for sale by debenture, largely ending up in the hands of Londoners and country gentlemen. Lands of delinquents were given in lieu of payment to officers of the New Model Army, a fact that Christopher Hill argues widened the gulf between the army and the common people, creating in the people irreconcilable distrust of their new leaders. Although much of this small redistribution of wealth was to be reversed during the Restoration, in the 1650s it seemed to indicate the emergence of a new elite rather than a transformation of society—just enough to frighten traditionalists and frustrate radicals.[8] The pattern of land transfers reveals that many participants in the revolution—common people, soldiers, junior officers, small tradespeople, radicals, and other supporters—were being left behind by their leaders, closed out of not only the political process but also the benefits of what social change had occurred. The Cromwellians had turned their backs on a potentially huge constituency.

While abandoning one group, the new leaders continued to confront another—implacable royalists. This group rebelled on three major occasions in the 1650s: under Charles II in 1651, with Penruddock in March 1655, and with Booth in August 1659. With the exception of Penruddock's Rising, all the participants of the royalist revolts hoped for reinforcements from Presbyterians and others alienated from Cromwell. The revolts were planned by small groups of Cavaliers, and failed because they lacked local support. Further, they also increasingly alienated many royalists. Heavy penal taxes, provoked by the revolt of 1655, prompted older and more propertied families into passive conformity. As a result, while Booth's Rising was better planned than previous efforts and was theoretically better able to take advantage of the political situation, it was easily crushed by John Lambert since many of its potential supporters proved unwilling to risk themselves and their property. From the middle of the decade, leadership of the royalists passed to younger sons who had nothing to lose and who were much more ready to resort to violence to achieve their ends.

---

7. *State's Servants*, 276–81.

8. *Puritanism and Revolution: Studies in Interpretation of the English Revolution of the 17th Century*, 178–80.

Unsuccessful militarily, the Cavaliers nevertheless achieved two major political ends—one inadvertent, one planned. The first occurred when, alienated and frightened by Cavalier violence as much as by social anarchy, moderates came to believe that only a king could restore order in the country. The second was that the Cavaliers' single-mindedness rendered reconciliation of factions in the traditional ruling class impossible. As historian David Underdown has written, "The existence of an unreconcilable Royalist party was a fundamental cause of the impermanence of all republican regimes from 1649 to 1660. . . . As long as the Cavaliers remained unconverted, a freely elected Parliament was impossible unless the republicans were willing to sign their own death warrants."[9] Or, perhaps, unless they were willing to open the franchise to others outside the traditional political nation, who may have not only outnumbered but also opposed the royalists. This step, however, was one that the Cromwellians apparently never considered. Such an action would have first required a fundamental transformation of society—something which radical pamphleteers urged but which the Cromwellians decidedly did not want. Their position alienated too many on both ends of the political spectrum. Ultimately, they became a center that could not hold.

With the end of the rule of the major-generals came a virtual end to governmental attention to the localities. Increasingly, political events focused on Westminster and the fierce, continuous struggles among factions there. As Austin Woolrych indicates, 1657 brought two principal conservative victories—the return of civilian government and the adoption of a revised Petition and Advice. Woolrych maintains that both asserted the power of Parliament and achieved a balance among Protector, Council, and Parliament.[10] However satisfactory in theory, the settlement in practice depended upon the personality of Oliver Cromwell for implementation. It failed to please numerous radicals and soldiers and finally collapsed after Richard Cromwell succeeded as Protector.

Even before Oliver's death, there were many signs of instability in the conservative settlement. The elections of January–February 1658 returned many republicans to Parliament, while many of the leading Cromwellians were removed to the new "Other House." Moreover, the Cromwellians began to divide among themselves. "New" Cromwellians—conservative civilians, traditional in outlook and representing old families and the old

---

9. *Royalist Conspiracy in England, 1649–1660,* 331.
10. "Last Quests for a Settlement, 1657–1660," 183–86.

social order—aligned themselves against the "old"—chiefly the military. Radicals and junior officers both opposed the army's grandees and the entire tone of Cromwell's court. They allied themselves with Sir Henry Vane the younger, Sir Arthur Haslerigg, and the republicans in attacking the settlement. Succeeding as Protector on September 3, 1658, Richard Cromwell confronted a wide range of factions, and he inadvertently provoked dissention by relying obviously on the new Cromwellians. He thus alienated both the republican factions and the army grandees.

In November, Richard called for a new parliament. The elections returned a tremendously diverse group, from royalists to republicans, described by Thurloe as "so great a mixture no one knows which way the major part will incline."[11] The new Parliament began on January 27, 1659. From the start, factions warred against each other and among themselves. In March, a serious split occurred in the army faction that ultimately provided the catalyst for the fall of the Protectorate. The officers divided into two groups: the republicans and the supporters of the grandees, known from their meeting place as the "Wallingford House group." This group adamantly opposed compromise and began plotting in April to take strong measures against royalists, who were gradually filtering back into political life. Attempting to head off this plot, their opponents developed their own plan to kidnap the leaders of the Wallingford House group. Richard Cromwell objected and tried to influence Parliament to gain control of the army. In defiance of Parliament and Protector, Charles Fleetwood, one of the principal leaders of the Wallingford House group, called on April 21 for a rendezvous of the army. Powerless to counter him, Cromwell dissolved the Parliament the following day.

In the next two weeks, political activity erupted, taking inspiration from the virtual anarchy in the central government. Both junior officers and their civilian counterparts pressed for a restoration of the Commonwealth. Numerous anonymous writers raised the cry for the Good Old Cause and the return of the Rump. Many offered alternative solutions, proposing new structures of government. From this point until April of the following year, the political scene was in constant turmoil as effective government totally dissolved.

On May 7, in one of his final acts as Protector, Richard Cromwell recalled the Rump. The next day, forty members appeared at the House of Commons and immediately declared their intentions to restore the Com-

11. Quoted in Roots, *Commonwealth and Protectorate,* 235.

monwealth. Eventually, a total of one hundred and twenty members rejoined the Parliament and, on the twenty-fifth, Richard Cromwell resigned as Protector. From the moment of their return, members of the Rump began the search for a final settlement, establishing their own limitations by declaring that they would not sit beyond May 7, 1660. They discussed many possible models for the new government, including James Harrington's *Oceana* of 1656.[12]

Meanwhile, the army grandees, now led by Lambert, urged a split in legislative power to be shared between elected representatives and a "select Senate." They found an ally in Vane, who endorsed the idea of a "Body of Elders" to be composed of the "saints." Vane and his followers, however, proved to be a minority in the Rump, the larger group being led by Haslerigg, who adhered to strict republican principles and opposed the power of the army. Under Haslerigg's leadership, the Rump attempted to purge the army and in so doing enraged Lambert, who threatened a military coup.[13]

Debate continued through the summer, although by that time the Rump was further than ever from agreement. After the brief interruption of Booth's Rising, Haslerigg totally broke with Vane, who alone could successfully deal with the army. The army, bolstered by its victory over Booth, began to petition for reforms and pay, but the altercation between Vane and Haslerigg prevented any action on these requests. On October 10, the Rump received a new petition from the army, while Lambert and others canvassed for support in defiance of Parliament. In response, the Rump began a purge of the army, but not in time. On the thirteenth, the army interrupted the Rump and brought all government, such as there was, to a halt.

At this point, General Monck, with his army in Scotland, declared his support for the Rump and opposition to Lambert, stating that he would act to preserve civil authority. As an act of good faith, he purged his own forces. In Westminster, on October 27, and with the help of a few civilians, the army grandees established a Committee of Safety with the ostensible purpose of shaping a constitution without a House of Lords or rule by a single person. By November 1, a subcommittee including Vane was set to work on the constitution. On the fifteenth, it prepared a draft treaty to be presented to Monck and Lambert—a treaty composed amid widespread

12. Blair Worden, *The Rump Parliament*, 364–84, noting Cromwell's conservative design of the Rump from its beginning.

13. Violet A. Rowe, *Sir Henry Vane the Younger: A Study in Political and Administrative History*, 228–31.

dissention in the army and rioting apprentices in London. Prompted by this confusion, the General Council of Officers met on December 6 and agreed to call a new parliament with two houses, one of them a senate. Ludlow proposed also that in the meantime they appoint twenty-one "conservators of liberty" to keep the peace. Although it agreed, the council exacerbated existing problems by appointing only Wallingford House men to these positions.

Open revolt flared. By December 13, the army in Ireland declared for the Rump, and Fairfax, withdrawn from politics since 1649, broke his silence by affirming his support for Monck. Anthony Ashley Cooper and others seized Portsmouth by persuading its garrison to call for a parliament. Amid the anarchy, trade collapsed and the London Common Council joined the call for a free parliament and new elections. In response to the growing demand and the disintegration of the army, on the twenty-sixth the Rump reassembled in Westminster. Four days later, Monck and his army crossed the border into England. From the point of view of many observers, anything could happen. The year 1660 began with an extremely volatile political situation—a spectrum of proposals, riots, rebellions, and anarchy. Pamphleteers of whatever stripe saw a field wide open for uninhibited debate. They could not, however, clearly see an audience.

In the light of contemporary events, the lack of any clearly defined audience is not surprising. In the first five months of 1660, the political situation completely reversed itself. General Monck crossed the Scottish border at the beginning of January and began a march to London. Monck operated completely independent of the Rump, a fact that became fairly widely known as people addressed petitions to him demanding action against the ostensible governing body. The Rump, meanwhile, planned for recruiter elections to bring up their strength while continuing to sit. On February 1, the army mutinied, and in this troubled atmosphere Monck arrived in London on the third. Defying a request from the Rump to reduce the size of the army, Monck countered with a suggestion that that body "enlarge" itself. Facing Monck's army, the Rump did just that. On the twenty-first it permitted the secluded members to return. Also in compliance with Monck's demands, the Rump called for writs for the election of a new parliament to meet on April 20.[14]

At this point, Monck was still openly committed to a commonwealth.

14. Austin Woolrych, Historical Introduction to *The Complete Prose Works of John Milton*, rev. ed., 7:156–62, 171–77.

When the secluded members returned, he ordered his officers to suppress any risings for Charles II. To hopeful pamphleteers, the first three weeks of February seemed to indicate that a republic was still possible. By the end of that month, however, all hope had evaporated. Monck had been in communication with Charles and his supporters throughout the month, and by March the general's intentions were clear. On March 16, the Long Parliament dissolved itself while Monck advised Charles to go to Breda to issue terms for Charles's return. At the same time, the elections began. No one was to be barred from voting, so there was little doubt about results. A Presbyterian majority was returned to the House of Commons, along with some overt royalists, while most regicides and republicans lost their seats. Some radicals were returned—a sign that there was no absolute rejection of either them or their principles. On April 25, this diverse group assembled for what became known as the Convention Parliament.

This body ultimately set no conditions for Charles's return. G. E. Aylmer believes that there were two major reasons for this refusal. First, the division between the Presbyterian majority and the republican minority was deep and extensive enough that they could not agree on a set of terms. Second, the Presbyterians, buoyed by the elections, were "overconfident of getting their way" with the new king.[15] In the Declaration of Breda, issued on May 1, Charles stated his intentions, which should have warned all nonroyalists what they could expect. Presenting all points in only the most general terms, Charles concealed his specific plans and carefully put off any resolution of the most pressing issues—the scope of pardons, the religious settlement, the redistribution of sequestered lands, and the army's arrears in pay.

All of these crucial questions were thus unanswered when the Parliament proclaimed Charles II king on May 8. From that date onward, his more well-to-do subjects sponsored public demonstrations and rump-burnings in his honor, while great crowds turned out to meet him when he landed at Dover on the twenty-fifth. From Dover, Charles made a progress to London, entering the city on the twenty-ninth. Although there were many open displays of welcome for Charles, there also remained people who never turned royalist. Charles continually coped with local plots and uprisings. Milton, of course, never capitulated and, as Aubrey remembered, neither did Harrington: "He severall times . . . sayd, Well, the King will come in. Let him come-in, and call a Parliament of the greatest Cavaliers in England, so they be men of Estates, and let them sett but 7

15. *Struggle for the Constitution,* 160–62.

yeares, and they will all turn Commonwealthe's men."[16] His prediction would come true, but not as or when he expected.

From a rhetorical perspective, two points emerge from a survey of research concerning the decade of the 1650s. First, there is a sense of rapid, directionless change. No solution lasted long, while every proposal except the last met with fervent opposition. And, as the Clarendon Code and later events were to prove, even the Restoration was by no means universally popular. Each proposal could be regarded as experimental, each pamphlet or speech a random suggestion made for the sake of argument. More so than at any other time during the revolution, each pamphlet may be regarded as dynamic, in flux—not an object, but an act.

Second, one senses the isolation of political actors in 1659. Increasingly, they focus their attention on the events in and around Westminster. The leading figures especially appear abstracted from the country as a whole and practically unaware of any but their own immediate struggles. Significantly, the decisive action of 1659 and 1660 was taken by Monck, a general who had been totally uninvolved in the daily political activities of the grandees of the General Council of Officers. Under such circumstances, it was impossible for a writer to decide with any certainty where the political community was, of what interests it was composed, or who its chief members were.

The pamphlets thus divide along broad generic lines as well as into ideological camps. Brief, topical arguments appear beside long, careful, and learned expositions of theory, all attempting to locate and mobilize readers. Republican pamphleteers bore the triple burden of being at once rhetoricians, politicians, and philosophers, presenting to the general reader relatively new and alien theories. This special difficulty confronted both Milton and Harrington. Royalists faced an easier responsibility, having the advantage of being able to defend the past forms and practices that many readers did not remember firsthand. Nevertheless, they too presented philosophical arguments, refusing to assume too much goodwill from their readers. Throughout 1659 and in the first five months of 1660, the political community repeatedly collapsed and regrouped, giving all the more urgency to public debate and public action. Much more than in either 1642 or 1649, writers had to build solid, formal bridges to their diverse, undefined audience. The multiplicity of genres and the increase in philosophical tracts reveal the pamphleteers' growing uncertainty about both their audience and their own roles in public discourse.

16. *Aubrey's Brief Lives*, 284.

EIGHT

Order Restored: The Monarchists

By 1659, significant debate between monarchists and radicals had completely disappeared. Both groups faced the tremendous burden of reconstructing an entire political vision in language that supported it. The two visions so differed that they could not share any of the same conventions of public discourse. This lack of commonality was in part a result of the fundamental change in perception accelerated by the revolution. As many intellectual historians have recognized, the mid-seventeenth century in England brought essential transformations in political thought, language, and conventions that moved all political discourse from the religious sphere to the rational. Even such dedicated royalists as Sir Robert Filmer began to justify absolutism as a manifestation of natural law. As historian Quentin Skinner argues, the rate of both ideological and linguistic change accelerated during the middle of the century, with theory and language altering in dialectical relation to the course of events and each term of the equation constantly affecting the other.[1] Especially in the 1650s, events and arguments changed so rapidly that they undermined remaining community values and conventional discourse. In the anarchy, there ultimately was no community. Under such conditions, nothing was conventional.

Monarchists as well as radicals, then, had to create a climate of opinion ready to receive their ideas. And, as diarists noted at the time, that climate was extremely volatile. On November 7, 1659, John Evelyn recorded that it was still dangerous to speak or write for the king. Six months later, on May 2, 1660, Samuel Pepys observed a recent order of Parliament commanding the burning of "all books whatever that are out against the Government of Kings, Lords, and Commons."[2] Yet, despite the public

---

1. "Some Problems in the Analysis of Political Thought and Action." Cf. J. A. W. Gunn, *Politics and the Public Interest in the Seventeenth Century.*

2. Evelyn, *The Diary of John Evelyn*, 3:235; Pepys, *Diary and Correspondence*, 1:50.

demonstrations for Charles II that began in March, most monarchists remained anxious about the extent of their king's popularity. As self-evident as their cause seemed, monarchists believed that its reception was by no means sure.[3]

In 1659 and 1660, the monarchists needed an integrative discourse capable of reaching beyond their own party and of being as inclusive as possible. As in 1649, they collectively abandoned the royalist tropes and court culture of the 1630s to reach Presbyterians and others frightened by the anarchy. But, much more than they did in 1649, the monarchists also needed to reconstruct a systematic vision of monarchy that would appeal to a wide audience. As traditionalists, monarchist writers had been alarmed by the advent of the political theory of Thomas Hobbes and his followers, who defended absolutism as the only truly effective form of government.

No foes of absolutism in itself, especially as Charles I attempted to practice it, the monarchists as a group disliked and feared the implications of "Hobbist" thought, which ultimately contradicted all the premises of traditional English political discourse. Chiefly, of course, Hobbes aimed at a "scientific," not Christian, theory of politics. He thereby undermined many scriptural arguments in favor of monarchy. Further, and from the traditionalists' perspective even worse, was Hobbes's principle of political obligation—a principle that addressed each individual as an independent actor. As Skinner shows, conservative critics perceived that "as Hobbes grounded political obligation on calculations of rational self-interest, so he believed that a man became absolutely obliged to obey *any* government that could protect him." They also saw that "as Hobbes had made obligation depend on protection, so he had intended to add that when a subject was not adequately protected his obligation must cease."[4] These critics feared that Hobbes removed human beings from any social or communal obligations, making private interest the principal criterion for allegiance to government. Gone from Hobbesian theory was any notion of benefits and mutual obligation—the theory that had formed the basis for Western political thought since classical times. In the period from 1659 to 1660, most monarchists shared the diarist John Evelyn's disgust for both people

3. Recent Restoration scholarship emphasizes the high degree of anxiety evident in the literature of the 1660s. Restoration monarchists saw their task as only beginning when Charles II returned. See especially Nicholas Jose, *Ideas of the Restoration in English Literature, 1660–1671,* 1–16.

4. "The Ideological Context of Hobbes's Political Thought," 315, 308–11, 314–16. Skinner's emphasis.

and nations that "mind onely their profit, do nothing out of Gratitude, but collateraly, as it relates to their gaine, or security."[5]

Rhetorically, then, the monarchists attempted to reconstruct a middle ground of tradition between two extremes—the Hobbists and the radicals—that asserted the essential political autonomy of the individual. The monarchist rhetoric of 1659 and 1660 sought to develop a discourse that absolved the audience of the burden of active participation in the confusing, frightening world of contemporary politics. Instead, it was emphatically what Wayne C. Booth has identified as a "rhetoric of assent"—a rhetoric that demands not thought or analysis but agreement and assertion of belief.[6] Above all, the monarchists of 1659 and 1660 wanted a language that would reassure readers of the continuity of the world as they remembered and idealized it, after twenty years of continuous and tumultuous change.

The rhetoric the monarchists developed in 1659 and 1660 is supremely a discourse of belief. Generically, it is overwhelmingly epideictic even as it is applied in what would appear to be a deliberative situation. Indeed, the most distinctive feature of the monarchist rhetoric of 1659 and 1660 is generic displacement—the epideictic functions *as* deliberative rhetoric. Such discourse does certainly advocate a course of action, but its principal focus and chief purpose are to characterize and unify readers behind beliefs it presents as community values. Through their rhetoric, the monarchists advocate far more than a Stuart restoration; they aim at nothing less than the re-creation of the readers and all members of the political nation as ideal subjects, ready to submit willingly to a new order being carefully presented as the old.

As Richard Cromwell's Parliament and the restored Rump quarreled and split into factions, monarchists began their rhetorical reconstruction of order. Already in the first half of 1659, tracts were appearing that invoked the "*Halcyon* daies" under the rule of Charles I and the "happy Estate" of 1639.[7] These tracts and the ones to follow rarely focus on the past. Rather, the past functions as an undefined element, allowing each reader to supply his own specifics. Leaving the past undefined, monarchist

---

5. Evelyn in conversation with the Dutch ambassador, November 15, 1659, *Diary*, 3:236. See also Frederick Vaughan, *The Tradition of Political Hedonism: From Hobbes to J. S. Mill*, 69–80.

6. *Modern Dogma and the Rhetoric of Assent*, xii–xvi.

7. *A Pertinent Speech Made by an Honourable Member of the House of Commons*, March 16, sig. A3; *Loyal Queries*, June 14, sig. A4.

writers are able to present their vision not as their creation but as a revival of traditional values. All monarchist pamphlets share this perception, in which a monarchy constitutes the best government and organization of society, and a commonwealth or a republic constitutes the worst. Hence, any praise of monarchy becomes an implicit criticism of the present state of affairs, while any criticism of government, radicals, or commonwealth theory is a praise of monarchy.

The monarchical tracts fall into two broad categories that reflect the larger project of reconstructing the society. The first group I term "rhetorical" tracts, distinguished by the specificity of their arguments. The second, I term "philosophical," chiefly because their authors argue from general principles, with little overt application. Both insist that there is no workable or desirable alternative to the monarchical model, or indeed to the whole society they defend. Together, the two groups reveal a concerted effort to redefine their political perspective as they argue it.

The writers of the rhetorical tracts found their most persuasive approach to lie in reviving images of the past. Because they refer to the past, the images possess an aura of truthfulness and constitute a more appealing vision than the chaos of current events. These tracts are organized around that contrast—it in itself provides the proofs of the argument. The writers concentrate on three general topics: the disastrous present, praiseworthy values, and the personalities of political figures and groups. All three topics are interrelated and ultimately focus on one idea—that the only remedy for present ills, the only means to achieve the positive values, is embodied in Charles Stuart; it is not merely to be found in a restored monarchy. Charles himself thus provides a concentrated focal point for all the arguments, and he is the reason for the epideictic character of monarchist rhetoric.

Their presentation of the recent past immediately suggests the epideictic nature of the monarchists' rhetoric. Because their ultimate goal is to praise Charles II, the monarchists' presentation of history serves as a narration, the part both ancient and Renaissance rhetoricians considered the most crucial to the epideictic oration. And since one of the most common traditional tropes in praise of kingship is the picturing of the king as head of the body politic, the genre allows pamphleteers to revive this organic imagery as a vehicle for narration. All of recent history may thus be discussed in the language of disease. Richard Brathwaite's *Panthalia: Or, the Royal Romance,* a roman à clef on recent English history, characterizes the past twenty years of political struggle as a medical imbalance:

It seem *Candy,* said the Governess, became seaz'd of a violent Phrency. A constitution so distemper'd, requir'd a continued Purge. Bodies Politick being so full of vicious humors cannot be long healthful. It is most true, replied *Panthalia:* and you collect rightly the indisposition of *Candy.* It was a deep *Surfet* that first begat in my Country this informity. A *surfet* of peace, which caus'd her to be more remiss in the prudent managment of her State. (sig. N)

Brathwaite manages both to place blame squarely on the parliamentarians, restless men who disparage the gift of peace brought about by the admirable rule of Charles I, and to characterize the country in the most traditional of terms. In so doing, Brathwaite emphasizes the continuity of the old political community. In his work, the old rhetoric and its traditional metaphors reassure readers that their ways of understanding the world are still appropriate to contemporary politics despite events in Westminster.

Many other tracts also employ organic imagery in overt appeals to the old political nation. *The Londoners Last Warning* explicitly addresses the "traditional rulers" with property and social position, declaring that the people are "struck with a dead Palsie, . . . your Body, whose blood, life and spirits, are Laws, Liberties and Freedoms, is in every part so weakned, that it hath scarce strength for recovery" (sig. A). The cause of the sickness is "the wounds of your Head, which you received by your own neglect," and yet the people insist on turning for a cure to "Mountebanks, who rather make experiments how much your nature can suffer" (sig. A2) The *Vox Vere Anglorum* also accuses the present government of state-quackery. The people are sick with a "malady," and their leaders have employed "so much Phlebotomy and Scarification . . . and all to no purpose, but rather to encrease the dolour, and heighten the danger." The solution, however, is simple: we should "call for, and use this *Soveraign* cure" (sig. A2).

In the discourse of the monarchists, a restoration of the Stuarts becomes the only true means to, as *A Pertinent Speech* states, "lay a plaister to the wounds and Balsome to the sores of these distressed Nations" (sig. A4). Even Charles II, in a broadside speech made at Brussels, envisions his role as healer, his function being to "powre Balm into the wonnd [*sic*] of Our three Kingdoms." In these tracts, the writers not only employ the organic description of the state but also revive the notion of the king as both metaphorical and literal healer. The future Charles II himself touched victims of scrofula—the King's Evil—while on the Continent as part of his campaign to establish in the eyes of the people his right to be their monarch.[8]

8. Keith Thomas, *Religion and the Decline of Magic,* 204–6.

The pamphleteers' use of the figurative language of disease and healer immediately invoke the ordered, familiar world of the past and strongly imply a causal relationship between departure from that past and the current catastrophe.

The monarchists' complaints are naturally not limited to a sense of malaise. They frequently focus on change and disorder in the government. As the author of *Metamorphosis Anglorum* explains, there has been repeated upheaval: "From a King, to a House of Lords and Commons, from that to a House of Commons only; this routed they set up a Protector, then down goes a Protector, and up mounts the old House of Commons again, and now is that Extinct: so many Scenes have their been in the acting of the *English Tragedy,* which I fear me is not yet half consummate" (sig. D10). In the author's eyes, the opponents of monarchy have become a grotesque parody of the stage plays—another part of the idealized past—that they themselves had banned.[9] The theatrical imagery, the *theatrum mundi* of politics, is an additional part of the traditional discourse of the prewar period. In using it, this author shows himself to be a believer in the old way of life as well as the old ruling House.

Classical and religious imagery also aid in the reconstruction of traditional political language. *Englands Redemption* speaks of "the vexed Government of frantick *England,*" now a ship of state without a pilot guided by unskilled people (sigs. A2–A2v). *A Pertinent Speech* sees the constant changes in government as scourges of God, sent to punish the people for their abandonment of the king (sigs. A2v–A3). *King Charles the II: His Restitution* agrees: God has been angered by our "Idolatry" (sig. A2v) of Parliament and rebellion, our "vaine confidence in an arm of flesh, which is cursed" (sig. A3). As the prophet Isaiah warned, the country is now thrown into a state of chaos (sig. A3v). All these images invoke the idea of right order upset—people stubbornly and proudly refusing to submit to God's will. They also suggest that, as the anarchy is God's punishment for the people's wrongdoing, so the people must themselves return to the preordained path of government and society, rather than to trust of the Rump. The old language reinforces the rightness of the ideas. Like Scripture itself, the old political metaphors suggest stability and truth, familiar and comforting.

Traditional language and the epideictic genre also enable monarchist

9. See Nancy Klein Maguire, "The Theatrical Mask/Masque of Politics: The Case of Charles I," 6–9; and Lois Potter, *Secret Rites and Secret Writing: Royalist Literature, 1641–1660,* 184–93.

pamphleteers to mount a strong attack on the Rump. For confirmation, the epideictic genre demands only amplification, not logical proofs or examples. Therefore, simple allusions to the past activities of the Rump together with vituperative language command the assent of the readers, as pamphleteers create what amounts to a declaration of faith concerning the practices of their opponents. William Prynne, as single-minded as ever, invokes tradition in *The Re-publicans* as he denounces the *"Mock-Parliament,"* which first made Oliver Cromwell "a more absolute real, though not nominal King over us, than any of our antient Kings" and now seeks to become "*absolute*" (sigs. A3, A3v). *A Pertinent Speech* describes the desperation of the nation suffering under the severity of Parliament (sig. A2v). In language reminiscent of the parliamentarians of 1642, these monarchists lay claim to being the true opponents of absolutism, which they present as completely alien to England, the Personal Rule notwithstanding.

The author of *Vox & Votum Populi Anglicani* makes even more serious charges against the Parliament. He asserts that the Parliament is destroying the spirit of the nation by encouraging debate rather than gratitude and obedience. Now, he claims, everyone thinks himself qualified to hold forth on the correct form of government instead of examining where his true duty lies: "Alas, My Lord, Mysteries of State have, of late times, been so prostituted, we have got such a habit of talking at random, under our late Usurpers, who (rather like true Tyrants, than good States-men) enslaving our Persons, left our tongues at Liberty, That nothing can bridle our Extravagancies, in a time of Critical concernment, and impetuous Longings." Rather than show restraint and turn to Charles Stuart, everyone prefers to debate in taverns so that "all our meetings are now become Cabals" and they flounder in a "great gulf of Discourse" (sig. A2v). Each small group advances its own program, neglecting the good of the country as a whole. These groups, the author feels, create fantasies by insisting on looking only to the future, when the past is a more appropriate subject for discussion.

The past becomes the monarchists' key to the future and to the correct understanding of current events. As did the *Eikon Basilike* in 1649, monarchist pamphlets borrow from their traditional opponents' discourse—this time the Puritans' polemical history—to appeal to a broad audience that includes those potential opponents. Several pamphlets follow the example of the *Book of Martyrs* by invoking both recent and ancient history to place the present struggles in a larger pattern. But whereas the Puritans typically concentrate on actions and their interpretation, the monarchist tracts use history to provide material for attacks on the character of their opponents. *Panthalia* explains the first civil war by projecting the present back to 1642: "While some stood for an Anarchical Independency; Others for a Platonick parity, One for a democratick, another for an Aristocratick: others, and those of the Popular Leaders for an Oligarchick Power. Neither was it at all to be wondred, that the Members should become thus distracted, being from their Head divided." Further, these "Plebians" were able to use the "Publick Treasury" to recruit for their army, while the forces of "Rosicles," the prince, were ill-governed and "Libertines." Instead of keeping faith with their prince, the people pursued their own interests and brought about the wars. Moreover, the prince could not even trust his own advisers, who truly cared only to advance themselves (sigs. H4, H4v).

As a roman à clef, Brathwaite's *Panthalia* absolves itself of actual allegiance to historical events, which, as even many contemporary readers would certainly recall, bore no resemblance to the fictionalized description. Instead, it uses the vehicle of history to attack the members of the Rump for both their supposed low social origin and their pretensions as political theorists. As his list of illustrations makes clear, Brathwaite objects to *all* political debate. Those who argue in favor of "aristocratick" government are as laughable as the partisans of democracy. Through *Panthalia,* Brathwaite assails all manifestations of the new order, from the entry of "Plebians" into politics to the private interest of the prince's evil counselors. His is principally not a political but a cultural appeal—Brathwaite supports none but the prince. *Panthalia*'s attacks become covert praise of restoration. The fictional description thus serves as narration rather than example—its object is to establish the heinous behavior of subjects and the virtue of the king.

Many other monarchist tracts convert history to praise and vituperation. *Metamorphosis Anglorum* concentrates on the events of the 1650s, drawing parallels between English history and classical Rome. Anachronistically, it compares Richard Cromwell to Henry V eagerly snatching the crown from his dying father's head and, without further proofs, criticizes Lambert's "Caesarian Spirit" (sigs. B3, C7). The *Vox Vere Anglorum* challenges republican uses of conquest theory, not by citing laws or statutes but by charging that party with willful ignorance. Charles Stuart, it argues, does not draw his title simply from William I but from "Edgar Atheling, the then apparent and right Heir of the Crown, from whom a descent of title to this Prince is as manifestly deductible, as from that William, which all men conversant in true History cannot but know" (sig. A3v). *King*

Charles the II: His Restitution draws from biblical history to show patterns of God's judgment and punishment of the Israelites when they disobeyed their kings (sigs. A3v–A4v). *Three Propositions from the Case of Our Three Nations* surveys history from biblical, classical, and modern times, including the recent history of England, to show how changes in governments inevitably lead to wars, tyranny, and other catastrophes (sigs. A3v–A4). In all of these tracts, the writers concentrate on the wrongness of their opponents' actions, rather than the rightness of their cause. This history appears to be confutation by example—and thus suits the ultimate deliberative end of these tracts—but principally serves as amplification of charges against the Rump and radicals. In their use of history, then, the monarchist pamphleteers fuse the deliberative and epideictic genres. Their recommended course of action is praise of the Stuarts.

In all their efforts to describe and comment upon the current state of affairs, these writers look firmly backward. Their use of history, disease imagery, and allusions to fear and chaos stresses that the present disasters result from a departure from the norm of monarchy, an upset of the natural balance, a quest after novelty, a violation of law. From this perspective, it is irrelevant to discuss future plans, since a restoration of the past will restore all the values swept away by the "Great Rebellion." The deliberative end becomes epideictic. Significantly, this strategy is explicitly employed by King Charles himself. He makes few references to his own plans in *King Charles His Speech to the Six Eminent Persons.* Instead, he blandly expresses his happiness in seeing "our poor distressed and distracted Kingdoms in hopes of Settlement, and Restoration of its pristine Glory, by the Establishing of Our Self." His mere presence will set everything to right—a position a short step from "*L'état, c'est moi.*" But this is exactly the pamphleteers' point: he embodies the state, he is the head of the body politic. His return to the throne will mystically restore what all right-thinking men desire.

The tracts reflect Charles's approach to persuasion as they abandon specific proposals in favor of extensive characterization of traditional values—true religion, free parliaments, liberties, justice, and peace. In these tracts, Charles becomes the embodiment of those values while the Rump appears as their chief enemy. In discussions of religion, monarchist pamphleteers focus on the activities of the sectarians and their pretentious usurpation of the right to interpret scriptures. As the *Metamorphosis Anglorum* complains, chaos has permeated to religion: "No Cobler but presumes to make himself the head of a Sect or faction, and presumes to glory in thundring the most holy word of God out of his prophane lips; to whom his she Auditors (for so for the most part they are) listen to as to an Oracle, and hee presuming his confidence to be knowledg, carries himself as proudly as if he were their Ghostly Father" (sig. E5). With the conduct of James Nayler and the first Quakers in mind, the author claims that such sects and their supporters invert the natural hierarchy in many ways. Women gain power in the sects, as do men of humble social origins. Both threaten the traditional social order.

Worse, in the eyes of these pamphleteers, is the evidence that the government actually encourages such disruptions. *The Londoners Last Warning* decries a supposed plot by the Rump to help the Anabaptists and Fifth-Monarchy Men; the Rump "within these two dayes were ready to vote them a publique toleration of their Religion, while you shall have none, and if they had not been perswaded they were too great Friends to the House of *Austria,* the Petition had been granted." Moreover, there are rumors that the churches will all be closed within two weeks (sig. A2v). Prynne complains in *The Re-publicans* that his foes "give a free toleration, protection to all sorts of Sects and Religions whatsoever" and permit correspondence with papists, Jesuits, and "Jesuited Papists" (sig. A3v). All three tracts are clearly addressed to nonsectarians, to those who oppose toleration. While the *Metamorphosis Anglorum* links the sects with the lower classes and ridicules them, the other two tracts associate them with foreign powers and thus turn their members into potential traitors and spies.

This suggestion takes on greater significance when readers are told in other pamphlets how the English king has been the champion of the Protestant cause throughout the world. *Loyal Queries, Humbly Tendred to the Serious Consideration of the Parliament, and Army* asks whether a treaty between Prince Charles and the Parliament might present the best opportunity "to the Protestant Cause, and to strike a greater terrour into the hearts of all Popish Princes in Europe, than ever any yet did since the Reformation" (sig. A5). The *Vox Vere Anglorum* charges that disorder in the church opens the door for subversion by Jesuits (sig. A4). The broadside *No King but the Old Kings Son* presents Charles as a hero of Protestantism. His return to the throne will preserve the faith at home and abroad.

The true faith is, of course, the Church of England. As its head, Charles is its embodiment at home. Revival of the Church of England will signal the return of the traditional social order. To monarchist pamphleteers, church and state are inevitably linked, and harmony in one will prompt the same in the other. According to the broadside *Orthodox State-Queries,*

Charles himself can restore true religion if Parliament will make him "nursing Father to our deplorable and almost ruined Church." In *The Republicans,* Prynne employs identical imagery to argue that God has placed kings at the head of both church and state (sig. A2v). Other pamphlets directly link the restoration of Charles with true religion. *Three Propositions* states that the Stuarts are the only hereditary successors to the throne and "that it is due to them, Religion, Reason, and Law affirm unanimously" (sig. A4v). The broadside *A Declaration of the Knights and Gentry in the County of Dorset* brands all rebellion and dissention as "Unchristian Animosityes, which reigne in divers turbulent Spirits, even of our own Party"; the signatories declare that they wish to unite the country behind Charles by "an Indispensible Tye of Religious Charity." As the *Vox Vere Anglorum* points out, monarchy is the only government appointed by God, and the English people took their first oath at the outbreak of the first war to defend the king. It is therefore blasphemy to abjure him now (sig. A3v).

In all these tracts, the writers strive to identify the monarchy and specifically Charles with true, English religion and, by extension, all those who adhere to some form of Anglicanism with Charles. In so doing, they also attack their opponents, the sects, by suggesting that they are at best infatuated rabble, at worst foreign agents. "True religion" is patriotism—sectarianism is treason. Thus, these pamphleteers revive the religious model—and the political imagery—of the Tudors and early Stuarts, a vision in which the people ostensibly rallied in one body and with one spirit behind the simultaneously spiritual and temporal head of England. They identify orthodox religion with themselves, urging all readers who share their beliefs to join with them in supporting the king. They restrict their discussions of the meaning of "religion," emphasizing the forms, but not the substance, of the old church and ignoring all the questions concerning settlements and doctrine. Dissent of any kind, whether from sects or members "even of our own party," becomes both a religious and a political threat that must be silenced. Keeping the discussion general and confining their discourse to praise of the old faith, the pamphleteers hope to include everyone from Prynne himself to Archbishop Juxon, allowing the reader to construct for himself his own ideal settlement within the broad terms of God and king.

The principal political slogan of 1642 was "God, King, and Country." Just as they link God and king in their expositions of religion, so the monarchists of 1659 and 1660 identify king with country. In these pamphlets, *country* is defined in two ways—as "free parliament" and as limited monarchy. Both terms operate together in a vision of balance and unity. Many of the broadsides and shorter tracts, whether written in 1659 or 1660, call for a free parliament with free elections, declaring that they will obey such a parliament, which would then truly reflect the people's—that is, the traditional political nation's—wishes. Certainly, monarchist pamphleteers knew that many members of the traditional political nation had indeed been prohibited from voting during the last ten years. The Rump sitting in 1659 had in that sense not been freely elected. Hence, a call for free elections and free parliaments was almost inevitably a demand for the reassertion of monarchist political power. *We* thus means monarchists, but, since the pamphlets do not define the term, the *we* overtly appeals to many different kinds of readers. As *A Pertinent Speech* asks, "Shall the people have a free Parliament, or shall they not? If they shall have a free Parliament, then must they have free liberty to choose whom they please, if not, we do but follow former steps, and still endeavour to enslave them" (sig. A4v). *Vox & Votum* adds, "The House of Commons, . . . hath a trust, But it is to assent our Liberties, not abrogate our Lawes, Let them keep themselves to our trust, And we are satisfied" (sig. B4).[10] Within the context of the pamphlet itself, "our" liberties can be interpreted as the traditional liberties of any Englishman. Within the context of the monarchists' larger project, however, "we" are a much smaller group of the old political nation.

No tract denies the existence of Parliament or questions its desirability, but most offer definitions that restrict its function. Unlike their treatment of religion, the monarchists' discussion of Parliament receives specific exposition. These writers insist that the Parliament needs a control—as current events have demonstrated—and that control is the king. Some even argue that Charles should return to England without any restrictions placed upon him. *Vox & Votum,* which grants both voices and votes to the traditional political nation, declares that the country needs Charles's speedy return without condition (sig. B4); the broadside *The Royall Virgine* states that the writers ask for neither "a Free PARLIAMENT, a full PARLIAMENT, or a Piece of a PARLIAMENT, (We leave that to the discretion of him) who onely has Power to Call a PARLIAMENT."

More often, however, monarchist writers take pains not to appear to be slavish followers of absolute rulers. They concede to former parliamentarians the importance of the Parliament in the governing of the country.

10. Similar themes appear in the broadsides *Declaration and Address of the Gentry of the County of Essex* and *A Declaration of the Knights.*

Stressing apparent balance and reason, they discuss the role of Parliament in a limited monarchy, a strategy unthinkable to the royalists of 1642. The monarchist pamphlets of 1659 and 1660 argue that only a limited monarchy truly supports and defends English liberties and insures justice. Their authors stress moderation, carefully dissociating themselves from extreme royalists and the court of Charles I.

Employing a strategy that evokes the parliamentary discourse of 1642, the author of *No King but the Old Kings Son* subtitles his broadside "a Vindication of Limited Monarchy," explaining that republicans and other Commonwealthsmen "lost the substance of Liberty and happines in pursuit of the shaddow." He explains that the old government "included all the perfections of a Free State," being very similar to a commonwealth, since the senate proposed, the people resolved, and the magistrate executed. Before 1649 the Parliament did freely debate and consider important issues while it was able to hold the king accountable. Even exercising his highest prerogatives, the king could never be the sole legislator. The author further contends that monarchy—through a balance of liberty and majesty—gives the people the greatest freedom.

This discourse directly addresses the old opponents of Charles I with an ingenious strategy. Instead of urging specific proposals, it carefully praises the values of the Commonwealthsmen. In this tract, free states can indeed have "perfections," "the people" should participate in the government, and the government itself should preserve and encourage freedom. Moreover, the author takes 1649—not 1642—as the year in which England entered its crisis, which was not struggle in the political nation but rejection of its traditional form of government. Implicitly, then, the author praises his ostensible opponents for their desire to have "Liberty and happines," even if they did lose it through unfortunate choices.

Parliamentary values are a common theme in monarchist tracts. *Orthodox State-Queries* contends that the English monarchy is the best of all monarchies since its power is not absolute. The government is balanced— the prerogatives and dignity of the king defended by the privileges and freedoms of the Commons. *Loyal Queries* wonders whether there can be a better proposal to secure the exercise of the Protestant religion "in a just liberty, and a modest variety of opinions" than to restore a Protestant prince and both Houses of Parliament (sig. A5v). Other pamphlets, such as *Englands Redemption,* support monarchy by arguing that "it grew by Nature" (sig. A3) in England and that all English laws were designed with the assumption of a king; hence, concludes *Vox Vere Anglorum,* any divergence from monarchy can only be unnatural and a threat to the security guaranteed to Englishmen by their laws (sig. A3v).

The conciliatory tone of these tracts results from their adoption of the parliamentary rhetoric of 1642. In addressing the undefined, insecure audience of 1659 and 1660, these new monarchists offer the hope of stability and peace as they appear to endorse, not to fight, the goals of their former opponents. We agree with your ends, they say, but not with your means. If you want liberty, justice, and freedom—as we do—you may only achieve it through a government properly balanced and yet unified in the person of a king. Only rule by one person, held properly accountable, can achieve and maintain peace.

Charles himself declares that peace is his foremost object, as do the signatories of the monarchist declaration from Dorset. *The Declaration and Address of the Gentry of Essex* claims that with a proper settlement the diverse factions of the country will be reconciled. Far from wanting revenge, the gentry says, "we will thankfully submit and attend the Resolutions of the next ensuing *Parliament,* for a just and happy Settlement of *Church* and *State,* that so at last (by Gods blessing) those odious marks of Sides and Parties may for ever be blotted out, and a perfect Union may again be restored to this distressed Nation."[11] Peace is a nebulous value, treasured by all. Debate and conflict, in whatever form, are alien to peace.

In this rhetoric, the monarchists are the true upholders of all English values, values that even the Commonwealthsmen say they share. The writers imply also that none of these values is being advanced by the Rump, and they carefully show that there are only two possible choices—anarchy or monarchy, the present or the past. Couching their arguments in the familiar terms of the past, they exclude the other option, the present. Their language precludes anything but the idealized past, which by 1659 also means the language of the old parliamentarians. Charles himself offers nothing but praise of the old ways in his declaration. He cheerfully endorses all propositions that glorify God, the Protestant religion, the rights of the crown, the privileges of a free and full parliament elected by free consent, and the "Just Rights and Liberties of our Subjects." In place of specific examples and proposals, as in a traditionally deliberative tract, the future king and his supporters substitute the amplification of the epideictic confirmation. They list and praise values, hoping thereby to unify a fragmented audience weary of conflict.

11. Similar topics are covered in *Declaration of the Knights,* and *Three Propositions,* sig. A2v.

The epideictic nature of such a conciliatory strategy ironically appears best in the few overt vituperations of the Rump. The most lively of these— *The Londoners Last Warning,* written in the midst of the anarchy—urges an uprising of the disfranchised traditional rulers and others, crying, "How easy at this time it is for you to redeem, what will sodainly and assuredly be engaged almost to despair, your Religion, your Laws, your Liberties, your Freedomes, your Country from slavery, your Estates from oppression, injustice and rapine, and your Persons and Posterity from eternal ruine; a few dayes will snatch from you this happy opportunity, and you will then grieve and condemn too late your want of courage" (sig. A4). This salvo confirms what the conciliatory tracts merely suggest—that *unity* really means no dissent, that *freedom* means the liberties of the traditional ruling class excluded from the present government. *The Londoners Last Warning* uses the same themes as the conciliatory tracts, leaves the same terms undefined, and addresses the same audience. Only the tone is different. Whatever their tone, however, these tracts universally call for the traditional governing class to reassert itself. They urge the old understanding of freedom and liberty—a limited latitude for themselves and the freedom to obey for others.

Having defined the values of the community they hope to reconstruct, the monarchists devote most of their attention to praising Charles II and attacking his enemies. In these tracts, Charles is the embodiment of the proposed community, so praise of him becomes the plan of action— epideictic rhetoric becomes deliberative. Because he is the solution of all the problems discussed in the tracts, Charles himself often appears at the end of the authors' presentations. The conclusions thus become true epideictic perorations. Their primary function is to give pleasure—to confirm the readers in their values, to make them feel comfortable and secure. Only secondarily do they urge support of the Restoration. More often than not, that course of action is left implicit. The epideictic genre, with its focus on community, creates the impression that that community already exists.

In this discourse, the monarchists present themselves as the spokesmen for the political community. The Rump and radicals are the deviants. The monarchists do not even try to engage them in discussion: in their tracts, the only conceivable response of the radicals is silence. In Anthony Sadler's broadside *Maiestie Irradiant,* the idea of Charles alone crushes the opposition:

> The Name, is Renowned;
> The Title, Royal:
> So Renowned, is the Name:

So Royal, is the Title:
It makes, even—
Rhetorick, to be Silent:
Impudence, to be Asham'd:
and Treason, to be Amazed.

The *Vox & Votum* culminates in an almost religious vision of the monarchists' desires: "All, (as it were by Inspiration) crying aloud, for the King, not for his shadow; not for a King in title, . . . No, it must be a King, surrounded with Majestick Beams, consecrated with holy oyl, invested with inviolable Authority and Power, limited only by the Justice of ancient Laws; such a Prince, and nothing else, will answer our Expectations" (sig. A3v). The pamphlet explicitly mentions traditional restrictions on the monarch, but in language that invokes prewar court poetry and rhetoric. Once more, the king appears as a superhuman figure, standing apart from history and politics and offering stability to his people.

Poetic discourse appears commonly in the monarchists' tracts in order to cement their vision of the expected harmony of a Stuart restoration. *King Charles the II: His Restitution* borrows biblical language in calling the king the breath of our nostrils (sig. A3), while *Englands Redemption* describes him as the rising sun, lately hidden by the mists of treason but now shining his beams on an ungrateful country (sig. A3). To the author of *Loyal Queries,* Charles is almost saintly; readers are invited to consider "whether this truely English spirited Prince, hath not preferred penury and want of all things, (but of a good Conscience) before the Arms, Navies, and Armies, which have been tender'd him, by the Pope, and his Partizans, in his Assistance, for the Recovery of his right of Government, (with this Proviso) to renounce the Protestant Religion, and to conform to the Church of Rome?" (sig. A5). In these tracts, Charles becomes the embodiment of charity, loyalty, and true religion—all the values the monarchists wish to claim as their own as they attempt to unite the enemies of the Rump. With its contentiousness, changing leaders, and sectarians, the Rump appears as the antithesis of all these values; it is a collection of individuals, each seeking his own benefits.

As monarchist pamphleteers argue, only a king can truly desire the good of the entire country. The *Metamorphosis Anglorum* explains that "the Monarch first propoundeth honour then the publick good; and lastly, proprietary interest and profit. But the Popular EState [*sic*] evermore inverteth this order, for it hath private gain in the first intention, the common good in the second, and honour in the last: which diversity of proceeding ariseth not out of the different formes of their government, but out of their different natures that govern: so great odds there is between a Prince and a Citizen" (sigs. E2v–E3). Charles himself asserts his agreement with the people by explaining how he is "so sincerely affected with the same Pious desire of the Publick good." The monarchists argue that by nature the king is a public person and his interests are identical to those of the country. He is the country. Therefore, the pamphleteers and monarchists in general seek the public good in promoting their cause. Any opponent is not only selfish but also a public menace.

When they actually turn to their opponents, the monarchists most frequently resort to specific attacks on their characters. While the king appears dignified, modest, loyal, and public-spirited, the radicals and members of the Rump are "Popish Emmissaries and Jesuites," "New *Athenian Republican Tyrants,*" "oppressing Hypocrites," and "Traytors," picked "out of Corners and Goales, where they lay drenched in debt by luxury, and Ryot."[12] Several tracts select particular subjects. *Orthodox State-Queries* singles out the republican theorist James Harrington, asking "whether the Author of the *Vtopian* Commonwealth, stiled the *Rota,* may not be thought to have a rotation in his *Pericranium;* and whether it be not probable that his wit is wasting, and may be trussed up in an Egg-shell, since his books do pass but for waste paper." *Panthalia* attacks Milton, in the fictional character of Chalibetes, "an excellent Orator: One, who had Tongue enough, to fortifie an ill cause, and to cloath his pretences in any colour: but the indisposition of his body crossed the intention of his mind" (sigs. R–Rv).

Metamorphosis Anglorum offers fully drawn prose characters of several leading generals and Rump members. Vane, for example, "is a man of a turbulent Spirit, and working Brain; a strange composition of Choler and Melancholy: A Person who having given himself wholly to whmisies [*sic*] in Religion, will still find out Crochets in State too, and indeed the fittest may be to advance any interest to the rnine [*sic*] of a Government, who can but sooth him with the conceit that he is pleased with his Chimera's" (sigs. C8–C9). The personal attacks reduce legitimate or at least sincerely held and reasonable grievances to individual character flaws, isolated from the course of both history and politics as much as Charles is above them. By rhetorically reducing the opposition to a small collection of deviant person-

12. First quotation: *Orthodox State-Queries;* second: Prynne, *Re-publicans,* sig. A3; third: *King Charles the II: His Restitution,* sig. A3v; fourth: *Englands Redemption,* sig. A2v; fifth: *Vox Vere Anglorum,* sig. A3.

alities, the monarchists reassure readers of the basic stability of the country. Both it and the readers are unblemished. In these tracts, the current chaos is not a disease of the state but of only a few men; only remove them and order will be restored.

The monarchists typically amplify their charges against the Rump by examining its actions. But, rather than presenting specific examples, the monarchists attack in only the most general terms, allowing their readers to interpolate their own fears and anger stemming from current events. Prynne comes closest to a specific accusation when, in *The Re-publicans,* he lists the abuses of the Rump. He labels it an oligarchy and claims that it allows itself to subvert laws, execute people, seize their property, and "create new Treasons" (sig. A3v). *Loyal Queries* asks whether the Rump members reveal "a high degree of madnesse" in repeatedly trying new forms of government "when experience of so many Ages hath taught them, that the old form of government, is most safe, most honourable, most peaceable, and most Heaven-like?" (sig. A4). *Vox & Votum* denounces the opposition as "lovers of Anarchy" and asks, "What, I pray, can be more contumelious, than that many of the same Persons should, so perversely, deny their undoubted Sovereign the same Prerogative, which they, so tamely, graunted to the Vilest of Usurpers" (sig. B3). Aside from promoting monarchist values as the appropriate ones for the country, these generalized attacks on the sanity of the Rump members localize the chaos besetting the country. Simply portraying a malaise on the part of the traditional political nation could lead to despair, a fear that nothing could change. The monarchist pamphleteers preclude this possibility by focusing on a few men in high places. With them out of the way, England can have a stable government again.

Further, the localizing of the problem absolves readers of any guilt and fear they may have that the English people are being appropriately punished for their sins. The discourse of the monarchists gives readers the opportunity to redeem both themselves and their country by abandoning the Rump. After all, as *Englands Redemption* argues, the country itself and its people are sound; the Rump in its turmoil is "a Warning Piece to all Nations, that they never attempt to try and judge their King for what cause soever" (sig. A2v). *The Londoners Last Warning* tells readers to resist the Rump and not permit themselves "cowardly to be frightened into a perpetual Slavery to the worst of your fellow Subjects" (sig. A3v). Thus, support of Charles II becomes an act of individual and national heroism. Readers should reject their government to save their country.

The monarchists thus argue that the members of the Rump and the radicals—insane, self-seeking, destructive men—oppose the good of their country. The government of the Rump is motivated by private interest, that "innovation" of both Harringtonian and Hobbesian political theorists. Against these new and threatening ideas stand the monarchists, with their religious and traditional defense of kingship. The charge of "private interest" becomes their chief weapon in attacks on their opponents. The author of *Metamorphosis Anglorum* puts the argument most succinctly when he declares that the restoration of England to its "former renowne . . . can never be done by settlement of a Commonwealth, where every Member will regard his private profit" (sig. E2v). *Orthodox State-Queries* pursues a similar line, asking whether it is consistent with "religion, Equity, or common reason" that "free-born people of England, . . . should submit to a new kind of Government, by way of a Commonwealth, or otherwise, . . . merely to support the unjust interests of some particular men." The tract thus juxtaposes "interest" to religion, equity, and reason, which are the values its author assumes he shares with the readers. "Private interest," he suggests, is alien to the traditions of their country.

Ultimately, many monarchist tracts imply that disagreement of any kind is unpatriotic and un-English. *A Declaration of the Knights and Gentry* argues that anarchy and disorder are the direct results of jealousies between "a close, and malitious Faction of Separatists" and "a heady, and intemperate sort of People, which falsely terme themselves Royallists." *Vox Vere Anglorum* maintains that governmental chaos and the "malady" of the state are continued for the profit and ambition of the people who originally caused them (sig. A2). Both tracts essentially say that members of the true political nation—embodied in the readers—do not disagree and therefore have no reason to perpetuate the current government. The contending sides are completely out of touch with the country. Readers should thus show their public spirit by rejecting strife of all kinds and obeying their king.

Ironically, their praise of traditional values and "public spirit" put these monarchists close to the "Hobbists" in their understanding of the need for monarchy. The monarchists' conception of "public spirit" itself is fundamentally different from the classical ideal of individual men acting freely and autonomously in service to the state. The monarchists' arguments ultimately deny the possibility of such action in ordinary people. Their attacks on commonwealths and republics charge that such forms of government allow individuals to act independently; that is, simply to pursue their own interests. In these arguments, people themselves are held to be incapable of upholding and working for the nation as a whole. Only a king, since he embodies the nation, can be trusted to put the public good first, and he alone can truly see it. The king's public spirit stems from himself, growing out of his own nature. The people's is not natural but comes from and constitutes obedience to the king. The monarchist pamphleteers implicitly reject the idea that average human beings can internalize abstract ideals and draw public spirit from them. In this vision, human beings can only achieve collective good by taking direction from a qualitatively better man—by being controlled by an outside force.

Their conception of public good as an external rather than an internal force informs the monarchists' exposition of traditional values as well. *Religion* means an established church with extremely limited toleration. Whatever one's private feelings, one must conform to the outward order. *Liberties* and *freedom* are usually left undefined, but most often appear in discussions of taxes, trade, and property. At most, *freedom* sometimes refers to local elections in which all "the people"—that is, the traditional electorate with the necessary property qualifications—are permitted to vote. In the localities, those traditional forms of government, law, and religion had greater appeal than the house of Stuart. Hence, any defender of the Stuarts who truly wished to appeal to a wide audience needed to link Charles II to those traditions. In this context, writers can ignore personal conviction: those convictions are irrelevant to the question of formal stability. *Public consciousness* becomes nothing more than assent to and acceptance of traditional forms. *Public interest* becomes defining one's private interests within the scope of these forms. However individually active, the citizen thus becomes politically and publicly passive. However superficially lively the political debate, the participants must never challenge the fundamental forms and assumptions of government and society that keep certain classes in power.

This basic ideological assumption determines the monarchist rhetoricians' uses of genre. Ostensibly, they wish to persuade their readers to support the restoration of Charles Stuart—to deliberate about a particular course of action. Yet the reasoning and proofs they offer are reduced to narration and amplification in praise of the king and monarchy, and vituperation of the republicans, radicals, and the Rump within the context of the values and standards of the old social order. More than a blend of deliberative and epideictic genres as they appeared in the anti-regicide tracts, these pamphlets fuse the two genres. Both ends merge as readers are asked not to consider carefully all the arguments presented but to adopt a course of action by assenting to a specific vision of government and society. Since the writers do address a course of action, their tracts go beyond the scope of the purely epideictic genre, yet their focus is predominantly epideictic. Through their various techniques of presentation, they outline and imply the community values and attendant social and political structure of the past, which are abruptly contrasted to the present. The writers give their readers only two choices—accept or reject the proffered vision. To reject it is to find oneself beyond the pale, grouped with the supporters of the Rump. To accept it is to enter into a community, to take one's place within a group that shares values tacitly agreed upon. In persuading their readers, these monarchist pamphleteers re-create the community of the past and supply the missing context for isolated and alienated readers.

However confident their rhetorical tracts might sound, the monarchists did not regard their cause as a foregone conclusion. Some writers felt the need to explain more fully the general theory of monarchy, hoping to add their contribution to the wide pool of political philosophy. Of course, these works did have a wider rhetorical context—they tried to convince readers of the desirability of their subject—but their tone and techniques differ considerably from the rhetorical tracts. The philosophical tracts are non-specific and logical, individual and private in tone. But these facts are not evidence of the authors' sense of personal danger. Out of the six tracts discussed here, four appeared in the spring of 1660, when the return of monarchy was certain. As a group, they attempt to absolve monarchists of the charge of "private interest," since they try to present "objective" cases for the English limited monarchy. Believe as they might that such a form of government was best, in 1660 no writer could conclude that the idea was self-evident.

Philosophically as well as rhetorically, monarchist pamphleteers needed to claim as their own the discourse of God, King, and Country—the parliamentary language of 1642 that by 1659 evoked not opposition to the crown but familiarity and tradition. In contrast to the royalists' extremism, the monarchists' adoption of parliamentary rhetoric enabled these philosophical writers to develop a discourse of moderation. Forensic like radical pamphleteering and epideictic like royalist, this discourse often sounds new and contemporary even as it evokes the old order and community values. In so doing, it addresses only the traditional political nation, urging as "balance" the familiar imbalance of "natural" rulers and ruled.

This discourse of moderation reaches its peak in the writing of George Lawson. His major work, *Politica Sacra & Civilis,* composed beginning in 1657 and published immediately after the Restoration on May 16, 1660, aims at accomplishing for conservatives what Milton attempted for radicals—a complete synthesis of politics and religion in a justification of a particular form of government. Unlike his royalist contemporaries and like the republican James Harrington, Lawson understood that the old assumptions about the foundations of government could not be taken for granted and that theories of power needed a basis in more than scriptural argument.

Lawson undertakes a full investigation of government, positing from the start that God approves two kinds—that of men and that of angels. Lawson explains God as a monarch and Christ as the monarch of the church. Having outlined the divine source of both kinds and thereby distinguishing his thought from that of the "godless" Hobbists, Lawson then considers each kind independently. He presents the political government of men as a civil "community," distinct from the *plebs,* the common people, with two parts—a constitution and an administration. A commonwealth is by its very nature a hierarchy that, to Lawson, is synonymous with order. Politics institutionalize the hierarchy to preserve "love" within the community that is bound together by "affection."[13] As is the case with Milton, Lawson regards full membership in the community to be the result of men's innate qualities—their "affection" toward each other—rather than of more transient characteristics, such as property or interest.

Like Harrington, Lawson also distinguishes the form of government from the source of its sovereignty. Harrington locates power in land ownership and depicts government as arising from, and properly corresponding to, the distribution of property. Lawson sees community as the constant, the commonwealth (or hierarchy) arising out of it. Power always belongs to and resides in the community; the king retains power to be just. Like Harrington again, Lawson believes that the community itself can best be served by a form of government that preserves "balance" among the members. Lawson invokes this idea of balance to defend "mixed" government—government by king, lords, and commons—as the best guarantor of the commonweal. Therefore, in new language, Lawson defends the traditional form of English government as the most natural and logical

13. Julian H. Franklin, *John Locke and the Theory of Sovereignty: Mixed Monarchy and the Right of Resistance in the Political Thought of the English Revolution,* 53–84.

kind of government and the subjection of the populace as the best way of serving *salus populi,* the welfare of the people.[14]

To create his discourse of moderation, Lawson expresses deeply conservative ideas in a language deriving from the forensic rhetoric of radicals. Despite the similarities in their understanding of "community," Lawson replaces Milton's radical, dynamic interpretation with his own conservative, organic view. His is the voice of the old order, before the influence of either Hobbes or the Stuarts. Because he reacts to both the radicals and the extreme royalists, he can present his ideas as belonging to the rhetorical middle. His language adopts the forms and tropes of radical discourse. *Politica Sacra & Civilis* is profoundly forensic as it concentrates on definitions of terms, the ethos of the speaker, and logical proofs. Its discussion of *salus populi*—the slogan of regicides and republicans—and its quasi-Harringtonian insistence on balance and historical evidence make its author appear sympathetic to the arguments of his most prominent opponents. Behind the conciliatory stance is Lawson's demand for acquiescence. His discourse mirrors that of the rhetorical tracts in reassuring members of the traditional political nation that theirs is the only legitimate power.

To establish their moderation, Lawson and others overtly declare their nonpartisanship. They cultivate the ethos of disinterest, often writing as strictly private persons in letters to friends, declaring themselves moved by simple patriotism. Lawson maintains that his goals are truth and peaceful resolution to the conflict: "I am enemy to no man, yet professedly bent against errors; and that not only in others, but also in my self, if once I know them. I am not pre-engaged to any Party, but a servant unto truth, and devoted unto Peace. I wish I may not be prejudicate, or partial, or precipitate as many do, who contend to maintain a Party or a Faction, but do not care to search out the truth; these do not close up, but open the breaches amongst us, and make them wider, and leave others unsatisfied" (sig. B5v).[15] What follows, then, will be an investigation of the optimal form of government, not a political argument. To oppose such a discourse is to be an enemy of truth. Thus, Lawson's declared "moderation" precludes debate.

Other authors nullify opposition by co-opting it. *Monarchy Asserted, to be the Best . . . Form of Government* is presented as a report of a discussion held

---

14. Conal Condren, *George Lawson's "Politica" and the English Revolution,* 43–132.

15. The stance of neutrality appears elsewhere as well. *A Short Discourse Upon the Desires of a Friend* is presented as a private letter, not meant for general circulation.

in 1657 urging Oliver Cromwell to take the title of king. The preface explains that even the king's own enemies saw the perfection of monarchy: "The Name and Title of King a fit Liewer to take down that exorbitant power [the military], and knew, the government being once settled upon the old foundation, the law did limit the power of the Governour" (sig. A8). By insisting on the supremacy of law and the necessity of curbing the power of an institution, this writer abandons the old royalist position and evokes that of the Parliament of the 1640s and even of some discussions in the recalled Rump. In so doing, he appears to acknowledge his opposition even as he dismisses it. He uses their words to present his own argument while appearing evenhanded.

Part of creating the appearance of moderation is the authors' careful and legalistic insistence upon defining and rejecting "extremes" and "extremism." Lawson echoes republican theorists in his attack on absolute monarchy as "a very dangerous form of Government, and very inclinable and propense to Tyranny; and such a Sovereign, as is invested with such transcendent power, degenerates and turns Tyrant" (sig. K5v). The anonymous author of *De Monarchia Absoluta Dissertatio Politica* employs arguments similar to those of Milton and radical sectarians when he argues that such a monarchy is a great indignity to human nature, a perversion of normal government, and a threat to liberty (sigs. A2v, A3v). Both authors borrow "extremist" language to characterize another extreme position, thus distancing themselves from both Hobbes and the old royalists.

Others invoke the values of the old political nation as they attack democracy. *A Short Discourse Upon the Desires of a Friend* argues that democracy can only lead to chaos, which in turn leads to military rule (sig. B2). *A Discourse for a King and Parliament* complains that "the establishing of a *Free-State* is . . . desperate; and therefore it was the course that the prevailing Mechanicks among the *Swisses,* were inforc'd to take: How else shall we be levell'd to a *parity,* which is of the very essence of a Free-State? . . . Reduc'd must the Gentry be to the condition of the Vulgar" (sig. A4v). These writers address as well as reassure the "natural" leaders of England. They thereby insure that any subsequent arguments they make may be rightly understood by that group to mean power for itself. Thus, these writers can appear to be nonpartisan while actually adopting a political stance.

Further, their oversimplification of the free state allows an epideictic attack on the ideas of both radicals and absolute monarchists as foreign and threatening without losing their conciliatory tone. By characterizing free states as social levelers and absolute monarchies as oppressors of individual liberties, these writers indicate that the moderation they seek is not social but political. It is the kind of government that preserves "liberty" for the gentry, Lawson's definition of the "community," while protecting them from challenges from above and below. In these tracts, *liberty* carefully excludes the majority of the population. In turn, *tyranny* becomes anything that restricts the political action of the "community." In this context, *balance* becomes a code word for reestablishing the prewar polity.

Balance is the favorite theme of the philosophical tracts, with Lawson as its leading proponent. In these pamphlets, balance is an organic quality that exists in the presence of consensus. To Lawson, this consensus is equivalent to public interest. It is not simply the compilation of private interests—it arises from agreement. This agreement both is and preserves *salus populi anglicani.* The goal of government, then, should be to protect and encourage agreement. This goal, Lawson says, is best achieved through traditional English government—mixed government, which is the complete blending of monarchy, aristocracy, and democracy. With such elements interdependent, an advocate of any one form can only preserve it by agreeing with the other. Any upsetting of the balance destroys the whole (sigs. K8v–N7).[16]

These writers put their faith in institutions rather than individuals, whether the individuals are supreme magistrates or kings. Allegiance to the institutions becomes a way of diminishing and ultimately forestalling any debate. The institutions, once defined, are beyond question. As explained by *The Case Stated Touching the Soveraign's Prerogative and the Peoples Liberty,* both prerogative and liberty are absolutes, best preserved by institutions. The king's authority is not the power of an individual, but is *"Jure Divino,"* and the king has a "sacred" relationship with his people that is indissoluble by either party. Liberty of the subject is protected in the freedom of Parliament, secured by the Petition of Right, Magna Carta, and the law. To obey these principles brings peace, but criticism and questioning bring disaster: "Your Anti-governists will alwayes finde starting holes, upon the least discontent to shake off that Yoke, which is undoubtedly laid upon every Subject, as a necessary Tye of their Obedience and Loyalty to their Soveraign" (sigs. A2v–A4). The institutions exist and protect liberty as long as the subjects accept them. Indeed, such acceptance should ulti-

---

16. *De Monarchia,* sigs. B4v–Cv, presents a similar argument, stating that all men are by nature free and equal, and that the commonwealth is interdependent like a family.

mately eliminate the need for dissent, since, in the words of *A Short Discourse,* it should produce "such a Government as may compose all differences" (sig. B3). While to such radical contemporaries as Milton, liberty means freedom to dissent, to these "moderate" monarchists, liberty means freedom *from* dissent.

Despite this crucial distinction, the monarchist writers continue to echo the radicals rather than their royalist allies when they present their proofs. Like the radicals, these "moderates" discard heavy use of Scripture in favor of example and analogy. Lawson turns to current events to support his point that imbalance of power leads to violence. He explains that the civil wars broke out because Charles tried to hold sovereign power alone, deserted the Parliament, and defied the law. In response, the people, owing allegiance to the community of England, supported the just party, the Parliament (sigs. Bb2–Bb4v). Lawson and others also offer examples from ancient, biblical, and modern history to illustrate the consequences of adopting various forms of government. Rome, Carthage, Athens, the Netherlands, Venice, and Switzerland all furnish warnings about republican government and the growth of oligarchy.[17]

In offering evidence against democracy and absolute monarchy, these writers frequently turn to "natural" proofs of the rightness of a temperate hierarchy. *De Monarchia* states as an absolute principle the idea that all human beings are naturally free and equal and that government is nothing more than a large family which should, naturally, be governed by love and right subjection (sigs. A2v–A3). *The Case Stated Touching the Soveraign's Prerogative* continues the family analogy, claiming that the people take their anointed king for better or worse (sig. A3). *A Discourse for a King* presents advocates of democracy as champions of a system so unnatural as to be ludicrous: he that "delights in the Rule of *many,* let him begin a President *in his family,* and he may there possibly have *enough* to do" (sig. B2). The writers mean for these points to be self-evident, requiring no extensive shoring-up from quotations of Scripture or extensive examination of religious tenets.

But, fundamentally, these writers believe that no such proofs are necessary. Theirs is a vision so thoroughly grounded in the belief in the rightness of their position that they do not feel the need to establish first principles. Those principles are simply there—assumed—and therefore presumed to

---

17. The examples appear in *A Discourse for a King,* sigs. A4v–B; *Monarchy Asserted,* sigs. C4v–C5; George Lawson, *Politica Sacra and Civilis,* sig. K6v.

carry far more weight than any position requiring the support of scripture. To the author of *A Discourse for a King,* the ultimate proof of the need for kingship is the existence of only one God (sig. B2). *De Monarchia* refutes the defenders of absolutism by indicating that tyranny denies the image of God in all men and confines it to the prince, contrary to basic Christian principles (sigs. A4v–B). Lawson sees the confirmation of mixed government in the celestial order, given by God himself (sigs. B–Bv).

In Lawson above all, what finally emerges as the best reflection of divine order is the English polity before the Personal Rule. Sovereignty resides in the community, the "compleat" members of which are "Males of full Age, Free, Independent, have the use of Reason, and some competent Estate" (sigs. C5–C6). It is this community—not the commonwealth that arises from it—that insures propriety of goods, liberty of persons, and equality of the members. The commonwealth itself—the government—is "the order of superiority and Subjection in a community for the Publick Good." All "virtual" members—women, children, servants, strangers— are subject to the complete members, and they to each other. In explaining his fundamental principles of politics, Lawson assures his readers that there need be no social transformation.

The philosophical tracts are ultimately designed to uphold the traditional forms of government, and they do so in a much more absolute way than the rhetorical tracts ever could. These tracts argue by presenting philosophy as being above party labels—as Lawson says, "enemy to no man." Nevertheless, their surveys of first principles and their exposition of "balance" advocate a "moderate," "mixed" government that is actually a code for the dominant values of prewar England and a technique for excluding other theories, other points of view. As Lawson's definition of community shows, this philosophy severely restricts the actual range of thought and political action to a small group of people with presumably like values. "Public interest" is thus a result of restricting the public sphere to these people only.

The monarchist tracts of 1659 and 1660 present a powerful, integrated vision of a Church of England God, a Stuart king, and a traditional political nation. Despite its ultimately restrictive nature, this vision functioned integratively because it was articulated in the old, frequently more broadly interpreted parliamentary terms of 1642—God, King, and Country. Those familiar terms from the past—not their interpretations but the terms themselves—signaled stability. Leaving the terms undefined, writers enabled readers to infer whatever they desired from the arguments they read. The impression of stability arose from the presumption of shared values encouraged by the deliberately vague discourse.

Rhetorically, the monarchist pamphleteers achieved their impression of stability through generic displacement. They interpret epideictically what might appear to be a deliberative subject—the course of future political action. But for the monarchists of 1660, there really was no issue to deliberate. Assuming the values of their particular community to be the correct and only ones possible, their rhetorical ends could truly be only epideictic—to assert their beliefs and endorse their traditional institutions. The genre itself permitted the undefined terms and the use of opponents' former slogans. As English rhetoricians believed, the epideictic genre allowed the deemphasis or even omission of the confutation. Thus, the writer could keep his discourse completely positive and therefore constructive. Further, the genre demands strong emphasis on the narration. Through narration, the writer can literally tell the story of the society as he wishes it to exist, presenting it as if it already does exist. By attending to such a story, the reader assents to its vision.

This is the strategy behind the monarchists' apparent rhetoric of moderation. It depends upon the readers' presumption—not assertion—of common ground, and it promotes that presumption by co-opting the language of the opposition. The writer's position therefore appears moderate and conciliatory without actually conceding any point to his opponent. Such a strategy runs the risk of legitimizing the opponent's perception, if the opponent or the reader should be sufficiently alert to call the bluff. Such an event, however, requires considerable sophistication and detachment on the part of the opponent, and in 1660, as on many subsequent occasions, such detachment proved to be impossible.

The monarchist tracts of 1659 and 1660 present the old political nation regaining its voice, declaring its absolute right to determine what is best for the country. It is the voice of one class speaking for itself but claiming to speak for all. Amid radical calls for further experiments in government and for the transformation of individuals within a new society, monarchist writers confidently asserted the rightness, security, and totality of their vision.

NINE

Order Transformed: The Radicals

The rhetorical training of early seventeenth-century England well served the monarchists of 1659 and 1660. Their linkage of genre and ideology led monarchist writers, whose political vision required of readers simple assent, to the epideictic genre and to a discourse of moderation that was integrative and addressed the political public at large. That same training, however, led also to the failure of radical discourse. The ranks of the radical pamphleteers of 1659 and 1660 included the likes of John Milton and James Harrington—writers whom subsequent generations, from participants in the Glorious Revolution to twentieth-century scholars, have admired for the clarity and power of their language and argument. Yet the reading public of their own time was not persuaded. Contemporary readers continued to buy the *Eikon Basilike* while the recalled Rump debated republican theory.

As we have seen, it was not the power of monarchist arguments that swayed readers. The discourse of moderation depended little on logic or evidence, both of which radicals provided in abundance. Moreover, readers were not drawn to monarchist rhetoric because of the imminence of the Restoration. Until February 1660, even the staunchest royalists despaired of a return of the Stuarts, and the characteristics of monarchist discourse varied little, whether a tract appeared in 1659 or immediately before Charles's return.[1] What attracted readers was monarchists' rhetorical strategy, so it is to radicals' rhetorical strategy that we must look to comprehend the failure of their discourse.

Unlike the monarchists, the radicals could claim no all-encompassing vision. They were not one group but many—republicans, sectarians, Cromwellians, and anonymous others who opposed a Stuart restoration. With

1. Samuel Pepys notes in his diary on March 6, 1660, that "everybody now drinks the King's health without any fear, whereas before it was very private that a man dare do it" (*Diary and Correspondence,* 1:33). The previous week he and some friends were doing so in secret.

no common program, radicals adopted the backward-looking rallying cry of the "Good Old Cause," leaving readers to supply the specifics of what that cause might be. Whether he chose the negative path of resistance to the Stuarts or the positive path of advocating a particular government, no radical pamphleteer could automatically assume that great numbers of readers already shared his convictions. More than at any previous time, the radical pamphleteer needed to create an audience at the same time as he proposed its transformation in a new society.

This double burden is reflected in the tracts themselves. Like the monarchists, the radicals produced both rhetorical and philosophical pamphlets, the first variety addressing specific issues, the second attempting to establish universal and intellectual grounds for the proposed government. The rhetorical tracts appeared chiefly in April and May 1659, during the period of the factional fighting in Richard Cromwell's Parliament, the plotting of the Wallingford House group, and the first days of the recalled Rump. The philosophical tracts, including two representing Harrington's republican Rota Club discussions, span the whole period of the last days of the Commonwealth, dating from summer 1659 to January 1660, during the various assemblies of the Rump and the governance of the Committee of Safety in late fall 1659.

There is a third group, however, quite unlike anything the monarchists produced. This group provides the strongest evidence for the strain the rhetorical burden placed on the radicals. It is composed of what I call "mixed" tracts—those that attempt not only to address specific issues, and define and persuade readers, but also to make concrete proposals based on articulated philosophical principles. Figuring prominently among these are Milton's *The Readie & Easie Way to Establish a Free Commonwealth* and Harrington's *Pour enclouer le canon* and *Wayes and Meanes Whereby an Equal and Lasting Commonwealth may be Suddenly Introduced*. Most mixed tracts appeared during summer 1659, when the Rump was discussing possible forms of government. Yet some, including both editions of Milton's tract and Harrington's *Wayes and Meanes,* appeared in the Rump's last days, after the great debate was over. In fact, Milton and Harrington have the distinction of being the only radicals to write after January 1660.[2]

The authors of the mixed tracts take upon themselves a tremendous

2. The only other one I have found is Henry Fletcher's *The Perfect Politician* (February 1660), which is a fairly sympathetic biography of Cromwell, not an overtly argumentative tract.

rhetorical burden by adopting both the public, deliberative *role* of the classical *politikos*—the individual advising the state—and the forensic *discourse* of the private advocate, instructing readers how properly to conduct themselves in a commonwealth. With Harrington as one of their most prominent advocates, they developed a language that, like that of the monarchists, exhibits generic displacement. In radical discourse, forensic rhetoric displaces and substitutes for deliberative, and it replaces the deliberative public stance with a social stance. In classical terms, the *politikos,* through his new discourse, becomes a *rhetor*—the speaker for a client in a court of law. Despite the ostensibly deliberative circumstances in which they wrote, the radical pamphleteers signal in their language a retreat from the public sphere and a rejection of politics.

This shift in the nature of radical discourse had a contemporary observer. That was Milton. His *Readie & Easie Way*—especially the curious second edition—marks him as both participant in and perceptive critic of the direction his fellow radicals were taking. He published the first edition between February 23 and 29, 1660, while other writers were falling silent and even the Rota Club was disbanded. In so doing, he committed a defiant act, but his subsequent publication was truly extraordinary. The second edition, considerably revised and including a strident attack on Harrington, appeared between April 1 and 10—*after* the Council of State had ordered the arrest of Milton's publisher, Livewell Chapman, and elections had begun for what would become the Convention Parliament.[3] Milton considered his criticism of Harrington to be important enough to risk his life to publish it, even though both Harrington and republicanism itself had by that time fallen from favor. Milton's criticism indicated no less than his intuition that radical discourse, especially in Harrington's works, had betrayed radical ideals. This belief lay behind the revisions of the second edition and underscored its irony: as perceptive as he was, Milton himself proved to be unable to develop a discourse suitable to his arguments.

The great variety of critical reactions to *The Readie & Easie Way* has resulted from this central irony. Older opinions range from Arthur Barker's condemnation of the tract as "a crazy structure hastily raised from the

3. According to Woolrych's chronology in the Historical Introduction to *The Complete Prose Works of John Milton,* 7:166–76, 204–6, Harrington's *Wayes and Meanes* was published on February 8, 1660, when Milton began *The Readie & Easie Way.* Milton published his tract after the return of the secluded members on February 21. The second edition appeared after the Long Parliament had dissolved, on March 16. The proclamation for the arrest of Livewell Chapman was issued on March 28.

debris of the crumbling republic, weakly supported by appeals to the past and future, and founded on an idealism which could hardly withstand the terribly weakening force of facts," to Don M. Wolfe's endorsement of its "practical solution" for "maintaining the revolutionary program known as 'the Good Old Cause,'" and W. E. Gilman's praise of "Milton's mastery of the technique of persuasion."[4] Recent scholarship has retreated from both these absolutist positions. Critics now regard the tract as a public demonstration by a crowd of one in support of free discussion, noble intellect, and political independence, and they call attention to Milton's "prophetic" voice.[5] Most scholars who adopt this position describe a generalized "prophecy" only, the prophecy of the poet and visionary. But, in *The Readie & Easie Way*, Milton's change in voice appears as a response to very specific ideas, and the prophecy itself results from Milton's efforts to solve the rhetorical dilemma of the republicans.

The seventeenth century—especially the decade of the fifties—brought a rapid redefinition of political thought, a change that provoked serious problems for radical rhetoricians. According to the classical definition of man as a political animal, human life was divided between two spheres— the public and the private. The public sphere was the commonweal, in which each man was an independent actor. The private sphere was the household, in which inequality prevailed and members pursued their own interests. As Hannah Arendt and Richard Sennett have noted, the seventeenth century saw the rise of the social sphere, in which the public and private realms intersect. Within the social sphere, people behave rather than act. They become the objects of outside forces. In this context, Harrington emerges as a new theorist of the social sphere, rethinking politics and government in terms of public and private *interest*.[6]

4. Barker, *Milton and the Puritan Dilemma, 1641–1660*, 260; Wolfe, *Milton in the Puritan Revolution*, 297, 298; Gilman, *Milton's Rhetoric: Studies in His Defense of Liberty*, 168. Cf. Barbara Kiefer Lewalski, "Milton: Political Beliefs and Polemical Methods, 1659–1660."

5. See especially James Holstun, *A Rational Millennium: Puritan Utopias of Seventeenth-Century England and America*, 246–65; Kevin Gilmartin, "History and Reform in Milton's *Readie & Easie Way*"; Stanley Stewart, "Milton Revises *The Readie & Easie Way*"; Thomas N. Corns, *The Development of Milton's Prose Style*, 101–3; Christopher Hill, *Milton and the English Revolution*, 199–204; and Keith W. Stavely, *Politics of Milton's Prose Style*, 98–111.

6. Arendt, *The Human Condition*, 22–73; Sennett, *The Fall of Public Man*, 28–41, 56–63, 64–87; C. B. Macpherson, *The Political Theory of Possessive Individualism: Hobbes to Locke*, 160–93; J. C. Davis, *Utopia and the Ideal Society: A Study of English Utopian Writing, 1516–1700*, 205–20; Christopher Hill, *The Experience of Defeat: Milton and Some Contemporaries*, 197–201.

To Milton, the republicans' loss of public consciousness, together with the corresponding growth in their attention to the reconciliation of private interests, was incompatible with his ideas of civil liberties and human character. It denied his ideal of the orator and of deliberative oratory itself. Ultimately, to Milton, it put the republicans on the same philosophical basis as the monarchists. *The Readie & Easie Way* is his last effort before the Restoration to speak as a public man, as he had in *Areopagitica,* but this time he speaks not simply for Christian liberty but for the whole idea of a political public. In so doing, he also makes his last attempt to transform readers into similar public actors. Yet, despite his intuition as to the cause of the radicals' failure, Milton was unable completely to translate that perception into a full-fledged public discourse. Instead, like his radical contemporaries, he wrote a mixed tract, combining philosophy, rhetoric, and practical politics. He differs from his colleagues only in the degree to which he preserves some characteristics of deliberative discourse. Throughout his tract, Milton reveals his uncertainty about his audience: who and where they are, and even whether they exist. As a final irony, in addressing his crucial philosophical question, Milton's voice itself becomes increasingly privatized as it abandons the three genres of discourse in favor of prophecy. *The Readie & Easie Way* both defends and embodies the eclipse of Milton's public man.

By 1659, it had become commonplace for radical writers to concern themselves with questions of private interest. From the late 1640s through the 1650s, groups as diverse as the Diggers and the de facto theorists pivoted their discussions on the two axes of people and property. How writers treated property depended largely on their understanding of both human nature and human desires. In general, the more a writer emphasized human individuality, the greater his concern with the disposition of property. The greater his concern with the protection of private property, the more the writer ignored questions concerning the commonweal, the public sphere.

The exception that proves the rule appears in the works of Gerrard Winstanley, leader of the True Levellers, or Diggers, who practiced his ideals in Surrey from 1649 to 1650. Winstanley was one of the only writers of the period to design an ideal state that would advance and protect people as a community. He based his communal vision on the conviction that the spirit of God dwelt indiscriminately and equally within every living thing. *Reason* was the spirit of God working within the individual human being. *Religion* became a metaphorical presentation of ethics. Since all living things were equal, ethics were to be social rather than individual, cooperative rather than competitive. Winstanley's society would preserve equality by recognizing that each person had a right to subsistence. This right became the foundation of individual freedom.[7]

The conviction of individual freedom based on subsistence led to Winstanley's indictment of private property. The existence of private property, he argued, encouraged greed, covetousness, and the desire to advance oneself at the expense of others to the extent of denying others' right to subsistence. There could be no true democracy when people were being economically exploited. Therefore, personal gain could not be allowed to come at the cost of the public good. Winstanley's community vigorously separated the public from the private sphere. In what one scholar has called his "radicalization of Christian mysticism," Winstanley prophesied that individuals could achieve redemption on earth by serving the common good.[8] Thus, in Winstanley's works as in few others, freedom was associated with spiritual regeneration and the traditional, Christian commonweal.

At the opposite end of the radical spectrum were the de facto theorists, nonmonarchist followers or imitators of Hobbes. Like Hobbes, they rejected theological arguments of all kinds in an effort to ground political theory on rational, philosophical principles. Such writers as Anthony Ascham and Marchamont Nedham attacked the royalist code of honor and the Puritan belief in holy struggles, perceiving that both doctrines led to constant strife and insecurity. The de facto theorists valued peace and stability more than any particular form of government and believed that any government that could maintain order and protect its people deserved that people's allegiance. *Protection* meant more than safety from physical

7. On the Diggers, see Frank E. and Fritzie P. Manuel, *Utopian Thought in the Western World,* 350–55; and Davis, *Utopia and the Ideal Society,* 169–203.

8. T. Wilson Hayes, *Winstanley the Digger: A Literary Analysis of Radical Ideas in the English Revolution,* 63. Very few radical tracts discuss social justice or poor relief as a necessary condition of freedom. Two men who do discuss these matters wrote letters that appear in *Original Letters and Papers of State . . . among the Political Collections of Mr. John Milton.* The first is the otherwise unknown Mr. William Hickman, who urges equality of taxation in a letter to Cromwell dated November 16, 1650. The second is the equally anonymous Mr. Samuel Herring. In a letter to Parliament dated August 4, 1653, he suggests a thorough reformation of social customs in order to aid the poor, including the sale of church lands and the appointment of the deserving poor to public office.

harm, however. These writers understood it to mean the maintenance of an atmosphere in which people could reasonably pursue their own interests. Beyond this protection, they saw no need for public consciousness. The commonweal was nothing more than the totality of balanced, personal interests. People would do what was right if they could clearly see their own interest at stake, for, as Nedham explained it, *Interest Will Not Lie.*[9]

The radical writers best known before the late 1650s—the Levellers—combined theological arguments and principles derived from the common law with the new theory of public interest. Leveller writers such as John Lilburne, William Walwyn, and Richard Overton began with a notion of Christian liberty that granted spiritual equality and equal privilege within the church to all the regenerate. They connected these principles to the common lawyers' idea of "natural law," contending that all men were naturally equal and possessed inalienable rights, and they therefore should have equal political privilege. From these assumptions they derived the tenets of individuality, freedom of association, and equality before the law.

Translated into practical terms, these ideas meant individuality and private property. Their specific proposals aimed at protecting individual property owners from the rich and powerful. These principles formed the basis for the famous army debates at Putney from October 28 to November 11, 1647, in which the lower ranks, who supported individual rights, challenged the leadership and goals of the grandees, who wished to maintain the traditional privileges of the rich. The debates ended in political failure for the Levellers, who then turned to their special interest—the law. Beginning with the Large Petition of September 11, 1648, the Levellers composed documents that outlined specific proposals for a broad restructuring of society, politics, the law, and economics to grant greater freedom to the individual. These documents culminated in their proposed constitution, the Agreement of the People, the third and final version of which appeared on May 1, 1649. In all, the Levellers proposed supremacy of the Commons, equality before the law, freedom of conscience, freedom from tithes and conscription, extensive reforms in the law, and such economic reforms as would free individuals to compete in the marketplace—direct

9. The term *de facto* actually applies to the theorists of 1689, but Quentin Skinner shows in "The Ideological Context of Hobbes's Political Thought" how Hobbes's thought influenced these writers as well. On Ascham and Nedham, see also John M. Wallace, *Destiny His Choice: The Loyalism of Andrew Marvell,* 10–43.

taxation rather than excises, poor relief, prohibition and reversal of enclosures, and abolition of monopolies.[10]

Their discussions of principles made them some of the first theorists of "public interest." As J. A. W. Gunn notes, public interest "was something closer to the particular interests of private men than had normally been assumed. It consisted not so much in the use of *arcana imperii* to strengthen the state as in those conditions that would protect private rights."[11] With the emphasis on private rights, the Levellers abandoned the idea of commonweal. Their ideal was personal rather than collective. Choosing to fight legal battles instead of political ones, they considerably narrowed the sphere of individual action from public to social.

The public sphere also evaporated from the works of the republicans. In the few tracts that appeared before 1659, writers spoke for their particular party even as they attempted to offer political solutions to specific problems of the Protectorate and, later, the restored Rump. Such works as Sir Henry Vane the younger's *A Healing Question* (1656) offered proposals for restructuring the army and creating a national council to govern the country during parliamentary recesses. Vane's audience was not the whole of the political nation, but only "the honest party," which needed to be cleansed of "selfish concern" (17). The notorious *Killing Noe Murder* (1657) advocated tyrannicide as the remedy for the injustices of Cromwell's government and reminded readers that "our interest" was threatened by the growing powers of the protector (15). The writers of both tracts conceived of a limited audience even as they described public reforms. Their tracts are private discussions rather than public speeches.[12]

The social nature of republican discourse before 1659 is nowhere better illustrated than in the works of James Harrington. An original and independent thinker, Harrington derived several of the major tenets of his theory from such thinkers as Hobbes and Machiavelli, but he applied them to new ends. From Hobbes he took the mechanistic approach to politics

10. A. S. P. Woodhouse, Introduction to *Puritanism and Liberty: Being the Army Debates (1647–1649) from the Clarke Manuscripts with Supplementary Documents*, 69–72; Christopher Hill, *Puritanism and Revolution: Studies in Interpretation of the English Revolution of the 17th Century*, 72–73; William Haller and Godfrey Davies, Introduction to *The Leveller Tracts, 1647–1653*, 35–40.

11. *Politics and the Public Interest in the Seventeenth Century*, 30.

12. Perez Zagorin, *A History of Political Thought in the English Revolution*, 151–52; Violet A. Rowe, *Sir Henry Vane the Younger: A Study in Political and Administrative History*, 204–11.

and human motivations, grounding his theory on rational principles.[13] Like Hobbes, he saw human nature encompassing both reason and passion, which could be reconciled by interest. The best-functioning government balances interests and is, in fact, determined by them. As Harrington wrote in *A System of Politics,* "All government is interest, and the predominant interest gives the matter or foundation of the government."[14] From Machiavelli, Harrington borrowed the ideas that history was the source of the rational principles of government and that those principles endorsed republicanism as the best way to balance the powers of the One, the Few, and the Many.

In a major break from previous philosophers, Harrington focused on the economic foundations of power, and he added the balance of property to the balance of power as the condition for the well-being of the state. Harrington believed that sovereignty should be determined by the distribution of property. The land constitutes the base, the government the superstructure, and political disturbance inevitably arises when there is discord between the two. Hence, when property is owned by one, the government should be a monarchy; when by a few, an oligarchy; and when by many, a republic. Harrington observed that when it does not correspond to the base, the superstructure can only be maintained by force. Therefore, for the sake of peace and stability, and in the light of historical necessity—Harrington's chief principle, deriving from but not originated by Machiavelli—the superstructure must alter to suit the base. Harrington believed that order can only grow out of a system that protects most of the people's interests, and he believed further that, as wealth was redistributed, only a republic could truly secure the common public interest.[15]

On the basis of these principles, Harrington constructed *Oceana* (1656), designed to be a model for the government of England. While believing that rational action and virtue usually coincide, Harrington refused to assume that good men will make good laws. He therefore built his mythical republic on institutions derived from what he thought were immutable principles. Oceana was to possess a mixed government—a magistracy representing a monarchy; a senate, based on election by merit and serving

13. J. G. A. Pocock, "Historical Introduction," *The Political Works of James Harrington,* 68–69, and *The Machiavellian Moment: Florentine Political Thought and the Atlantic Republican Tradition,* 189–94, 364–71; James Cotton, "James Harrington and Thomas Hobbes."

14. *The Political Works of James Harrington,* 836. All references to Harrington in this chapter are to Pocock's edition and will be cited in the text by page numbers.

15. See also Holstun, *A Rational Millennium,* 187–201.

as a strictly advisory body, representing an aristocracy; and a representative body of the people (excluding servants) to vote on the advice of the senate, representing a democracy. The predominance of power resided in the people, and the state rested on fundamental and unchanging laws. As this state was perpetual, Harrington guaranteed balance in society by proposing two institutions: an agrarian law, limiting the ownership of land to maintain the base of power; and rotation of offices, with equity preserved by the secret ballot, to prevent the growth of private interest.[16]

Harrington's republic was decidedly aristocratic, based on the ideal of Venice, modified by ancient Rome. Harrington carefully divided the people into classes, excluding from citizenship all servants and women, as did the Levellers. He further divided the citizens into a military class, composed of those under the age of thirty, and a class of elders, to function as reserves in time of war. Both are further divided into "horse" and "foot" classes on the basis of a property qualification, those possessing at least one hundred pounds belonging to the "horse" class. These classes forever balance and require each other, since "an army may as well consist of soldiers without officers, or of officers without soldiers, as a commonwealth . . . of a people without a gentry, or of a gentry without a people" (183). In Oceana, the gentry advise, the people choose—the roles are forever fixed. The gentry, absolved of choice, are free to advise; the people, absolved of initiation and debate, are free to listen and choose the best advice.

The Harringtonian republic, then, is truly a government of laws, not men. It depends upon the machinery of government—not public consciousness—to maintain stability and equity. When a commonwealth worked best, men became part of the machine. As Harrington explained in *A Discourse upon this Saying*:

> At Rome I saw one [a pageant] which represented a kitchen, with all the proper utensils in use and action. The cooks were all cats and kitlings, set in such frames, so tied and so ordered, that the poor creatures could make no motion to get loose, but the same caused one to turn the spit, another to baste the meat, a third to skim the pot and a fourth to make green sauce. If the frame of your commonwealth be not such as causeth everyone to perform his certain function as necessarily as did the cat to make green sauce, it is not right. (744)

With this example, Harrington defines the social sphere. The members of his commonwealth do not act but behave. The laws and social structures

---

16. Pocock, *The Machiavellian Moment*, 83–113.

are the outside forces that influence their behavior. Making exceptions only for great men, Harrington relegates his people to the passive role of making choices rather than decisions.[17]

Despite their philosophical differences, the radical works of the 1640s and 1650s share a common feature—the re-creation of the audience. While the royalists demand identification and accommodation, the radicals call for self-examination and the questioning of fundamental principles. In challenging the established, public conventions of monarchist government, the radicals, true to their rhetorical training, abandon the conventions of public discourse as well, recasting their arguments in new language. The Levelers, with their emphasis on individual rights within the existing or slightly altered structure of society, model their discourse on that of the courts of law. The de facto theorists, in keeping with their focus on the protection of private interests, choose the language of the philosophical treatise. Harrington, aiming at a social and economic as well as a political transformation of England, chooses a genre that traditionally addressed all of these goals—the utopian. From the time of Plato onward, the genre of the utopia formed the discourse of small, social, elite groups discussing public issues among themselves. The Digger Winstanley, alone of all the writers surveyed here, demands both a transformed state and a transformed human being. Instead of simply adopting an existing language, his writing, visionary and transcendent in character, combines and radically alters conventional literary and religious genres to forge a new and truly radical discourse.[18]

These widely varying concepts of human nature and discourse greatly expanded the contexts of debate in the 1650s. Radical writers presented not only different sets of rights, responsibilities, and ethics—but they also created new human beings, all of whom needed to be invited to participate in society, not taught to obey. Yet in presenting new variations on public and private interests, society, and government, these writers collectively fragmented any notion of an unchanging, public community. In remaking

17. Harrington sees true greatness possible only in unusual people—his Megalator in *Oceana*—and in aristocrats; hence, his aristocratic senate. As I shall discuss below, Milton's attack on Harrington focuses on the passive role Harrington gives the people. "Decision" involves the process of consideration, "choice" merely the selection of options. Milton is thus one of the first writers who distinguishes the democratic process from the mere existence of elections.

18. Hayes, *Winstanley the Digger,* 109–12; Manuel and Manuel, *Utopian Thought,* 119–22, 250–60.

and focusing on either the individual or a transformed society, radical writers of the 1650s undermined the very conventions that advanced public discourse. With the loss of public discourse came the loss of the idea of public man—and the disappearance of any notion of public audience. Partly as a result of their own political convictions, the writers of the 1650s pursued an increasingly elusive audience. By 1659, pamphleteers spoke into a void.

The collapse of the public sphere accounts for the horrible anguish behind the rhetorical tracts of spring 1659. Written during a severe crisis of government and public order, these tracts reflect their writers' deep anxiety and fear. All search for some meaning to current events and cry out against the abandonment of the Good Old Cause. Acutely sensing the absence of a larger community or common purpose, these writers attempt to unify a party rather than urge a specific common goal for the future. They call to God and the "saints" somehow to resolve the crisis as they confront the end of their expectations. In place of the public discourse of deliberative rhetoric, these radical pamphleteers cling to an unfortunate mixture of the forensic and epideictic genres. They make extensive use of invective, but, instead of making it contrast to a proposed noble goal, they subordinate it to the purpose of defining that goal. Under such circumstances, the entire radical program is defined only by negation. In the rhetoric of its defenders, the Good Old Cause disappears in a cloud of inference.

Most pamphleteers fail to explain the Cause. To many writers, such as the author of *A Perambulatory Word to Court, Camp, City, and Country,* it is simply the alternative to "any single Soveraigne" (sigs. A2v–A3). To the authors of *The Humble Remonstrance of the Non-Commission Officers and Private Soldiers, To the Right Honourable the Ld. Fleetwood,* and *An Invocation to the Officers of the Army,* the Good Old Cause is a yardstick by which to measure the actions of the army, all finding it delinquent to some degree. *An Invocation* denounces army hypocrisy for failing to act: "What talk you of the Good Old Cause, whilst it and Equity, Religion and Reason, are voted out of the House of Commons by Courtiers and Cavaleers?" (sig. A2). *The Humble Remonstrance* and *To the Right Honourable the Ld. Fleetwood* call for a purge of officers not loyal to the Cause (sigs. A2 and A2v, respectively). The authors of the broadside *Twelve Plain Proposals* and *To His Excellency the Lord Fleetwood, and the General Council of Officers* use the Cause as a call for the army to cease its factional fighting and resume its old duties and functions (sig. A3). In these tracts, reference to the Cause is a general indictment of the grandees. Any reader may supply his own specifics.

In their attempts to define the Good Old Cause, these writers resort to exposition by negatives. By implication, the Cause is whatever the monarchy and Protectorate were not. *A Briefe Relation of Certaine Speciall and Most Materiall Passages* describes a king as "a favourer of iniquity; nay, . . . a settler of a Court, or nursurie of Whores, Rogues, Bawds and such like persons, as was evidently seen in former dayes at Whitehall" (sig. A2). The author suggests that all single-person governments degenerate into this condition, and he asks whether the protector's own court did not match this description. With invective echoed by *An Invocation* and *To the Right Honourable the Ld. Fleetwood*, *A Perambulatory Word* lists examples of ancient and biblical courtiers bringing countries to disaster, calling them "canniballs to their Countrey," and asking, "Shall not Crowns, Scepters, painted Sepulchers, and parasiticall Pageantries perish, or rather perpetuate the memory of their perfidious practices, whilst every passenger shall with a pointing-finger proclaim there lies a filthy carkasse under a fair stone, or an English Monster under a Marble Monument" (sigs. A2v, A3).[19] As powerful as this invective is, it has no true power of confutation, since in none of these tracts does an author contrast it to a clearly articulated, positive illustration of the Cause. Invective for its own sake becomes destructive. Without presenting an alternative, writers of invective can provoke their readers only to despair.

Such negative exposition continues in the pamphleteers' attacks on their opponents. While the monarchists unify their audience by praising the king, the radicals slide into despair as they berate former allies for betrayal and desertion. *To the Right Honourable the Ld. Fleetwood* accuses the army of being "exceedingly corrupted, by the endeavour of self-seekers" who design to "bring in upon us an Innundation of Tyranny and slavery both in things Civil and Religious" (sigs. A2–A2v).[20] *An Invocation* calls the grandees "prostituted Parasites, who have pawn'd their souls" (sig. A3), while *A Perambulatory Word* brands them and their civilian supporters "selfish and irreconcilable designers . . . who to advance their personall powers, and to paint the plumes of present oppressours, would rob us of the price and purchase of our bloody and dear-bought Liberties" (sigs. A4–A4v).

Absent from these tracts is any discussion of the specific liberties and

---

19. Cf. *An Invocation*, sig. A2v; *To the Right Honourable the Lord Fleetwood*, sig. A3v.

20. Similar sentiments appear in *The Humble Remonstrance*, sigs. A2–A2v; *A Perambulatory Word*, sig. A2; *Twelve Plain Proposals; Huc Ades, Haec Animae*, sig. A3.

ideals the army has betrayed. Since readers are left to supply their own definitions, these writers offer no coherent vision of the cause they defend. Their tracts attack the personal failings of individuals for the inability to achieve some better society, government, or other unspecified goal. Without a positive statement of principle, the pamphleteers fight a rearguard action. Focusing on the past—for accusations of betrayal are evaluations of a past action—their tracts are given a feeling of hopelessness, as no alternative to the chaos of the present is offered. They unify their readers with nothing but anger.

In true forensic fashion, the radical pamphleteers depend upon ethos to give power to their arguments. They attempt to influence readers by presenting the evidence for their past, sincere dedication to the Cause. In their address *To His Excellency the Lord Fleetwood, and the General Council*, the soldiers declare their support of that Cause for which they had committed such violent acts:

> And because our cousciences [*sic*] bears us witness that we dipt our hands in blood in that cause, & the blood of many thousands hath been shed by our immediate hands, under your commands in that Quarrel, we are amazed to think of the account that we must render at the great and terrible day of the lord, if by our silence the Freedoms of these Nations . . . should be lost & returned into the hands of that Family which God hath so eminently appeared against in his many signal Providences, little less then miracles. (sig. A2)

They have sealed in blood their own loyalty, they say. Readers hear behind the soldiers' words a plea to not be betrayed by the same cause that they were willing to kill and die for. They will be in danger—and not just from God—if their officers desert them. In pleading that the "disaffected" officers abandon private interests, they also demand, "Think of us" (sig. A2).

In projecting an ethos of sincerity and deep feeling, the radical writers also focus on private concerns—fear for themselves and for current suffering. Their language increasingly suggests powerlessness and despair. *Huc Ades, Haec Animae* points to the present division in the country and asks the army to consider the "dangerous inconveniencies" that might occur if no resolution is found (sigs. A2v–A3). The address *To the Right Honourable the Ld. Fleetwood* claims that God has abandoned both nation and army "since the interruption of that renowned victorious [Rump] Parliament, and the advancement of a private personal Interest, in stead of the Weal-publick," listing as evidence people's great loss of money, deaths, illegal imprisonment, and the possibility that England is "like to be made a prey to a foreign Enemy" (sig. A2v). Months later, the broadside *The Remonstrance of the Apprentices* decries the same problems, charging that, "We take no pleasure in the remembrance of our unhappy Valour, having wasted a great deal of brave Blood in the purchasing of our shame, and in serving the ambitious Designs of some Grandees, which nevertheless we have seen frustrated and disappointed as well as our good intentions deluded." In stressing their suffering and fear for themselves, these writers turn argument into complaint.

True to this focus on past and present, the radical writers offer no solution for the future but an appeal to God and his "saints." Many, such as the petitioning apprentices, confess to confusion about God's will. Others see the fate of the Stuarts as a divine judgment so strong that England must resist at any cost a restoration of monarchy. *The Humble Remonstrance* offers some hope in seeing God working through the faithful in the army (sigs. A2–A2v), while the broadside *Twelve Plain Proposals* urges any kind of resistance because "it is better to dye of the Remedy then the Disease." In a call to action, *Huc Ades* praises "those godly Lights," who have been shining examples of "Valour, Equity, Wisedom, Magnanimity, Dexterity, and other excellent Virtues" (sig. A2). All these tracts attempt to unify a party by praising the "saints" in the army. In so doing, they address only those that already identify themselves as such. The writers offer no coherent program, other than suggestive calls to the sects. They thus do not attempt to reach any uncommitted or wavering reader.

Only a handful of tracts concentrate on the future. The most notable, *The Declaration of the Faithfull Souldiers of the Army,* constructs its entire argument on the premise that God is watching over the faithful of the army and will help them protect the godly of the nation. The tract praises God for uniting so many people under the Good Old Cause and assures the godly that the soldiers pray for God's aid. In the end of the struggle, the writer promises, God will yet triumph in England: "We hope we shall with as unanimous courage shew our selves for our great God, for the *Good Old Cause,* and for the Good People of this Nation . . . Desiring the Lord to own us all, and to bring us to the wished Effects of our Spiritual and Temporal desires, for the Publick good of the Common-wealth; and in the end to eternalize us in the blessed union and fellowship of Himself in glory" (sigs. A2–A3v, A4). This writer presents the Cause in a positive light, making it not something lost or betrayed but a focal point for future aspiration to be achieved through devotion, faith, and struggle—like Heaven. While the

Basilike offered monarchists specific plans for the future, and Charles II outlined definite proposals to take effect after his return, *The Declaration of the Faithfull Souldiers*—the most positive of the radical rhetorical tracts— presents a nebulous, sectarian vision, integrative only to those who already possess some notion of what that vision might be in practice. *The Declaration of the Faithfull Souldiers,* like its companion tracts, preaches only to the converted.

Unsure of their audience and their community, the authors of these rhetorical tracts only define their cause by negation. They do want to indict their opponents for betrayal of the Cause—their readers should condemn such people for abandoning God. The problem with such an indictment, however, is that the writers cannot be specific about the nature of the crime. They offer broad innuendos concerning private interest, rule of single persons, and vanity. These are all charges that the writers hope their readers will agree to find reprehensible. Through the common rejection of these charges, the writers attempt to forge a community that will then unite to oppose monarchy. A set of rules may define a community that in turn presents an entity worth defending; commonly held anger, however, dissipates if not bound together firmly by some transcendent principles. Such principles the rhetorical writers do not supply. For them the Cause is nothing more at this point than a rallying cry—it is not a plan or a program. While monarchist rhetorical tracts can rely on the sentimentalized but well-defined idea of a Stuart restoration, radical works flounder in sectarian appeal.

The effort to outline a comprehensive political program is taken up in the radicals' philosophical tracts. Among all anti-monarchical pamphlets, these are the fewest in number and their tone is not as private or detached as that of corresponding monarchist works, such as those by Lawson and Wren. The radical philosophical works attempt to put forward a common set of reasonable principles that can convert anyone not already committed to monarchy. Two of these tracts, J. S.'s *Government Described* and William Sprigg's *A Modest Plea, for an Equal Common-wealth Against Monarchy,* consider not only the case for democracy, and against monarchy and aristocracy, but also the means by which society and individuals may be transformed to be full participants in the new government. The remaining tracts—two works by Harrington—assume as their starting point a basic alteration in property and focus their discussions on the proposed structures and operations of the government, taking into account certain fundamental beliefs about the nature of human beings. All of the tracts examine the problems of community, property, and individualism, as they translate the idea of public interest into concrete terms.

Both J. S. and Sprigg endorse a complete restructuring of society and redistribution of wealth to dissipate the social tensions that they believe caused the civil wars. Concentration of property in the hands of a few, they believe, led to the growth of competing private interests within a governmental structure unable to balance them. Both authors see monarchy as the worst form of government, since it concentrates wealth and power in the hands of one person who then perceives himself as different and separate from the rest of the people. J. S. complains that monarchy, "conspiring in behalf of its own Interest, against the Interest of the people, it thereby converteth it self into Tyranny" (sig. A2). Sprigg explains that a king "hath an Interest distinct from that of the people, [and] must be most apt to degenerate, and have the greatest propensity to Tyrannie and Oppressions." Further, monarchies corrupt those who aspire to service of the Court, including "Orators and Poets, the constant Parasites of Princes," who use their talents to serve themselves rather than their country (sigs. A3–A8).[21]

Aristocracy, as practiced in Venice, is almost equally objectionable. J. S. argues that the interest remains private, but less concentrated, with the result that it begets violent factionalism. To Sprigg, promotion of and government by aristocracy makes its members proud and ready to advance at any cost "that diversity of Preying Interests, that are the source and spring of all our miseries" (sigs. C–Cv, K2–K3). J. S. also sees private interest at work in proposals for oligarchies of "saints." Such specially privileged groups, he explains, are "unconstant, unlimited, spiritually proud, and notoriously ignorant; who think none to have Right in Government but themselves" (sigs. A2–A2v). As Milton will be shown to do in *The Readie & Easie Way,* these writers define tyranny as private interest linked to great power. But, while Milton turns to public consciousness and community as bulwarks against tyranny, these writers endorse Harringtonian property reform as the basis for equitable government.

Both writers explain democracy in Harringtonian terms. J. S. defines it as the most natural and best form of government, since rotation of office keeps the governors honest (sig. A2v). Sprigg argues that such a form—with the hereditary nobility abolished and property equally distributed—will insure peace, stability, and public interest. Imbalance of wealth, he

21. See also Davis, *Utopia and the Ideal Society,* 254–65.

believes, creates private interest, since many people cannot adequately pursue their own good. When such people are inhibited from honestly shifting the balance of wealth for themselves, social problems arise which inevitably lead to strains on the public and finally to a collapse of the basic structures in society. Sprigg provides the illustration of an elder brother reaping the full benefits of primogeniture, spending his patrimony "on Whores and Sycophants, while his more ingenuous Brethren, are either roosted under the ruines of some smoaky old Cottage, or exposed as Pensioners to be maintained by the old Charity of a wretched miserable world" (sigs. G4–G4v).

The only way to true public interest, both writers believe, is to free each family, not just the few, to pursue their own interests. Then, each man will understand himself to be part of the nation and will be eager to serve it. J. S. sees in democracy the ideal balance of communal and individual interests. Such a form of government, he says, allows equal status of all families as groups, while it "will animate an hundred . . . to put themselves forth to acquire Parts, and to fit themselves with Abilities to serve the Publique, either by Councel or Arms" (sig. A3). Sprigg, more sympathetic toward the gentry, still feels that an equal commonwealth will insure toleration and open more careers to more people. Younger sons will not be forced into trades, the church, or the universities, while all occupations will be open to merit. Citing Bacon's *The Advancement of Learning,* Sprigg argues that a thorough reformation of education will make it possible for young men to be trained to serve the public and to identify their interest with that of their country (sigs. I5–I6v). Transformed through education or through the acquisition of property, each individual thus plays an important role in his society. J. S. and Sprigg give their readers a distributive vision for the future, one that readers may achieve by revaluing themselves and seeing themselves worthy of power.

The means for achieving that vision, rather than the vision itself, are the chief focus of Harrington's tracts *Valerius and Publicola* and *The Rota.* The first of these tracts is a dialogue, the form having been selected, Harrington explains, because it is "the clearest and most effectual for the conveying a man's sense unto the understanding of his reader" (782). The second announces itself to be the result of discussions held at the Rota Club, which met from November 1659 to February 1660 to discuss what John Aubrey described as "aerie modells" of government.[22] Harrington

<hr>

22. *Aubrey's Brief Lives,* 284; the standard treatment of the Rota Club is still that of H. F. Russell Smith, *Harrington and His Oceana: A Study of a 17th Century Utopia and Its Influences in America,* 101–8.

presents both tracts as objective discussions. Valerius and Publicola are depicted as foreigners evaluating events in England. The Rota Club refers almost exclusively to "Oceana"—an ideal state rather than a specific one. As such, Harrington presents them as philosophy, not argument.

In these two pamphlets, Harrington explains not only the nature of man, but also the basis and structure of government, the examples justifying government, and a proposal for creating an ideal government. Both tracts revive arguments first presented in *Oceana*. As *The Rota* explains, the basis for government is the "overbalance of property": whatever group holds the overbalance determines the form (808). Discord arises from the equal balance of property. To Harrington, this is the fundamental fact underlying all government and social structure. The idea of community, as defended by the monarchists, is simply absurd: "To hold that government may be founded upon community is to hold that there may be a black swan or a castle in the air; or that what thing soever is as imaginable as what hath been in practice must be as practicable as what hath been in practice" (808). Especially in *Valerius and Publicola*, Harrington provides extensive examples to show that his proposals are indeed practicable and based on observable facts.

After having established his fundamental principles, Harrington demonstrates how his ideal government corresponds to both man's nature and his interest. He declares in *The Rota* (809) that his basic set of principles and his constituent assemblies are so truly representative and reflective of social structure that they cannot be improved: "Two assemblies thus constituted must necessarily amount unto the understanding and the will, unto the wisdom and the interest of the whole nation; and a commonwealth, where the wisdom of the nation proposeth and the interest of the people resolveth, can never fail in whatever shall be farther necessary for the right constituting of itself" (810). Constructing a government that provides for the exercise of both, Harrington believes he has resolved the conflict between public and private interest.

More than other radicals, Harrington clearly explains how an equal commonwealth allows the individual to connect his own interest with that of the country. *Valerius and Publicola* explains that "if the power of the people be committed to a single person, the common interest is submitted unto that of a family: and if it be committed to a few, it is submitted to the interest of a few families" (785). Therefore, if power is committed to all, it can be made up of everyone's interest, weighed and considered by all. In a properly representative assembly, each person may clearly see his interests in relation to those of the whole country. Publicola admits, however, that the people can only see the identity of private and public interests when they are "under good orders"—a well-regulated society and government— for "it is not modest that you or I, or any particular man or party, blinded with self, should pretend to see with such a constitution" (798–99). Harrington's institutions will insure people's selflessness.

Harrington's faith in and dependence on forms inevitably lead him to give in every pamphlet a careful explanation of the form his government will take. The form is everything, for it is "a form that must preserve their [the people's] liberty" (795). When the form corresponds to the balance of property, "and the power thence naturally deriving," there will be a perfect government, since the form "necessarily" arises from the base (802–3). Harrington's proposals—identical in *Valerius and Publicola* (801–2) and *The Rota* (810–21)—are absolute, the institutions mechanistic and therefore unchangeable. To Harrington, the right institutions eliminate the need for individual transformation. Hence, in these tracts he makes no comment on education. He trusts the individual reader to recognize his own interests, see the truth, and follow suit.

All these writers agree on general ends: they wish for an equal commonwealth, and they agree that a representative form of government reconciles public and private interest. Sprigg believes that through proper education individuals may come to see the value of a representative government as a truth. Harrington insists that this truth can only be instilled through institutions maintaining the external aspects of society. Both, however, wish to restructure the base of society by redistributing either some (Sprigg) or all (Harrington) lands and building new institutions. Because of this central fact, they cannot appeal to any native traditions. Their examples, though demonstrable, are foreign. Their proofs, based on transformed human nature or logic, are dry and intellectual. Sprigg attempts to shore up his arguments with emotional appeals; Harrington does not. These philosophical tracts establish basic principles, but, unlike the monarchists' works, they remain on an abstract level. *The Rota* is truly "aerie" since it is complete and self-contained. It, like the other philosophical tracts, remains a private discussion.

Several points emerge from the survey of the rhetorical and philosophical tracts. First is the predominance of Harrington. His ideas and language influence the works of many other writers. Second is the radicals' growing association of the idea of "community" with obedience and monarchy, an association which in turn reinforces their endorsement of equality and individualism. Finally, continuing from 1649, there is among radical writers a suspicion of rhetoric and language itself, most conspicuous in Sprigg's condemnation of orators and poets as "the constant Parasites of Princes."

The combination of these points suggests a growing and fundamental problem with radical discourse in 1659 and 1660: What happens to persuasion, and political discourse itself, when writers reject—as Harrington and his followers do—the idea of community as the basis for government, and develop simultaneously a deep suspicion of integrative discourse? The sectarians did have an integrative vision, however exclusive. Ideologically distributive, the republican theorists and others did not have their own rhetoric of integration to replace the sectarian rhetoric they abandoned. The visionary language of *The Declaration of the Faithfull Souldiers* stands alone amid the rhetorical tracts. Among the philosophical tracts, Sprigg's *A Modest Plea* is vigorously epideictic in its vituperation of existing social structures, and yet it loses its strength when it offers its own alternative.

The authors of the mixed tracts attempt to provide both an overall vision and a specific plan for reforming government and society, but they undercut their effectiveness through the same rejection of epideictic rhetoric. The topics they all share—careful presentation of the authors' ethos, definition of desirable values, exploration of public interest, and presentation of specific plans of action—ally them firmly with forensic and deliberative discourse. In these tracts, all other topics are subordinate to the specific plan as authors become advocates addressing a limited audience. Suspicious of community, they address readers as individuals and deemphasize political freedom in the name of social equality. Heroism is possible only for the few, while the many should concentrate on the protection and furtherance of their interests.

Milton—orator and poet—shares the four general subjects of his radical contemporaries, but with a decided difference: he inverts their emphasis. While in both editions of *The Readie & Easie Way* he does present a plan, he subordinates it to his discussion of public men, not public interests. From the first edition to the second, he increasingly stresses his convictions that political freedom underlies and enables every social benefit, that liberty is located in the act of dissent, and that true individuality and even heroism are possible only when a free individual exercises his power to debate within a public community. Both editions of his tract, but especially the second, embody Milton's effort, through rhetoric, to remake his readers in the image of his ideal public man.

In true forensic manner, the writers of mixed tracts take pains to define their ethos, and most project one that is both logical and disinterested. In *Pour enclouer le canon,* Harrington presents his defense of a republic as simply a logical conclusion to his study of the first principles of government. His tract is an effort to educate "the many" not to fear a commonwealth by showing them that the three alternatives—monarchy, tyranny, and oligarchy—are fundamentally unsound and unstable, and therefore cannot lead to lasting peace (729–30). He matches his logical explanations with declarations of disinterest, beginning *Wayes and Meanes* with this short poem:

> I do not pack, nor cog my dice,
> But show my game; is this a vice?
> Or where's the fault, when all is done,
> If I have lost, or you have won? (824)

By presenting his ideas as both a lesson and a game, Harrington denies emotional engagement with his subject. He demands of his readers similar cool-headed readings of his tracts. The quick display of emotion is a trait of the monarchists, and only emotion can stand in the way of the logical and therefore right conclusion Harrington advocates. His discourse associates dispassionateness with the public good.

Other radical writers employ a similar strategy. They consciously set themselves apart from both public chaos and linguistic violence, even as they attack their opponents. The signatories of *To the Officers and Souldiers of the Armies of England, Scotland, and Ireland* and *The Remonstrance of the Noble-men . . . of the Late Eastern, Southern, and Western Associations* depict the army and Parliament as the only valid alternatives to, in the words of *To the Officers and Souldiers,* "our present bondage, dangers, schisms, Confusions, frequent Rotations of publique Government" (sig. A2). True seekers of stability must therefore accept the supremacy of these bodies. The author of *A Commonwealth, and Commonvvealths-men, Asserted and Vindicated* protests his serious commitment to reason and practical proposals while he distances himself from contemporary pamphleteers: "In this time of general scribling, and dayly impregnating the Press with no less seditious then ridiculous Pamphlets, it cannot but be thought an Act accountable to discretion, for any one of a sober Spirit & settled Principles to appear in Print among such lewd Company, or to offer any thing of seriousness, in a way now rendered so unagreeable for business of that nature" (sig. A2). *Speculum Libertatis* overtly rejects the practice of vituperation, assuring the reader, "*Dear Country Man,*" that it contains "not Obscoenity, Scurrillity Sedition, or Calumny," but only a sincere proposal for founding "a reall Common-wealth" (sig. A2). In declaring their public-spiritedness and use of moderate language, these writers all demand rational consideration for their proposals. They attempt to unify by forswearing linguistic passion and striving to be inoffensive.

Milton, on the other hand, reveals his engagement in his subject by employing vituperation and indicting both his readers and others for their failure to rise to the republican occasion. He offers a plan, but declares it to be relatively unimportant—"And so the same end be persu'd, not insisting on this or that means to obtain it."[23] He explains that he is not concerned with specific proposals, or even the impending restoration, but with "this unsound humour of returning to old bondage" (355). The fault lies in individuals, led astray by "cunning deceivers," "bad principles," and "fals apprehensions" (355). The people themselves are not thinking clearly and need to be shown the proper way to act. He will not instruct them; he will instead offer himself as an example of what he desires. Through reading his tract and seeing the discourse of a free man, the readers themselves, Milton hopes, will insist on liberty.

"Liberty" is one of the most popular topics in the radical exposition of values. Even in 1659 and 1660, radical writers could not assume with any confidence that readers would immediately understand their values, so their tracts bear extensive expositions of what important terms mean. *Liberty* usually means religious freedom, as it does in *No Return to Monarchy, To the Officers and Souldiers,* and *A Common-vvealth or Nothing. No Return* addresses both "true Freedom to the Nation in general" and "true Liberty to the Saints under their several Forms and Judgments," strongly suggesting that one is impossible without the other (sig. A2). *To the Officers and Souldiers* endorses the restoration and supremacy of the Long Parliament, arguing that it founded "*Liberty of Conscience*" (sig. A2v). *A Common-vvealth or Nothing* asks, What will guarantee civil liberty if it is separable from liberty of conscience (sig. A2v)? In identifying civil liberty and liberty of conscience, these authors declare to all sects that they must have a commonwealth if they want toleration. In so doing, they make an overt appeal to the sectarians' interest and urge them to seek a commonwealth.

---

23. *Complete Prose Works,* 7:355. Except as noted, all references are to the first edition of *The Readie & Easie Way.* Most of the material in the first edition reappears in the second. Both appear in vol. 7 and will hereafter be documented in the text by page numbers.

Other tracts extend the meaning of liberty to include political freedom and equality, especially in a representative assembly. The *Speculum Libertatis* looks to a representative government as the best guarantor of liberty, which it defines as "all that right equity and justice, both in reason and religion, that a free people, and under no force, but of their own in their representatives, chosen and elected by themselves, can think or devise to bestow upon themselves to make the constitution of their government more just, equitable, and easy" (sig. A3). *The Honest Design* defines liberty as *"populi salus & utilitas"*—the well-being and advantage of the people—suggesting that a "self-denying Representative" examine all proposals to select the one that best suits that end (sig. A4). In *Wayes and Meanes,* Harrington concentrates on equal elections, equal representation, and a free parliament (824).

More often, following Harrington's lead, pamphleteers identify liberty with the equal distribution of property and equality before the law. The Harringtonian pamphlet *Chaos* advocates a total restructuring of economics and law to insure justice for all, which will constitute the real public good (sig. A4). In *Pour enclouer le canon,* Harrington himself argues that property and law are inseparable and that injustice is inherent in "unequal commonwealths: they pretend to be governments of laws, and at the same time defer unto some one or few men such power, prerogative and preeminence, as may invade and oppress laws" (729). *A Commonwealth, and Commonvvealths-men* quotes Harrington with approval, adding that, as England is now "upon a Popular balance," any government other than a commonwealth could only violate the laws, committing "violence" and "force" against property (sig. A4). *Speculum Libertatis* advocates reform of the law to protect each person's private interest (sigs. Av–B3), while *The Honest Design* suggests that people tend to become slaves to their property when the law does not properly protect it (sigs. A2v–A3v).

Only a few tracts extend the definition of civil liberty beyond the protection of property. *No Return* praises freedom of speech, endorsing the present as "a time of great Liberty, where every one takes upon him, to speak a word for his Country" (sig. A2). *The Remonstrance of the Noble-men* defines liberty as independence, urging Parliament to pass laws for the defense of "Persons, Lives, Liberties, Properties of the Subjects, against illegal Imprisonment, Banishments, Restraints, Confinements, Corporal punishments." Yet both tracts call upon Parliament to take action while urging readers to be logical and refrain from partisanship. The writers' visions of liberty carefully avoid the possibility of contention. All speak "for" their country in the presence of proper laws. These writers, like their peers, equate freedom with the protection of private interest. Freedom is thus best preserved through the mechanism of law, as it is created by Parliament and interpreted by the courts. Freedom also, then, does not need extensive exposition, since each individual will have his own interest.

Instead of trusting in laws, Milton depends upon public spirit. To set his readers along the path to correct interpretation, he extensively explains both religious and civil liberties. Religious liberty is "libertie to serve God and to save his own soul, according to the best light which God hath planted in him to that purpose, by the reading of his reveal'd will and the guidance of his holy spirit" (379). It should be, therefore, a wholly private matter. Any attempt to make it public is a "cause of much hindrance and disturbance in publick affairs" (380). Moreover, the association of politics and religion can lead otherwise devout people to the pursuit of power rather than their own salvation: "If ther were no medling with Church matters in State Counsels, . . . I verily suppose ther would be then no more pretending to a fifth monarchy of the saints" (380). Power, Milton suggests, is always ultimately hostile to the truly religious.

In the second edition, Milton severely reduces his discussion of religious liberty, devoting more attention to exposition of the consequences of making religion a public matter. One of the most fearsome aspects of monarchy, Milton explains, is its inevitable fusion of church and state. He quotes the *Eikon Basilike* to show "the antipathie which is in all kings against Presbyterian and Independent discipline" (458). Milton also suspects the Presbyterians of seeking political power at the expense of other Protestants in their bargaining with Charles II. In mentioning several religious groups, Milton suggests to readers the danger of allowing religion into politics. The best protection for each person's religious beliefs is to remove religion from the public sphere. The individual may then *exercise* his beliefs freely. Without that opportunity to act, there is no religious freedom.[24]

Milton also departs from his contemporaries by devoting extensive

24. This separation is the source for G. S.'s criticism of Milton in *The Dignity of Kingship Asserted*. G. S. attacks Milton for not considering God or God's will when he criticizes servitude to a single person: "Among the three persons, *Christ the Sonne,* and the *Holy Spirit,* who are God blessed for evermore, are both *Subordinately* related as *Persons* to the *Father,* and yet there is that blessed freedome and Liberty, that among them is *unity*" (70). Milton, like Machiavelli, does consider religion, but makes it wholly a matter for the private sphere. This is how Milton assures freedom of conscience.

attention to civil liberty, which he defines as "the civil rights and ad-vanc'ments of every person according to his merit" (383). Every avenue should be open, and Milton sees the best guarantee of this freedom not in laws but in public action and participation in government. To this end, he urges that every county be made "a little commonwealth" (383), since "nothing can be more essential to the freedom of a people, then to have the administration of justice and all publick ornaments in thir own election and within thir own bounds, without long travelling or depending on remote places to obtain thir right or any civil accomplishment" (384–85). Milton gives a political definition of liberty. It is not protection of private interests but the exercise of public spirit in the general advancement of a commonwealth.

Milton's emphasis on the public character of civil liberty becomes more pronounced in the second edition. True freedom will exist, he says, when we have "our forces by sea and land, . . . in our own hands . . . publick accounts under our own inspection, general laws and taxes with thir causes in our own domestic suffrages, judicial laws, offices and orna-ments at home in our own ordering and administration, all distinction of lords and commoners, that may any way divide or sever the publick interest remov'd" (461). When the people truly participate in public affairs as public men, they will attain freedom and liberty. When all participate, justice is assured. Property too will be protected. Milton adds a brief comment denigrating Harrington's attention to property, assuring readers that when all people put the public good over private, "no man or number of men can attain to such wealth or vast possession, as will need the hedge of an Agrarian law" (445).

In both editions, Milton warns readers of those people who want a king to protect their trade. This is pure private interest, he claims—they want people to prefer private luxury to the "frugalitie" that goes with public spirit. Private enrichment can threaten religious and civil liberty. It can become an "idol queen" when, for the sake of personal profit, individuals urge the people to "forgoe and set to sale religion, libertie, honour, safetie, all concernments divine or human to keep up trading" (387). Private interest leads to the neglect and even the injury of others. True public spirit advances the welfare of all.

Milton's contemporaries ally themselves to the public *interest*. Their understanding of such interest determines the plans they propose for settling the government. All claim to represent and support the public interest while accusing their opponents of private interest. To the petitioners of *To the Officers and Souldiers,* one's primary work should be "that *great work* of the Nation" (sig. A2v), while the author of *No Return* admires the fact that so many pamphleteers seek the public good, however varied their proposals (sig. A3v). *A Common-vvealth or Nothing* urges all readers to consider "what kind of settlement is safest and most suitable to the preservation or promotion of publick, popular freedom" (sig. A3). *Speculum Libertatis* asserts that in forming a new government, we should insure that all interests are subsumed into the common interest, to the "good and benefit" of the whole (sig. A3). While Milton provides a detailed exposition of what he means by "public good," these writers leave the term undefined and unexplored. In these tracts, it appears and functions as a disclaimer, assuring readers that the plans the writer is about to propose take into account each kind of interest.

In their expositions of private interest and enemies, these tracts resemble their rhetorical counterparts—the exposition of private interests provides an opportunity for invective. To the signatories of *To the Officers and Souldiers,* monarchists are "the flesh-pots of a single person," while Cromwellians are out only to save themselves when the king is restored: "It cannot be imagined they value the family of the *Cromwels,* except that family designe the Kingdom for *Charles,* thereby to make themselves glorious, (as they may suppose) and save themselves and posterities in the ruines of the *good old* Cause, and the good people of *England,* that stood by it" (sig. A2v). Not only are such people self-serving, but they are also not ashamed to advance themselves through the ruination of others or even of the whole country. *Speculum Libertatis* questions the integrity of anyone who wishes, by design or inattention, to "expose this poore Nation (in the eye of humane reason) to irreconcileable vassallage and slavery" (sig. A2v).

Other tracts link politics and religion. *A Common-vvealth or Nothing* suggests that monarchists "have still a Pope in their bellies, or a spite to popular Government" (sig. A4), while *The Remonstrance of the Noble-men* proposes to devise means to rid the country of "*Romish* Emissaries, or Seducers." Like such monarchists as William Prynne, these pamphleteers accuse their opponents of being foreign dupes or agents, supporters of religious and political slavery. They thus polarize the discussion, allowing no middle ground. The alternative to the plans they suggest is slavery. Such tracts demand the readers' assent rather than consideration.

One exceptional tract, Marchamont Nedham's *Interest Will Not Lie,* provides a careful analysis of interest as the basis for an argument in support of the recalled Rump. The tract is a detailed response to the monarchist pamphlet *The Interest of England Stated,* which attempts to win the sympathies of radicals by using their arguments.[25] Locating the common interest in the king, the tract declares that a restoration of monarchy will be in everyone's interest and that interest is the most persuasive argument he can use: "Men do not use to be importuned to leave their torment or disease, or want rhetorical Enducements, after the pleadings of Interest and Profit" (16). Like the de facto theorists, this writer implicitly denies the importance of public consciousness. To him, even the common discourse of rhetoric is irrelevant.

Nedham takes exception not to the author's analysis of interest as a motive force, or his assumption that interest is a valid consideration, but simply to the conclusion the author reaches. Nedham constructs a forensic refutation, his points governed by both the structure and the nature of the opponent's argument. So dependent is he on the tract he refutes that Nedham provides no formal conclusion to his tract. He divides his tract into two parts—the first a survey of the various interests at work in the country (3–26), the second a praise of Parliament that employs philosophical and legal arguments to justify the supremacy of the Rump (27–42). Characterizing it as each man's "little Commonwealth within himself" (9), Nedham defines interest in terms of self-protection, trade, and property rights. While Milton will attack monarchy for what it does to people's character, Nedham fears "the yet unknown Taxations which must needs be . . . entailed upon the whole English posterity, to maintain the pomp and pride of a luxurious Court, and an absolute Tyrannie" (8–9). Nedham appeals to his readers' emotions and their sense of self-protection as he urges support of the Rump, but at the core of his argument—the legality of the Rump—he cites Baxter, Grotius, and biblically based covenant theory in a closely written, logical presentation. Ultimately, his plan is simply to support the status quo.

Nedham's plan thus bears a resemblance to those of many radical but non-Harringtonian writers. Like Nedham, each of these writers uses his own analysis or mention of interest to introduce his own plan, which appears as the climax of the tract. *To the Officers and Souldiers,* published on April 30, 1659, calls for a restoration of the Long Parliament, the only true representative assembly, which, as it provided the Good Old Cause, will be faithful to it now (sigs. A2v–A3). *No Return* claims that Parliament should

25. The argument urging interest was highly atypical of monarchists. The only exceptions appear among the admirers of Hobbes and Hobbes himself.

be entrusted with sovereign power since it is composed of the true representatives of the people, in whom all power finally resides. There need be
only two restrictions: first, there should be freedom of conscience; second,
it should be made impossible for Parliament to convert the government
into rule by a single person (sig. A3v). *A Common-vvealth or Nothing* recommends that there be successive parliaments that sit no longer than a year,
and that the militia be freed from the control of one person or a council
(sigs. A3–A3v). All these writers assume that Parliament itself, with very
few restrictions, can reach a just settlement. The only changes they urge are
those that would prevent such actions as the establishment of the Protectorate or the rule of Lambert.

Harrington and several other writers are not so sanguine about the
reliability of any existing parliament. They propose more sweeping changes.
In both *Pour enclouer le canon* (732–33) and *Wayes and Meanes* (824–25),
Harrington outlines in detail the pattern for elections to be held in England. Drawing from his general plan as proposed in *Oceana,* he bases the
elections on local elections in fifty "shires" for an upper and a lower house
of Parliament. In *Wayes and Meanes,* he gives instructions for conducting the
elections and a timetable and system for resolving the government:

> Let what was . . . proposed by the senate, or house of knights, and resolved
> by the people, or house of deputies, be the law.
>
> In this constitution these councils must of necessity contain the wisdom
> and the interest of the nation.
>
> In this method, debate must of necessity be mature.
>
> If it be according unto the wisdom and the interest of the nation, upon
> mature debate, that there be a king, let there be a king.
>
> If it be according unto the wisdom and interest of the nation, . . . that there
> be a commonwealth, two assemblies in this order are actually a common-
> wealth. (824–25)

In any case, the people should decide, and they will have their way.
Through these elections, through debate and decision in Parliament,
through the institutions themselves, the people will reach a just, equitable
settlement. To Harrington, these procedures will insure peace and stability, regardless of the eventual outcome. Logical and detached, Harrington feels no need to employ any rhetorical colorations or emotional
appeals in support of his position. His position is right; therefore, it needs
no persuasion.

Harrington's concern for the franchise and the structure of government
reappears in the tracts of his followers. *A Commonwealth, and Common-*

vvealths-men essentially repeats Harrington's ideas and refers readers to Harrington's works (sigs. A4–Bv). *A Model of a Democraticall Government* and *Idea Democratica* endorse bicameral legislatures and rotation of offices. Both tracts would also limit the franchise. *A Model* urges the exclusion of those who oppose the establishment of a commonwealth (3–8); *Idea Democratica* suggests a property qualification for office, and further proposes that Parliament sit perpetually and that the members of the upper house be elected by those in the lower (1–2).

Several writers express some doubt about the enforcement and acceptance of their plans. *Idea Democratica* insists that all members of its Parliament be compelled to sign their agreement to the principles of government, hence giving official consent to its inception (5–6). *The Remonstrance of the Apprentices* would require all members of Parliament and government officials to swear an oath to preserve "the Fundamental Laws, Liberties, Franchises of the Free-men of *England.*" *Speculum Libertatis* proposes a written charter for the government, to be kept in every parish church bound up with the Bible and to be read to the people quarterly by the minister on the penalty of losing his livelihood (sigs. A4–A4v, C2–C2v). None of these authors has Harrington's confidence in the trustworthiness of the voters or in the power of his proposal. All look to safeguards built into it to protect the system from the vagaries of the political nation.

Aside from Milton, there was one other radical pamphleteer who suspected his fellows' reliance on mechanisms alone to preserve the Commonwealth. This was Sir Henry Vane the younger, who published anonymously *A Needful Corrective or Ballance in Popular Government, . . . to Iames Harrington*. Basically sympathetic to Harrington, Vane agrees that "genuine" power arises from "the right of consent and free gift by the common vote of the whole Body" (3). There are also "right of conquest," by which absolute monarchs rule, and "mixed right," sought by those "who not being able to be free men, are resolved to do their utmost not to be slaves" (4). To settle a government on genuine power, the nation must first be composed of people prepared to choose rightly.

Up to this point, Vane's arguments sound much like Milton's, but Vane's plea is strictly sectarian, as he addresses his suggestions only to the "godly" (1). People prepare to choose right by turning to God (7); therefore, the franchise should be restricted to the faithful, the remainder of the people to be "cast into a military order and discipline" (8). Vane rejects Harrington's careful, philosophical justifications for republican government. As Vane understands it, the pattern of government was revealed by

God to Moses (1–2) and was foretold in scripture (9–11). In appealing to the sects, Vane adopts an apocalyptic tone as he cites appropriate biblical texts. Neither public consciousness nor legal mechanisms but the faith of the "saints" is to preserve a commonwealth from private interest and monarchy.

To Milton, the distinction between public and private is not simply an introduction to a plan—it is the philosophical basis for his entire work. It underlies every argument he makes, every conclusion he draws. It determines his rhetorical strategy. Like his counterparts, he rises to the heights of invective in denouncing private interests, which he links inextricably to both vice and monarchy, revising his tract to add further exposition and examples. Unlike his fellows, Milton gives public-spiritedness full discussion. Here is the true emphasis of his tract. When individuals become public men they will inevitably usher in, defend, and uphold a free commonwealth. His first step, then, in establishing a free commonwealth, is to transform the reader into a public man.

He begins by describing the effect of monarchy on the character of the people. To Milton, monarchy is morally, not simply politically, wrong because it undermines and corrupts human nature. A king encourages the worst in human nature by being himself a public display of unbridled pride and selfishness:

> A king must be ador'd like a Demigod, with a dissolute and haughtie court about him, of vast expence and luxurie, masks and revels, to the debaushing of our prime gentry both male and female; nor at his own cost, but on the publick revenue; and all this to do nothing but bestow the eating and drinking of excessive dainties, to set a pompous face upon the superficial actings of State, to pageant himself up and down in progress among the perpetual bowings and cringings of an abject people. (360–61)

Like Nedham, Milton decries the expense of the court and the inevitable impoverishment of the people, but Milton is far more concerned about the possibility of people debasing themselves to worship a fellow human being and destroying their minds in the process. The aim of kings is "to make the people, wealthy indeed perhaps and wel-fleec't for thir own shearing, and for the supply of regal prodigalitie; but otherwise softest, basest, vitiousest, servilest, easiest to be kept under; and not only in fleece, but in minde also sheepishest" (384). Ultimately, it is not tyranny Milton fears, but the perversion of people's noble character by private interest and the promise of riches.

In revising *The Readie & Easie Way,* Milton adds further and more emphatic examples of the effect of monarchy on human aspiration. Hollow honors and money will make people prefer slavery to freedom, Milton claims. He mocks the rhetoric of the monarchists and their unifying vision of the paternalistic love of the king. He asks, "Can the folly be paralleld, to adore and be the slaves of a single person . . . is it such an unspeakable joy to serve, such felicitie to wear a yoke? to clink our shackles" (448). Aspiring to public office is noble, Milton believes, but monarchies perversely accord more prestige to court service, so that the best people in the country strive to be "grooms, even of the close-stool" (425). Worst, Milton sees the English people rejecting the destiny God intends for them. As he closes the second edition, the English are choosing a captain back to Egypt, refusing the struggle for their own freedom (463).

Against this portrayal of human debasement, Milton offers in the first edition his vision of an English people "flourishing, vertuous, noble and high spirited" under the Commonwealth (384). When each person is free, and free to participate in public life, he may aspire not only to nobility of soul but also to true heroism. In the second edition, Milton offers just such a vision in his portrait of himself. Acting as a public individual, Milton secured international fame for himself and his country by writing the Defences of the English People:

> Nor was the heroic cause unsuccessfully defended to all Christendom against the tongue of a famous and thought invincible adversarie; nor the constancie and fortitude that so nobly vindicated our liberty, our victory at once against two the most prevailing usurpers over mankinde, superstition and tyrannie unpraisd or uncelebrated in a written monument, likely to outlive detraction, as it hath hitherto convinc'd or silenc'd not a few of our detractors, especially in parts abroad. (421)

The Commonwealth provided the opportunity for someone not rich, powerful, or prominent to become great and urge greatness on his country. Milton was a public man defending a free nation. In *The Readie & Easie Way,* Milton presents himself as his own integrative vision of a free commonwealth. He achieved heroism once, and in the act of writing *The Readie & Easie Way,* he shows readers how free men may become heroes again.

Milton locates freedom in the act of debating publicly. This essential fact forms the basis for both his proposals and his attack on Harrington. The proposals themselves, especially as they appear in the first edition, are not particularly original. As Barbara Kiefer Lewalski has shown, they reflect many contemporary ideas.[26] Milton's call for a perpetual Council of State, chosen by a representative assembly (368), echoes a similar suggestion in *Idea Democratica*. His demand for ideological tests for membership in the assembly (368) appears also in *No Return* and *A Model*, as well as in Vane's works. A notable difference, however, appears when Milton justifies the perpetual council as a means of preventing factionalism and private interest (369). Far more detailed than any exposition in contemporary tracts, Milton's plan insists that the chief threat to freedom is neither the monarchy nor the private interests of only the monarchists and Presbyterians, but rather the private interests of the English people themselves.

In the second edition, Milton adds an attack on Harrington. This disagreement emphasizes the originality of the reasoning behind Milton's ideas. By 1660, Milton truly was the only author voicing his concern for the preservation of public consciousness through the preservation of free and extensive debate.[27] This principle underlies Milton's objections to four of Harrington's most important ideas: simple local elections, a legal system of checks and balances, the rotation of office, and a bicameral government. Under Harrington's system, Milton suspects there will be no need and little opportunity for independent public action.

Milton's revised model in the second edition addresses each of these points. In place of local balloting, Milton proposes a federal system in which each county is "a kinde of subordinate Commonalitie or Commonwealth" (458). Marchamont Nedham used the phrase to characterize individual interest, but in Milton's tract it suggests a public group as an extension of the individual. At the local level, more people will have the opportunity to participate in public discussions. In contrast to Harrington's elaborate system of checks and balances, Milton proposes a pyramidal structure of government with indirect representation and limitation of the franchise to "only those of them who are rightly qualified" (443). By limiting the franchise, Milton would insure an assembly in which debate would be practical. It is such an exercise of free speech that will "make the people fittest to chuse, and the chosen fittest to govern" (443). Public spirit can exist only through active expression.

The need for this expression prompts Milton's suspicion of Harring-

26. "Milton: Political Beliefs and Polemical Methods," 191–202.

27. By 1659, as far as I have yet been able to determine, no other radical writer was making Milton's argument about public consciousness. A survey of both the Clarke Papers and Thomas Burton's parliamentary diary reveals plenty of comments about public interest, but nothing about the commonweal.

ton's schemes for rotation of office and bicameral government. Milton's own proposals for the operation of government specifically call for perpetual consultation and debate. His Council of State must be perpetual to set the example of public service as the regular business of everyday life: "The day of counsel cannot be set as the day of a festival; but must be readie alwaies to prevent or answer all occasions" (433). Interruption of government is dangerous, since it is a break in public life. The people themselves must always be aware of their governors' actions and be capable of holding them to account. To insure accountability, Milton provides for armed revolt (435). The maintenance of a free government is a public concern, so people must be vigilant.

Milton further challenges Harrington's proposal of a huge popular assembly charged only with choosing one of the proposals presented by an upper house. Such a popular assembly, Milton believes, would be "unweildie with thir own bulk, unable in so great a number to mature thir consultations as they ought, if any be allotted them, and that they meet . . . to sit a whole year lieger in one place, only now and then to hold up a forrest of fingers, or to convey each man his bean or ballot into the box, without reason shewn or common deliberation" (441).[28] To Milton, such a plan mocks the very idea of the public man. A representative with no voice is as "sheepish" as a king's favorite subject. Milton's public man must be able to act, to think, to exercise his public consciousness. To Milton, only through debate and real public action can anyone truly develop the public consciousness that maintains liberty. One's spirit must be constantly challenged, exercised, questioned, and rebuilt. Otherwise, the spirit stagnates and accepts slavery.

Ironically, this very quality of constant debate is what attracted contemporary notice to *The Readie & Easie Way.* The monarchist tract *The Censure of the Rota* mocks Milton through the character of a fictitious Harrington and his famous club, suggesting that Milton fears "such admirable eloquence as yours, would be thrown away under an Monarchy, (as it would be) though of admirable use in a Popular Government, where Orators carry all the Rabble before them . . . for all your Politiques are derived from the works

28. Milton's emphasis on Harrington's apparent obsession with the mechanisms of voting is an accurate characterization. Almost all of Harrington's tracts include detailed explanations of mechanisms, especially *The Manner and Use of the Ballot* (362–67); *Brief Directions Showing How a Fit and Perfect Government May be Made, Found, or Understood* (584–98); and *Pour enclouer le canon* (728–33). All appeared between 1656 and 1659.

of Declamers, with which sort of Writers, the Ancient Common-wealths had the fortune to abound" (8). But, of course, that is the whole point. To Milton, the ancient orators were his ideal of the public man in action, and they were all the proof he needed of the greatness of the ancient republics.

Milton's politics, like his religion, mitigate against any kind of resolution. Both demand the daily remaking of the heart, the reexamination of political convictions, the questioning of one's own actions. The one essential element of Milton's free commonwealth is the continually changing debate. The process of debate insures freedom, but it is more—it is also Milton's vision of the moral life. Thus, the theories of his fellow republicans were not foolishness—they were a betrayal of his most dearly held beliefs. Milton's is one of the last protests of a radical of the old order to the rise of "public interest," and one of the few efforts to resolve the constant tension between individual and public good. This was the burden his rhetoric carried as he strove to develop a revolutionary discourse that would create public men.

What the radicals needed, and what Milton perceived that they needed, was an integrative, public discourse. Compared to Milton's writing, the tracts of his radical contemporaries are frequently dry and often simply boring. In addressing lists of proposals to specific persons or groups, the radicals ignore their readers, with whom Milton strives to establish a common purpose. He expresses that purpose in a discourse based on deliberative rhetoric, conveyed by the figure of the orator, Milton's vehicle for integration.

Deliberative rhetoric is certainly appropriate for the government Milton desires. Conventionally, it is the discourse of individuals, acting as public men, advising a governing body. By adopting the deliberative genre, Milton places his readers in the position of the members of that governing body. In effect, he asks them to take on the role of public men by reading the tract and by evaluating its arguments. In the act of reading, the readers may see themselves as worthy of the kind of government Milton proposes. In giving careful consideration to the tract, the reader may assure himself that he is indeed "rightly qualified" to participate in a "little Commonwealth."

Milton's revisions enhance the deliberative nature of his tract. According to seventeenth-century rhetoricians, the deliberative exordium should make a clear statement of accusation or defense. In his revised preface, Milton's famous plea for "Shroving-time" and his lament that this is his last chance to speak freely define the tract as a defense of his ideals. The tract itself becomes a speech-act, its existence a defense of free political expression. Milton's revised confirmation (the exposition of his plan) and confutation (the attack on kingship and Presbyterians) are packed with historical and biblical examples, which classical and Renaissance rhetoricians agree are essential to deliberative proofs. The revised edition also increases the sheer amount of Milton's invective, which he uses to strengthen his confutation.[29] The confutation is crucial to the effectiveness of the overall deliberative argument. Finally, in his peroration, Milton continues to add examples, a practice appropriate only for deliberative orations.

In adopting the deliberative genre, Milton addresses readers as those who already share his basic principles, especially his exposition of liberty and his assumption of the desirability of public character. His epideictic additions—the invective of the confutation and his praise of the "vertue, temperance, modestie, sobrietie, parsimonie, justice" of participants in a commonwealth—reinforce those principles (443). In ridiculing the close-stools of the royalists and the sweating tubs of the Presbyterians, Milton shows that he excludes them from his potential audience. When he asks, "Is it just or reasonable, that most voices against the . . . main end of government should enslave the less number that would be free?" (455), Milton admits he speaks to the small number that may share his ideals.

To integrate and unify this small audience, Milton chooses the vehicle of the figure of the orator. In using the first person throughout the tract, he addresses readers as fellow orators, capable of appreciating his argument. By calling attention to his own rhetorical achievements in the Defences, Milton underlines the heroic potential of every act of public speech and invites readers to become equally heroic. In contrast to his contemporaries, most of whom take pains to declare their disinterest and restrict their discourse to logical and legal expositions, Milton dominates his tract with his own ethos. His extensive use of epideictic oratory calls attention to his rhetorical skill. His voice becomes visionary as it expresses political proposals in terms of Scripture and sacred history—a rarity in the radical discourse of the moment. By giving such importance to his ethos, a strategy appropriate to forensic discourse, Milton steps outside the bounds of the deliberative genre.

While presenting himself as an orator, Milton modulates his voice into

29. I agree with Corns, *Development of Milton's Prose Style,* that Milton's rich use of metaphor and modification is a virtue, especially when we compare him to the monarchists. They are his real rhetorical competition. Modification is an ally of the epideictic genre, and often has an integrative effect, so Milton is right in using modification to attempt to unify his audience.

that of a prophet. As Stanley Stewart observes, Milton's proposals place the English people "in relation to the covenant ordained by God for his people throughout history, from the Old Testament past to the New Testament dispensation, which extends as far into the future as any prophet can see."[30] In so doing, Milton ultimately undermines his discourse. He catches himself between two of his own lines of argument—civil liberties, which are public and the exponents of which are orators, and religious liberties, which Milton himself says are private and the exponents of which are prophets. Prophecy has a historical and public *context*, but its discourse is traditionally unrelated to the *conventions* of political discourse.

In choosing the individualistic figures of first the orator and then the prophet as his vehicles for integration, Milton unintentionally subverts his political goal. Conventionally, the figure of the orator, most commonly employed in forensic discourse, does not serve to unify his audience in consideration of community values. His arguments and peroration may do so, but to emphasize values the orator must move the attention of the audience away from himself. Conventionally, the figure of the prophet stands outside the political establishment. His power lies in his individuality—he speaks not for the community but for God, often against the community. Though speaking publicly, the prophet is not a public man in the classical sense of the word. So, in spite of himself, Milton develops a rhetoric that is divisive. He addresses readers as individuals, in individualistic language, asking for *consent* with discourse better suited to *assent*. Milton's attempt at a new, public, integrative, radical discourse ultimately fails because he fails to break completely with the rhetorical conventions of his times.

The mixed tracts of 1659 and 1660 offer proposals and endorse deliberation, but, with the exception of Milton's, they are not primarily deliberative. They concern themselves with definitions—of liberty, freedom, public interest—and praise and blame. The plans, when proposed, appear as logical conclusions drawn from the premises given. Most of the plans—Milton's and Harrington's excluded—actually do little else than endorse the inevitable. They generally do not challenge the basic structures or functions of Parliament. Instead, they praise the ideal parliament as an institution insuring all desirable values. Their actual techniques now resemble those of their monarchist opponents—they outline and praise what they consider to be worthy values, create a world of absolutes in which

30. "Milton Revises *The Readie & Easie Way*," 222.

their own party embodies the public interest, and ask their readers to choose. As they present their arguments, there is not truly a choice at all.

Superficially, the rhetoric of the monarchists and radicals has converged. But on one essential point it has not. The radicals devote the bulk of their energies to definitions, to outlining for readers their vision of society. This is primarily a forensic procedure designed to inform and persuade a presumably neutral jury. These writers cannot, then, assume that their readers know what republicans, for example, believe or want. They must, after ten years, explain. While monarchists safely assume their claim to tradition, the antimonarchists assume a void. This void makes their praise and vituperation take on a particular meaning. Normally, epideictic oratory reinforces community values. In these tracts, it becomes supporting evidence for the definitions. These writers thus praise personal values—their own—instead of communal ones.

The ultimate goal of revolutionaries is to transform society. Only secondarily do they consider recruitment and persuasion. The first goal depends upon their vision of the future; the second, in contrast, depends upon their successful manipulation of existing conventions of discourse. To reconcile the two, revolutionaries must discover ways of transforming those conventions so that they successfully communicate a radical message in a form the audience accepts. At times, however, radical writers' understanding of language and persuasion can make this effort an impossible task. Such writers view the conventions of discourse as inseparable from the society they wish to change. Thus, they view with suspicion the existing linguistic bridges to their audience. As a result, however brilliant their language, their rhetoric will fail to persuade. In 1659 and 1660, the suspect bridge was the epideictic genre. Because the monarchists successfully used it integratively, the genre became, in effect, monarchist discourse. The only integrative alternative available to the radicals—prophecy— could not, as they presented it, function politically. Even Milton was defeated by his understanding of the conventions of public discourse. Committed to transforming the individual, he was ideologically unable to transform the language of the political order.

The tracts of 1659 and 1660 are the most diverse of any in this study. Writers on both sides react to political events in rhetorical tracts and try to shape coherent visions of society in philosophical works. Monarchists, knowing that they can depend upon a hazy collective memory of the past to support their arguments, write as though their values are already universally held and shortly to be put in practice. They urge a course of events, but their deliberative oratory merges with epideictic to define and unify the community of readers. Even in 1659, the monarchists write as if they know who holds the balance of power and what those people's values are.

Not even the most extreme anti-monarchist can endorse any of the settlements of the 1650s. Each is either a step back or a stopping place on the way to the ideal government. The only constant in radical tracts is the advocacy of change. While the monarchists focus on a king, most radicals turn to the institution of a reformed parliament in the future, and yet there was little agreement among radicals on what reforms that might entail. Milton himself, the last vocal opponent of restoration, looks to the individual and the long process of education, not any immediate solution. In 1659 and 1660, the monarchists' vision was whole and unified, the radicals' fragmented and diffuse. The radicals could not make any safe assumptions about their audience. They could not integrate either the audience or themselves.

The monarchists had successfully laid claim to the public voice. They revived the language of 1642, which contained the assumptions of traditional institutions, and combined it with the focal point of 1649—the integrative vision of the king. Through these techniques, they presented their ideas and interests as if they actually were those of the readers and the entire country. Their use of traditions, conventional language, and the combination of genres that best conveyed them made their position appear both right and inevitable.

The anti-monarchists of 1659 and 1660 were still defining and arguing. Their language had not become conventional. Despite their claims and best efforts, they finally spoke only to themselves. Their vision was distributive. They envisioned a society in which everyone may benefit and pursue his own interests and yet never harm or compromise the public good. While an admirable goal philosophically, the distributive vision has little rhetorical power in times of political distress. It provides no rallying points, no tenets of popular wisdom. For it to succeed, it must engage the mind and prompt courage, not comfort.

Ultimately, the radicals' dilemma resulted from both political and rhetorical failure. As numerous monarchists gleefully pointed out, their opponents had had ten years to institute their proposals and had failed. Or rather, the proposals had not really been attempted. The Commonwealth's failure to take action in the years from 1649 to 1653, noted by Milton, insured that the rhetoric of its defenders would never become truly conventional and could not perform an integrative function in 1659 and 1660. Successful rhetoric is advanced and confirmed by at least a few tangible political achievements. The revolution did finally insure the power of parliaments and the demise of divine-right monarchy in England, and yet those results could not be known in 1660. Ironically, Milton and the radical pamphleteers could not rhetorically exploit the victories their fight had won.

Bibliography

Primary Sources

Note: Codes following certain tracts indicate shelf marks of materials in the Thomason Collection, British Library.

Acts and Ordinances of the Interregnum, 1642–1660. Edited by C. H. Firth and R. S. Rait. 3 vols. London: His Majesty's Stationery Office, 1911.

Aphthonius. *Progymnasmata.* 2d ed. Edited by Reinhard Lorich. London, 1572.

An Apologetick for the Sequestred Clergie of the Church of England. [London, 1649]. E.554.(7.)

Arber, Edward. *A Transcript of the Registers of the Company of Stationers of London, 1554–1640 A.D.* 5 vols. New York: P. Smith, 1950.

Aristotle. *"Art" of Rhetoric.* Translated by J. H. Freese. Loeb Classical Library. London: Heinemann; Cambridge: Harvard University Press, 1975.

Articles of High Treason, and Other High Misdemeanors, Against the Lord Kymbolton, Mr. Denzil Hollis, Sir Arthur Haslerig, Mr. John Pym, Mr. Iohn Hampden, Mr. William Strode. London, [1642]. E.131.(2.)

Aubrey, John. *Aubrey's Brief Lives.* Edited by Oliver Lawson Dick. 1949. Reprint. Harmondsworth, England: Penguin, 1978.

Bastwick, John. *A Briefe Relation of Certaine Speciall and Most Materiall Passages, and Speeches in the Starre-Chamber, Occasioned and Delivered the 14th Day of Iune, 1637.* [London], 1638.

———. *The Letany of John Bastwick, Doctor of Phisicke.* [London], 1637.

[Bate, George.] *Elenchus Motuum Nuperorum in Anglia. Simul ac Iuris Regii et Parliamentarii Brevis Enarratio.* Paris, 1649. E.1759.(2.)

[Bayley, Thomas.] *The Royal Charter Granted unto Kings by God Himself.* London, 1649. E.1356.(1.)

[Bennet, Robert.] *King Charle's Triall Iustified.* London, 1649. E.554.(21.)

[Brathwaite, Richard.] *Panthalia: Or, the Royal Romance.* London, 1659. E.1791.

Brinsley, John. *A Consolation for Our Grammar Schools, (1622).* Edited by Thomas Clark Pollock. New York: Scholars' Facsimiles and Reprints, 1943.

————. *Ludus Literarius, (1612)*. Menston, England: Scolar Press, 1968.

British Museum. Department of Printed Books. Thomason Collection. *Catalogue of the Pamphlets, Books, Newspapers, and Manuscripts Relating to the Civil War, the Commonwealth, and Restoration, Collected by George Thomason, 1640–1661*. 2 vols. London: Trustees of the British Museum, 1908.

Burton, Henry. *An Apology of an Appeale*. [London], 1636.

Burton, Thomas. *The Diary of Thomas Burton, Esq. Member in the Parliaments of Oliver and Richard Cromwell, from 1656 to 1659*. Edited by John Towill Rutt. 4 vols. London: Henry Colburn, 1828.

Butler, Charles. *Oratoriae libri duo*. Oxford, 1633.

————. *Rhetoricae libri duo*. 5th ed. London, 1621.

Calendar of State Papers, Domestic Series, of the Reign of Charles I, 1625–1649. Edited by John Bruce and Mr. W. D. Hamilton. 22 vols. London: Longmans, 1858–1893.

Calendar of State Papers, Domestic Series, of the Reigns of Edward VI, Mary I, Elizabeth and James I. Edited by R. Lemon and Mary A. E. Green. 12 vols. London: Longman [sic], 1856–1872.

The Case Stated Touching the Soveraign's Prerogative and the Peoples Liberty. London, 1660.

The Censure of the Rota Upon Mr. Miltons Book, Entituled, The Ready and Easie Way to Establish a Free Common-wealth. London, 1660. E.1019.(*5.) Reprinted in William Rily Parker, *Milton's Contemporary Reputation: An Essay together with a Tentative List of Printed Allusions to Milton, 1641–1674, and Facsimile Reproductions of Five Contemporary Pamphlets Written in Answer to Milton*. Graduate School Studies, Contributions in Language and Literature, 7. Columbus: Ohio State University Press, 1940.

Chaos. [London, 1659]. E.988.(22.)

Cicero, Marcus Tullius. *Brutus*. Translated by G. L. Hendrickson. In *Brutus, Orator*, 1–293. Loeb Classical Library. London: Heinemann; Cambridge: Harvard University Press, 1939.

————. *De Inventione*. Translated by H. M. Hubbell. In *De Inventione, De Optima genere oratorum, Topica*, 1–346. Loeb Classical Library. London: Heinemann; Cambridge: Harvard University Press, 1949.

————. *Orator*. Translated by H. M. Hubbell. In *Brutus, Orator*, 297–509. Loeb Classical Library. London: Heinemann; Cambridge: Harvard University Press, 1939.

————. *De Oratore*. Translated by E. W. Sutton and H. Rackham. 2 vols. Loeb Classical Library. London: Heinemann; Cambridge: Harvard University Press, 1942.

————. *Partitiones oratoriae*. Translated by H. Rackham. In *De Oratore, Book III; De Fato; Paradoxa Stoicorum; Partitiones oratoriae*, 306–421. Loeb Classical

Library. London: Heinemann; Cambridge: Harvard University Press, 1942.

Clarendon, Edward Hyde, Earl of. *The History of the Rebellion and Civil Wars in England Begun in the Year 1641.* Edited by W. Dunn Macray. 6 vols. 1888. Reprint. Oxford: Clarendon Press, 1958.

Clarke, John. *Formulae oratoriae.* 4th ed. London, 1632.

The Commons Petition to the King in Defence of Mr. Pym. London, 1642. E.181.(43.)

A Commonwealth, and Commonvvealths-men, Asserted and Vindicated. London, 1659. E.988.(19.)

A Common-vvealth or Nothing: Or, Monarchy and Oligarchy Prov'd Parallel in Tyranny. London, 1659. E.986.(17.)

[Cook, John.] *King Charls his Case: Or, an Appeal to all Rational Men, Concerning his Tryal at the High Court of Iustice.* London, 1649. E.542.(3.)

Cox, Leonard. *The Arte or Crafte of Rhethoryke* [1532]. Edited by Frederic Ives Carpenter. 1899. Reprint. Chicago: University of Chicago Press, 1971.

The Declaration and Address of the Gentry of the County of Essex, who have Adhered to the King, and Suffered Imprisonment, or Sequestration, during the Late Troubles. London, [1660]. 669.f.25.(1.)

A Declaration and Protestation of the Peers, Lords, and Barons of this Realme, against the Late Treasonable Proceedings, and Tyrannical Usurpations of some Members of the Commons House. London, 1649. 669.f.13.(84.)

A Declaration and Protestation of Will. Prynne and Cle. Walker, Esquires, Members of the House of Commons. [London], 1649. 669.f.13.(72.)

A Declaration of the Faithfull Souldiers of the Army, to the Honest People of the Nation. London, 1659. E.980.(7.)

A Declaration of the House of Commons, touching a Late Breach of their Priviledges, and for the Vindication thereof, and of Divers Members of the Said House. London, 1642. 669.f.3.(32.)

A Declaration of the Knights and Gentry in the County of Dorset, who were in his Late Majesties Army. London, 1660. 669.f.24.(66.)

De Monarchia Absoluta Dissertatio Politica. Oxford, 1659. E.980.(4.)

D'Ewes, Sir Simonds. *The Journal of Sir Simonds D'Ewes from the First Recess of the Long Parliament to the Withdrawal of King Charles from London.* Edited by Willson Havelock Coates. New Haven: Yale University Press; London: Oxford University Press, 1942.

A Discourse for a King and Parliament. London, 1660. E.1021.(12.)

A Discreet and Learned Speech, Spoken in the Parliament, on Wednesday, the 4th of January, 1641 {1642}, by Mr. Hampden. London, 1642. E.199.(54.)

A Divine Tragedie Lately Acted. [Amsterdam], 1636.

Documents Relating to the Proceedings Against William Prynne, in 1634 and 1637.

Edited by John Bruce and Samuel Rawson Gardiner. Camden Society, n.s. 18. 1877. Reprint. New York: Johnson Reprint, 1965.

Dugard, William. *Rhetorices elementa.* 1648. Reprint. Menston, England: Scolar Press, 1972.

Eikon Alethine: The Povrtraitvre of Truths Most Sacred Majesty Truly Suffering, though Not Solely. London, 1649. E.569.(16.)

Eikon Basilike: The Pourtraicture of His Sacred Maiestie in His Solitudes and Sufferings. London, 1649. c.59.a.24.

Eikon Episte: Or, the Faithfull Pourtraicture of a Loyall Subject, in Vindication of Eikon Basilike. [London], 1649. E.537.(7.)

Englands Redemption: Or, a Path Way to Peace. London, 1660. E.1019.(1.)

Erasmus, Desiderius. *De duplici copia verborum et rerum commentarii duo.* London, 1569.

———. *De Ratione studii ac legendi interpretandique auctores.* Translated by Brian McGregor. Vol. 24 of *Collected Works of Erasmus: Literary and Educational Writings,* edited by Craig R. Thompson. Toronto: University of Toronto Press, 1978.

Evelyn, John. *The Diary of John Evelyn.* Edited by E. S. de Beer. Vol 3. Oxford: Clarendon Press, 1955.

Eye Salve to Anoint the Eyes of the Ministers of the Province of London. London, 1649. E.542.(16.)

Farnaby, Thomas. *Index rhetoricus.* 1625. Reprint. Menston, England: Scolar Press, 1970.

Fenner, Dudley. *The Artes of Logicke and Rhethorike.* London, 1584.

Filmer, Sir Robert. *Patriarcha and Other Political Works.* Edited by Peter Laslett. Oxford: Basil Blackwell, 1949.

Fletcher, Henry. *The Perfect Politician.* London, 1660.

Foxe, John. *The Ecclesiasticall History: Containing the Acts and Monuments of Martyrs: With the Persecutions Stirred Up by Romish Prelates in the Church.* 8th ed. London, 1641.

Fraunce, Abraham. *The Arcadian Rhetorike.* 1588. Reprint. Menston, England: Scolar Press, 1969.

Gauden, John. *The Religious & Loyal Protestation of John Gauden, Dr. in Divinity.* London, 1649. E.538.(11.)

Giffeheyl, Lodowick Frederick. *Two Letters Directed to the Mighty Ones of England, Scotland, and Ireland.* London, 1649. E.537.(23.)

Gil, Alexander, the elder. *Logonomia Anglica (1619).* Translated by Bror Danielsson and Arvid Gabrielson. 2 vols. Stockholm Studies in English, 27. Stockholm: Almquist and Wiksell, 1972.

God and the King: Or the Divine Constitution of the Supreme Magistrate. [London, 1649]. E.550.(2.)

Goodwin, John. *Ubristodikiai: The Obstructions of Justice.* London, 1649.
  E.557.(2.)

[Hammond, Henry.] *To the Right Honourable the Lord Fairfax and His Councell of
  Warre.* London, 1649. E.540.(18.)

*A Hand-Kirchife for Loyall Mourners or a Cordiall for Drooping Spirits, Goaning for the
  Bloody Murther, and Heavy Losse of our Gracious King.* London, 1649. E.541.(6.)

Harrington, James. *The Political Works of James Harrington.* Edited by J. G. A.
  Pocock. Cambridge: Cambridge University Press, 1977.

*His Majesties Declaration and Speech Concerning his Comming from Windsor to
  VVhite-Hall.* London, 1649. E.537.(13.)

His Majesties Declaration Concerning the Charge of the Army. London, 1649.
  E.536.(25.)

His Majesties Reasons Against the Pretended Iurisdiction of the High Court of Iustice.
  [London, 1649]. 669.f.13.(81.)

His Majesties Speech, in the House of COMMONS. London, 1642. E.199.(52.)

The Honest Design: Or, the True Commonwealths-man. London, 1659. E.980.(11.)

Hoole, Charles. *A New Discovery of the Old Art of Teaching Schoole.* Edited by
  Thiselton Mark. Syracuse: Bardeen, 1912.

Huc Ades, Haec Animae. London, 1659. F.980.(3.)

*The Humble Advice and Earnest Desires of Certain Well-Affected Ministers, Lecturers
  of Banbury in the County of Oxon, and of Brackly in the County of Northampton.*
  London, 1649. E.540.(12.)

*The Humble Remonstrance of the Non-Commission Officers and Private Soldiers of
  Major General Goffs Regiment (so called) of Foot.* London, 1659. E.979.(6.)

Hutchinson, Lucy. *Memoirs of the Life of Colonel Hutchinson.* Edited by James
  Sutherland. London: Oxford University Press, 1973.

Idea Democratica, Or A Common-vveal Platform. London, 1659.

*The Interest of England Stated: Or a Faithful and Just Account of the Aims of all Parties
  Now Pretending.* [n.p.], 1659.

*An Invocation to the Officers of the Army, Preventing their Own, and the Ruine of the
  Good Old Cause at the Very Door of Destruction.* London, 1659. E.979.(1.)

James I. *The Political Works.* Edited by Charles Howard McIlwain. Harvard
  Political Classics, 1. Cambridge: Harvard University Press; London:
  Humphrey Milford, Oxford University Press, 1918.

Killing Noe Murder: Briefly Discourst in Three Quaestions. London: 1656.

*King Charles His Speech to the Six Eminent Persons vvho Lately Arrived at Brussels, to
  Treat vvith His Majesty touching His Restoration to the Royal Throne and Dignity of
  His Father.* Antwerp, 1660. 669.f.24.(36.)

King Charles the II: His Restitution. London, 1660. E.1019.(8.)

*King Charls {sic} His Speech Made Upon the Scaffold at Whitehall-Gate, Immediately
  before his Execution.* London, 1649. E.540.(17.)

*The Last Damnable Designe of Cromwell and Ireton, and their Junto, or Caball,
    intended to be Carried on in their Generall Councell of the Army.* [London, 1649].
    669.f.13.(76.)

Laud, William. *The Works of the Most Reverend Father in God, William Laud,
    D.D.: Sometime Lord Archbishop of Canterbury.* Vol. 6, pt. 1. Oxford: John
    Henry Parker, 1857.

Lawson, George. *Politica Sacra & Civilis.* 2d ed. London, 1689.

The Londoners Last Warning. [London, 1659]. E.993.(24.)

*Loyal Queries, Humbly Tendred to the Serious Consideration of the Parliament, and
    Army.* London, 1659. E.986.(15.)

Master Hollis His Speech in Parliament . . . January. London, 1642. E.199.(55.)

Master Hollis His Speech in Parliament . . . March. London, 1642. E.200.(42.)

*Master Pym His Speech in Parliament, on Wednesday, the Fifth of January, 1641
    {1642}.* London, 1642. E.200.(4.)

Master Strowd His Speech in Parliament. London, 1642. E.199.(50.)

A Message from the Royall Prisoner at Windsor, to the Kingdom of Scotland. London,
    1649. E.537.(1.)

*Metamorphosis Anglorum, or Reflections Historical, and Political, Upon the Late
    Changes of Government in England.* London, 1660. E.2109.(1.)

Milton, John. *The Complete Prose Works.* General Editor Don M. Wolfe. 8 vols.
    New Haven: Yale University Press, 1953–1982.

*Mr. Glyn, His Speech in Parliament, Upon the Reading of the Accusation of the House of
    Commons against Mr. Herbert the Kings Attorney.* London, 1642. E.200.(31.)

*Mr. Pym His Vindication in Parliament of the Accusation of High Treason, Exhibited
    Against Him.* London, 1642. E.116.(29.)

*A Model of a Democraticall Government, Humbly Tendred to Consideration, by a
    Friend and Wel-wisher to this Common-Wealth.* London, 1659.

*Monarchy Asserted, to be the Best, Most Ancient and Legall Form of Government, in a
    Conference had at Whitehall, with Oliver, Late Protector.* London, 1660.
    E.1853.(1.)

Nedham, Marchamont. *Interest Will Not Lie.* London, 1659.

A New Declaration Concerning the King, from the Commons of England. [London,
    1649]. E.537.(28.)

Newes from Ipswich. [Edinburgh, 1636?].

A New-Yeeres Gift for the Kings Most Excellent Majesty Now at Windsore. London,
    1649. E.536.(26.)

No King but the Old Kings Son: Or, a Vindication of Limited Monarchy. London,
    1660. 669.f.24.(30.)

No Return to Monarchy. London, 1659. E.985.(16.)

*Original Letters and Papers of State . . . among the Political Collections of Mr. John
    Milton.* Edited by John Nickolls. London, 1743.

Orthodox State-Queries, Presented to All Those who Retain Any Sparks of their Ancient Loyalty. [London, 1660]. 669.f.24.(2.)

Peacham, Henry. *The Garden of Eloquence.* 1577. Reprint. Menston, England: Scolar Press, 1971.

Pepys, Samuel. *Diary and Correspondence.* 4 vols. London: George Bell, 1889.

A Perambulatory Word to Court, Camp, City, and Country. London, 1659. E.980.(15.)

A Pertinent Speech Made by an Honourable Member of the House of Commons, Tending to the Establishment of Kingly Government. London, 1660. E.1017.(18.)

[Philipps, Fabian.] *King Charles the First, No Man of Blood but a Martyr for his People.* [London], 1649. E.531.(3.)

[Philodemus, Eleutherius.] *The Armies Vindication.* London, 1649. E.538.(3.)

[Prynne, William.] *A Briefe Memento to the Present Vnparliamentary Iunto.* London, 1649. E.537.(7.)

————. *Mr. Pryn's Last and Finall Declaration to the Commons of England.* [London, 1649]. E.537.(12.)

————. *The Re-publicans and Others Spurious Good Old Cause, Briefly and Truly Anatomized.* London, 1659. E.983.(6.)

The Questions Propounded to Mr. Herbert the Kings Attorney General. London, 1642. E.132.(12.)

Quintilian. *Institutio oratoria.* Translated by H. E. Butler. 4 vols. Loeb Classical Library. London: Heinemann, 1921–1922.

Rainolde, Richard. *A Booke called the Foundacion of Rhetorike.* Edited by Francis R. Johnson. New York: Scholars' Facsimiles and Reprints, 1945.

Rectifying Principles. London, [1649]. E.537.(5.)

[Redingstone, John.] *Plain English to the Parliament and Army, and to the Rest of the People.* London, 1649. E.538.(4.)

The Remonstrance of the Apprentices In and About London. [London, 1659]. 669.f.22.(10.)

The Remonstrance of the Noble-men, Knights, Gentlemen, Clergy-men, Free-holders, Citizens, Burgesses and Commons of the Late Eastern, Southern, and Western Associations. [London, 1659]. 669.f.22.(11.)

The Resolver, Or, a Short Word, to the Large Question of the Times. London, 1649. E.527.(10.)

Rhetorica ad Alexandrum. Translated by H. Rackham. In Aristotle, *Problems 22–38, Rhetorica ad Alexandrum,* 258–449. Loeb Classical Library. London: Heinemann, 1937.

Rhetorica ad Herennium. Translated by Harry Caplan. Loeb Classical Library. London: Heinemann; Cambridge: Harvard University Press, 1954.

The Right Honourable the Lord Kimbolton His Speech in Parliament. London, 1642. E.199.(51.)

The Royall Virgine: Or, the Declaration of Several Maydens In and About the Once Honourable City of London. London, 1660. 669.f.23.(36.)

S., G. *The Dignity of Kingship Asserted: In Answer to Mr. Milton's Readie and Easie Way to Establish a Free Commonwealth.* London, 1660. E.1915.(2.) Reprint as Facsimile Text Society, 54. New York: Columbia University Press, 1942.

[S., J.] *Government Described: Viz. What Monarchie, Aristocracie, Oligarchie, and Democracie, is, Together with a Brief Model of the Common-Wealth, or, Free-State of Ragouse.* London, 1659. E.985.(7.)

Sadler, Anthony. *Maiestie Irradiant, or the Splendor Displayed, of Our Soveraigne King Charles.* London, 1660. 669.f.25.(4.)

Sherry, Richard. *A Treatise of Schemes & Tropes.* Edited by Herbert W. Hildebrandt. Gainesville: Scholars' Facsimiles and Reprints, 1961.

A Short Discourse Upon the Desires of a Friend. London, 1660. E.1016.(15.)

A Short-Title Catalogue of Books Printed in England, Scotland, and Ireland: and of English Books Printed Abroad 1475–1640. 2d ed. Edited by W. A. Jackson et al. 3 vols. London: The Bibliographical Society, 1976.

Sir Arthur Haslerigg His Speech in Parliament. London, 1642. E.199.(53.)

Six Great Matters of Note. London, 1642. E.135.(32.)

Speculum Libertatis Angliae Re Restitutae: Or, the Looking-Glasse of Englands Libertie Really Restored. London, 1659. E.989.(19.)

A Speech Made in Parliament by Mr. Glyn. London, 1642. E.200.(3.)

[Sprigg, William.] *A Modest Plea, for an Equal Common-wealth Against Monarchy.* London, 1659. E.1802.(1.)

[T., N.] *The Resolver Continued: Or, a Satisfaction to Some Scruples about the Putting of the Late King to Death.* London, 1649. E.546.(17.)

Three Propositions from the Case of Our Three Nations. London, 1659. E.985.(17.)

To His Excellency the Lord Fleetwood, and the General Council of Officers of the Armies of England, Scotland, and Ireland. London, 1659. E.974.(5.)

To the Kings Most Excellent Majestie: The Humble Petition of the Inhabitants of the County of Glocester . . . Whereunto is annexed Sir Edward Hales, his worthy Speech in Parliament. London, 1642. E.133.(7.)

To the Kings Most Excellent Majestie: The Petition of the Inhabitants of the County of Buckingham. London, 1642. E.131.(21.)

To the Officers and Souldiers of the Armies of England, Scotland, and Ireland: The Humble Petition and Advice of Divers Well-Affected to the Good Old Cause, Inhabitants In and About the Borough of Southwark. [London, 1659]. E.980.(1.)

To the Present Visible Supreame Power Assembled at VVestminster. [London, 1649]. 669.f.13.(75.)

To the Right Honourable the Ld. Fleetwood, to be Communicated to the Officers of the Army. London, 1659. E.979.(5.)

A True Relation of the Kings Speech to the Lady Elizabeth, and the Duke of Gloucester, the Day Before His Death. [London], 1649. 669.f.14.(9.)

Twelve Plain Proposals Offered to the Honest and Faithful Officers and Souldiers of our English Army. London, 1659. 669.f.21.(26.)

The Two Petitions of the County of Buckingham, as They were Presented to Both Houses. London, 1642. E.181.(29.)

Two Speeches Spoken in Parliament, by Sir Edward Hales, and Sir William Wroth. London, 1642. E.200.(17.) (18.)

Vane, Sir Henry, the younger. *A Healing Question*. London, 1656. Reprint. *Old South Leaflets*, 1, no. 6. Boston: Directors of the Old South Work, Old South Meeting House, n.d.

[————.] *A Needful Corrective or Ballance in Popular Government, . . . to Iames Harrington*. [London, 1660?].

Vicars, Thomas. *Cheiragogia sive manductio ad artem rhetoricam*. London, 1628.

Vox & Votum Populi Anglicani. London, 1660. E.1025.(2.)

Vox Vere Anglorum, or Englands Loud Cry for their King. [London], 1659. E.763.(3.)

Wallington, Nehemiah. "Historical Notices." In *Politics, Religion and Literature in the Seventeenth Century*, edited by William Lamont and Sybil Oldfield, 47–53. London: Dent; Totowa, N.J.: Rowman and Littlefield, 1975.

Wilson, Thomas. *The Arte of Rhetorike*. 1567. Contains both the 1553 and the 1560 editions. Edited by Robert Hood Bowers. Gainesville: Scholars' Facsimiles and Reprints, 1962.

Secondary Sources

Arendt, Hannah. *The Human Condition*. Chicago: University of Chicago Press, 1955.

Austin, J. L. *How to Do Things With Words*. 2d ed. Edited by J. O. Urmson and Marina Sbisà. Cambridge: Harvard University Press, 1975.

Aylmer, G. E. *The State's Servants: The Civil Service of the English Republic, 1649–1660*. London and Boston: Routledge and Kegan Paul, 1973.

————. *The Struggle for the Constitution, 1603–1689: England in the Seventeenth Century*. 2d ed. London: Blandford, 1968.

Barker, Arthur. *Milton and the Puritan Dilemma, 1641–1660*. 1942. Reprint. Toronto: University of Toronto Press, 1956.

Booth, Wayne C. *Modern Dogma and the Rhetoric of Assent*. University of Notre Dame Ward-Phillips Lectures in English Language and Literature, 5. Notre Dame and London: University of Notre Dame Press, 1974.

Brown, Peter. *The Cult of the Saints: Its Rise and Function in Latin Christianity*. Haskell Lectures on History of Religion, n.s. 2. Chicago: University of Chicago Press, 1981.

Brunton, D[ouglas], and D. H. Pennington. *Members of the Long Parliament.* London: George Allen and Unwin, 1954.

Bruyère-Robinet, Nelly. *Méthode et dialectique dans l'oeuvre de la Ramée: Renaissance et age classique.* Paris: Vrin, 1984.

————. "Le statut de l'invention dans l'oeuvre de la Ramée." *Revue des Sciences Philosophiques et Théologiques* 70 (1986): 15–24.

Bush, Douglas. *English Literature in the Earlier Seventeenth Century, 1600–1660.* 2d ed. The Oxford History of English Literature. Edited by Kenneth Allott and Norman Davis. Vol. 5. London: Oxford University Press, 1973.

Cable, Lana. "Milton's Iconoclastic Truth." In *Politics, Poetics, and Hermeneutics in Milton's Prose,* edited by David Loewenstein and James Grantham Turner, 135–51. Cambridge: Cambridge University Press, 1990.

Christianson, Paul. *Reformers and Babylon: English Apocalyptic Visions from the Reformation to the Eve of the Civil War.* Toronto: University of Toronto Press, 1978.

Clark, Donald Lemen. *John Milton at St. Paul's School: A Study of Ancient Rhetoric in English Renaissance Education.* 1948. Reprint. New York: Columbia University Press, 1964.

Clark, Peter. *English Provincial Society from the Reformation to the Revolution: Religion, Politics and Society in Kent, 1500–1640.* Hassocks, Sussex: Harvester Press, 1977.

————. " 'The Ramoth-Gilead of the Good': Urban Change and Political Radicalism, 1540–1640." In *The English Commonwealth, 1547–1640: Essays in Politics and Society,* edited by Peter Clark, Alan G. R. Smith, and Nicholas Tyacke, 167–87. New York: Barnes and Noble, 1979.

Clyde, William M. *The Struggle for the Freedom of the Press from Caxton to Cromwell.* London: H. Millford, Oxford University Press for St. Andrews University, 1934.

Coltman, Irene. *Private Men and Public Causes: Philosophy and Politics in the English Civil War.* London: Faber and Faber, 1962.

Condren, Conal. *George Lawson's "Politica" and the English Revolution.* Cambridge: Cambridge University Press, 1989.

Cope, Esther S. *Politics without Parliaments, 1629–1640.* London: Allen and Unwin, 1987.

Corns, Thomas N. *The Development of Milton's Prose Style.* Oxford: Oxford University Press, 1982.

Cotton, James. "James Harrington and Thomas Hobbes." *Journal of the History of Ideas* 42 (1981): 407–21.

Cressy, David. "Levels of Illiteracy in England, 1530–1730." *Historical Journal* 20 (1977): 1–23.

————. *Literacy and the Social Order: Reading and Writing in Tudor and Stuart England.* Cambridge: Cambridge University Press, 1980.

Daly, James. *Sir Robert Filmer and English Political Thought.* Toronto: University of Toronto Press, 1979.

Davies, Godfrey. *The Early Stuarts, 1603–1660.* 2d ed. Oxford: Clarendon Press, 1959.

Davis, J. C. *Utopia and the Ideal Society: A Study of English Utopian Writing, 1516–1700.* Cambridge: Cambridge University Press, 1983.

Derrida, Jacques. "The Law of Genre." Translated by Avital Ronell. *Critical Inquiry* 7 (1980): 55–81.

Douglas, A. E. Introduction to *Brutus,* by Marcus Tullius Cicero. Edited by A. E. Douglas. Oxford: Clarendon Press, 1966.

Douglas, Richard M. "Talent and Vocation in Humanist and Protestant Thought." In *Action and Conviction in Early Modern Europe: Essays in Memory of E. H. Harbison,* edited by Theodore K. Rabb and Jerrold E. Seigel, 261–98. Princeton: Princeton University Press, 1969.

Duncan, J. L. "The End and Aim of Law: Legal Theories in England in the Sixteenth and Seventeenth Centuries." *Juridical Review* 47 (1933): 157–77; 50 (1938): 257–81, 404–38.

Eisenstein, Elizabeth L. *The Printing Press as an Agent of Change: Communications and Cultural Transformations in Early-Modern Europe.* 2 vols. in 1. Cambridge: Cambridge University Press, 1982.

Elton, G. R. Introduction to *The Divine Right of Kings,* by John Neville Figgis. 2d ed. New York: Harper Torchbooks, 1965.

Eusden, John Dykstra. *Puritans, Lawyers, and Politics in Early Seventeenth-Century England.* Yale Studies in Religious Education, 23. New Haven: Yale University Press, 1958.

Everitt, Alan. *The Community of Kent and the Great Rebellion, 1640–60.* Leicester: Leicester University Press, 1966.

Figgis, John Neville. *The Divine Right of Kings.* 2d ed. 1914. Reprint. New York: Harper Torchbooks, 1965.

Firth, Katherine R. *The Apocalyptic Tradition in Reformation Britain, 1530–1645.* Oxford: Oxford University Press, 1979.

Foucault, Michel. *The Order of Things: An Archaeology of the Human Sciences.* New York: Vintage, 1973.

Frank, Joseph. *The Beginnings of the English Newspaper, 1620–1660.* Cambridge: Harvard University Press, 1961.

Franklin, Julian H. *John Locke and the Theory of Sovereignty: Mixed Monarchy and the Right of Resistance in the Political Thought of the English Revolution.* Cambridge: Cambridge University Press, 1978.

Fumaroli, Marc. *L'Age de l'éloquence: Rhétorique et 'res literaria' de la Renaissance au seuil de l'époque classique.* Geneva: Droz, 1980.

Gardiner, Samuel Rawson. *History of England from the Accession of James I to the*

Outbreak of the Civil War, 1603–1642. 10 vols. London: Longmans, Green, 1884.

Geertz, Clifford. *The Interpretation of Cultures.* New York: Basic Books, 1973.

Gilman, W. E. *Milton's Rhetoric: Studies in His Defense of Liberty.* Columbia: University of Missouri, 1939.

Gilmartin, Kevin. "History and Reform in Milton's *Readie and Easie Way.*" *Milton Studies* 24 (1988): 17–41.

Goldberg, Jonathan. *James I and the Politics of Literature: Jonson, Shakespeare, Donne, and Their Contemporaries.* Baltimore: Johns Hopkins University Press, 1983.

Gray, Charles. "Reason, Authority, and Imagination: The Jurisprudence of Sir Edward Coke." In *Culture and Politics from Puritanism to the Enlightenment,* edited by Perez Zagorin, 25–66. Berkeley: University of California Press, 1980.

Greg, Sir Walter Wilson. *Some Aspects and Problems of London Publishing between 1550 and 1650.* Oxford: Clarendon Press, 1956.

Gregg, Pauline. *Free-born John: A Biography of John Lilburne.* London: George G. Harrap, 1961.

Griffin, Leland M. "The Rhetoric of Historical Movements." *Quarterly Journal of Speech* 38 (1952): 184–88. Reprinted in *Methods of Rhetorical Criticism: A Twentieth-Century Perspective,* edited by Robert L. Scott and Bernard L. Brock, 346–52. New York: Harper and Row, 1972.

Gunn, J. A. W. *Politics and the Public Interest in the Seventeenth Century.* London: Routledge and Kegan Paul; Toronto: University of Toronto Press, 1969.

Haller, William. *Foxe's Book of Martyrs and the Elect Nation.* Bedford Historical Series. London: Jonathan Cape, 1967.

Haller, William, and Godfrey Davies. Introduction to *The Leveller Tracts, 1647–1653,* 1–50. 1944. Reprint. Gloucester, Mass.: Peter Smith, 1964.

Hast, Adele. "State Treason Trials during the Puritan Revolution, 1640–1660." *Historical Journal* 15 (1972): 37–53.

Hayes, T. Wilson. *Winstanley the Digger: A Literary Analysis of Radical Ideas in the English Revolution.* Cambridge: Harvard University Press, 1979.

Helgerson, Richard. "Milton Reads the King's Book: Print, Performance, and the Making of a Bourgeois Idol." *Criticism* 29 (1987): 1–25.

Hexter, J. H. *The Reign of King Pym.* Cambridge: Harvard University Press, 1961.

Hill, Christopher. *The Experience of Defeat: Milton and Some Contemporaries.* New York: Viking, 1984.

———. *God's Englishman: Oliver Cromwell and the English Revolution.* Harmondsworth, England: Penguin, 1970.

———. *Milton and the English Revolution.* Harmondsworth, England: Penguin, 1979.

————. "Parliament and People in Seventeenth-Century England." *Past and Present,* no. 92 (1981): 1–30.

————. *Puritanism and Revolution: Studies in Interpretation of the English Revolution of the 17th Century.* New York: Schocken Books, 1964.

————. *Some Intellectual Consequences of the English Revolution.* Madison: University of Wisconsin Press, 1980.

————. *The World Turned Upside Down: Radical Ideas during the English Revolution.* Harmondsworth, England: Penguin, 1974.

Hirst, Derek. *Authority and Conflict: England, 1603–1658.* Cambridge: Harvard University Press, 1986.

————. *The Representative of the People? Voters and Voting in England under the Early Stuarts.* Cambridge: Cambridge University Press, 1975.

Holdsworth, Sir William Searle. *A History of English Law.* 17 vols. London: Methuen; Boston: Little, Brown, 1903–1972.

Holstun, James. *A Rational Millennium: Puritan Utopias of Seventeenth-Century England and America.* New York and Oxford: Oxford University Press, 1987.

Howell, Wilbur Samuel. *Logic and Rhetoric in England, 1500–1700.* New York: Russell and Russell, 1961.

Jose, Nicholas. *Ideas of the Restoration in English Literature, 1660–71.* Cambridge: Harvard University Press, 1984.

Judson, Margaret A. *From Tradition to Political Reality: A Study of the Ideas Set Forth in Support of the Commonwealth Government in England, 1649–1653.* Studies in British History and Culture, 7. Hamden, Conn.: Archon Books for the Conference on British Studies and Wittenberg University, 1980.

Kantorowicz, Ernst H. *The King's Two Bodies: A Study in Mediaeval Political Theology.* Princeton: Princeton University Press, 1957.

Kishlansky, Mark A. *Parliamentary Selection: Social and Political Choice in Early Modern England.* Cambridge: Cambridge University Press, 1986.

Knafla, Louis A. *Law and Politics in Jacobean England: The Tracts of Lord Chancellor Ellesmere.* Cambridge: Cambridge University Press, 1977.

Lamont, William M[ontgomerie]. *Marginal Prynne, 1600–1669.* London: Routledge and Kegan Paul; Toronto: University of Toronto Press, 1963.

————. *Richard Baxter and the Millennium: Protestant Imperialism and the English Revolution.* London: Croom Helm; Totowa, N.J.: Rowman and Littlefield, 1979.

Laqueur, Thomas. "The Cultural Origins of Popular Literacy in England, 1500–1850." *Oxford Review of Education* 2 (1976): 255–75.

Lewalski, Barbara Kiefer. "Introduction: Issues and Approaches." In *Renaissance Genres: Essays on Theory, History, and Interpretation,* edited by Barbara Kiefer Lewalski, 1–12. Harvard English Studies, 14. Cambridge: Harvard University Press, 1986.

————. "Milton: Political Beliefs and Polemical Methods, 1659–60." *PMLA* 74 (1959): 191–202.

Loewenstein, David. "'Casting Down Imaginations': Milton as Iconoclast." *Criticism* 31 (1989): 253–70.

McIlwain, Charles Howard. Introduction to *The Political Works of James I,* edited by Charles Howard McIlwain. Harvard Political Classics, 1. Cambridge: Harvard University Press; London: Humphrey Milford, Oxford University Press, 1918.

Macpherson, C. B. *The Political Theory of Possessive Individualism: Hobbes to Locke.* Oxford: Oxford University Press, 1962.

Madan, Francis F. "Milton, Salmasius, and Dugard." *The Library,* 4th series, 4 (1924): 136–43.

————. *A New Bibliography of the Eikon Basilike.* Oxford Bibliographical Society Publications, n.s. 3 (1949). Oxford: Oxford University Press for Oxford Bibliographical Society, 1950.

Maguire, Nancy Klein. "The Theatrical Mask/Masque of Politics: The Case of Charles I." *Journal of British Studies* 28 (1989): 1–22.

Manning, Brian. *The English People and the English Revolution 1640–1649.* London: Heinemann, 1976.

Manuel, Frank E., and Fritzie P. Manuel. *Utopian Thought in the Western World.* Cambridge: Belknap Press/Harvard University Press, 1979.

Marcus, Leah S. *The Politics of Mirth: Jonson, Herrick, Milton, Marvell, and the Defense of Old Holiday Pastimes.* Chicago: University of Chicago Press, 1986.

Meerhoff, Kees. "Pédagogie et rhétorique ramistes: le cas Fouquelin." *Rhetorica* 5 (1987): 419–29.

————. *Rhétorique et poétique an XVIe siècle: Du Bellay, Ramus el les autres.* Studies in Medieval and Reformation Thought, 36. Leiden: E. J. Brill, 1986.

Milner, Andrew. *John Milton and the English Revolution: A Study in the Sociology of Literature.* Totowa, N.J.: Barnes and Noble, 1981.

Morrill, J. S. *The Revolt of the Provinces: Conservatives and Radicals in the English Civil War, 1630–1650.* Historical Problems: Studies and Documents, 26. London: George Allen and Unwin; New York: Barnes and Noble, 1976.

Murphy, James J. Introduction to *Peter Ramus, Arguments in Rhetoric Against Quintilian: Text and Translation in Peter Ramus's Rhetoricae Distinctiones in Quintilianum,* translated by Carole Newlands, 1–76. DeKalb: Northern Illinois Press, 1986.

Ong, Walter J., S.J. *Ramus, Method, and the Decay of Dialogue: From the Art of Discourse to the Art of Reason.* Cambridge: Harvard University Press, 1958.

————. "Tudor Writings on Rhetoric." *Studies in the Renaissance* 15 (1968): 39–69.

Orgel, Stephen. *The Illusion of Power: Political Theater in the English Renaissance.* Berkeley: University of California Press, 1975.

Parkin-Speer, Diane. "Robert Browne: Rhetorical Iconoclast." *Sixteenth Century Journal* 18 (1987): 519–29.

Parry, Graham. *The Golden Age Restor'd: The Culture of the Stuart Court, 1603–42.* New York: St. Martin's Press, 1981.

Patterson, Annabel M. *Censorship and Interpretation: The Conditions of Writing and Reading in Early-Modern England.* Madison: University of Wisconsin Press, 1984.

————. "The Civic Hero in Milton's Prose." *Milton Studies* 8 (1976): 71–101.

Pearl, Valerie. *London and the Outbreak of the Puritan Revolution: City Government and National Politics, 1625–43.* [London]: Oxford University Press, 1961.

————. "London's Counter-Revolution." In *The Interregnum: The Quest for Settlement 1646–1660,* edited by G. E. Aylmer, 29–56, 216–19. London: Macmillan, 1972.

Perlette, John M. "Milton, Ascham, and the Rhetoric of the Divorce Controversy." *Milton Studies* 10 (1977): 195–215.

Petegorsky, David. W. *Left-Wing Democracy in the English Civil War: A Study of the Social Philosophy of Gerrard Winstanley.* London: Victor Gollancz, 1940.

Plumb, J. H. "The Growth of the Electorate in England from 1600 to 1715." *Past and Present,* no. 45 (1969): 90–116.

Pocock, J. G. A. *The Ancient Constitution and the Feudal Law: A Study of English Historical Thought in the Seventeenth Century.* Cambridge: Cambridge University Press, 1957.

————. *The Machiavellian Moment: Florentine Political Thought and the Atlantic Republican Tradition.* Princeton: Princeton University Press, 1975.

————. A Retrospect from 1986 to *The Ancient Constitution and the Feudal Law: A Study of English Historical Thought in the Seventeenth Century. A Reissue with a Retrospect,* 306–34. Cambridge: Cambridge University Press, 1987.

Potter, Lois. *Secret Rites and Secret Writing: Royalist Literature, 1641–1660.* Cambridge: Cambridge University Press, 1989.

Reames, Sherry L. *The "Legenda aurea": A Reexamination of Its Paradoxical History.* Madison: University of Wisconsin Press, 1985.

Roots, Ivan. *Commonwealth and Protectorate: The English Civil War and Its Aftermath.* New York: Schocken, 1966.

Rosmarin, Adena. *The Power of Genre.* Minneapolis: University of Minnesota Press, 1985.

Rowe, Violet A. *Sir Henry Vane the Younger: A Study in Political and Administrative History.* London: University of London, Athlone Press, 1970.

Ruff, Lillian M., and D. Arnold Wilson. "The Madrigal, the Lute Song, and Elizabethan Politics." *Past and Present,* no. 44 (1969): 3–51.

Russell, Conrad. "The Theory of Treason in the Trial of Strafford." *English Historical Review* 80 (1965): 30–50.

Russell Smith, H. F. *Harrington and His Oceana: A Study of a 17th Century Utopia and Its Influences in America.* Cambridge: Cambridge University Press, 1914.

Sachse, William L. "English Pamphlet Support for Charles I, November 1648–January 1649." In *Conflict in Stuart England: Essays in Honour of Wallace Notestein,* edited by William Appleton Aiken and Basil Duke Henning, 149–68. London: Jonathan Cape, 1960.

Samuel, Irene. "Milton on the Province of Rhetoric." *Milton Studies* 10 (1977): 177–98.

Seigel, Jerrold E. *Rhetoric and Philosophy in Renaissance Humanism: The Union of Eloquence and Wisdom, Petrarch to Valla.* Princeton: Princeton University Press, 1968.

Sennett, Richard. *The Fall of Public Man.* New York: Vintage, 1978.

Sharpe, Kevin. "The Personal Rule of Charles I." In *Before the English Civil War: Essays on Early Stuart Politics and Government,* edited by Howard Tomlinson, 53–78. New York: St. Martin's Press, 1984.

———. "An Unwanted Civil War?" *New York Review of Books* 29, no. 19 (December 2, 1982): 43–45.

Shawcross, John T. "The Higher Wisdom of *The Tenure of Kings and Magistrates.*" In *Achievements of the Left Hand: Essays on the Prose of John Milton,* edited by Michael Lieb and John T. Shawcross, 142–60. Amherst: University of Massachusetts Press, 1974.

Siebert, Frederick Seaton. *Freedom of the Press in England 1476–1776: The Rise and Decline of Government Controls.* Urbana: University of Illinois Press, 1952.

Sirluck, Ernest. Introduction to *The Complete Prose Works of John Milton,* vol. 2., 1–216. New Haven: Yale University Press; London: Oxford University Press, 1959.

———. "Milton's Political Thought: The First Cycle." *Modern Philology* 61 (1964): 209–24.

Skerpan, Elizabeth P. "Rhetorical Genres and the *Eikon Basilike.*" *Explorations in Renaissance Culture* 11 (1985): 99–111.

Skinner, Quentin. "Conventions and the Understanding of Speech Acts." *Philosophical Quarterly* 20 (1970): 118–38.

———. "Hermeneutics and the Role of History." *New Literary History* 7 (1975–1976): 209–32.

———. "The Ideological Context of Hobbes's Political Thought." *Historical Journal* 9 (1966): 286–317.

———. "Some Problems in the Analysis of Political Thought and Action." *Political Theory* 2 (1974): 277–303.

Sloane, Thomas O. *Donne, Milton, and the End of Humanist Rhetoric.* Berkeley: University of California Press, 1985.

Smuts, R. Malcolm. *Court Culture and the Origins of the Royalist Tradition in Early Stuart England.* Philadelphia: University of Pennsylvania Press, 1987.

Stavely, Keith W. *The Politics of Milton's Prose Style.* Yale Studies in English, 185. New Haven and London: Yale University Press, 1975.

Stewart, Stanley. "Milton Revises *The Readie and Easie Way.*" *Milton Studies* 20 (1984): 205–24.

Stone, Lawrence. *The Crisis of the Aristocracy, 1558–1641.* Oxford: Clarendon Press, 1965.

———. "Literacy and Education in England, 1640–1900." *Past and Present,* no. 42 (1969): 69–139.

Thomas, Keith. *Religion and the Decline of Magic.* New York: Scribner, 1971.

Thorpe, Malcolm R. "Catholic Conspiracy in Early Elizabethan Foreign Policy." *Sixteenth Century Journal* 15 (1984): 431–48.

Todorov, Tzvetan. *Les Genres du discours.* Paris: Éditions du Seuil, 1978.

———. "The Origin of Genres." *New Literary History* 8 (1976): 159–70.

Tomlinson, Howard. "The Causes of War: A Historiographical Survey." In *Before the English Civil War: Essays on Early Stuart Politics and Government,* edited by Howard Tomlinson, 7–26. New York: St. Martin's Press, 1984.

Underdown, David. *Pride's Purge: Politics in the Puritan Revolution.* Oxford: Clarendon Press, 1971.

———. *Revel, Riot and Rebellion: Popular Politics and Culture in England, 1603–1660.* Oxford: Clarendon Press, 1985.

———. *Royalist Conspiracy in England, 1649–1660.* New Haven: Yale University Press, 1960.

———. *Somerset in the Civil War and Interregnum.* Newton Abbot, Devon: David and Charles, 1973.

Vann, Richard T. "Literacy in Seventeenth-Century England: Some Hearth-Tax Evidence." *Journal of Interdisciplinary History* 5 (1974): 287–93.

Vaughan, Frederick. *The Tradition of Political Hedonism: From Hobbes to J. S. Mill.* New York: Fordham University Press, 1982.

Wallace, John M. *Destiny His Choice: The Loyalism of Andrew Marvell.* Cambridge: Cambridge University Press, 1968.

Walzer, Michael. *The Revolution of the Saints: A Study in the Origins of Radical Politics.* Cambridge: Harvard University Press, 1965.

Webber, Joan. *The Eloquent "I": Style and Self in Seventeenth-Century Prose.* Madison: University of Wisconsin Press, 1968.

Wedgwood, C. V. *The Great Rebellion.* Vol. 1, *The King's Peace, 1637–1641;* Vol. 2, *The King's War, 1641–1647.* London: Collins, 1955–1958.

———. *The Trial of Charles I.* London: Collins, 1964.

Weiner, Carol Z. "The Beleaguered Isle: A Study of Elizabethan and Early Jacobean Anti-Catholicism." *Past and Present,* no. 51 (1971): 27–62.

White, Stephen D. *Sir Edward Coke and the "Grievances of Commonwealth," 1621–1628.* Chapel Hill: University of North Carolina Press, 1979.

Wolfe, Don M. *Milton in the Puritan Revolution.* 1941. Reprint. New York: Humanities Press, 1963.

Woodhouse, A. S. P. Introduction to *Puritanism and Liberty: Being the Army Debates (1647–9) from the Clarke Manuscripts with Supplementary Documents,* 2d ed., edited by A. S. P. Woodhouse, 11–100. Chicago: University of Chicago Press, 1974.

Woolrych, Austin. Historical Introduction to *The Complete Prose Works of John Milton,* vol. 7, rev. ed., edited by Robert W. Ayers, 1–328. New Haven and London: Yale University Press, 1980.

———. "Last Quests for a Settlement, 1657–1660." In *The Interregnum: The Quest for Settlement, 1646–1660,* edited by G. E. Aylmer, 183–204. London: Macmillan, 1972.

Worden, Blair. *The Rump Parliament.* Cambridge: Cambridge University Press, 1974.

Zagorin, Perez. *The Court and the Country: The Beginnings of the English Revolution.* New York: Atheneum, 1971.

———. *A History of Political Thought in the English Revolution.* London: Routledge and Kegan Paul, 1954.

Index

Absolutism: Fulmer's justification of, 169; Hobbes's defense of, 170

Agrarian law: in Harrington's *Oceana*, 205–6; in Miltonian commonwealth, 272

"Agreement of the People," 203

Ahab, King, 115

Anabaptists, 178

Anarchy, 174

Anglicanism, 89, 97

Anti-Catholicism: Laud's rituals depicted as, 49; in parliamentarian tracts, 74; broadside linking Charles I to, 78; doctrine of pope's indirect power as source of, 91; in N. T.'s *The Resolver Continued*, 141; in Prynne's *The Republicans*, 178; monarchist writings of 1659–1660, 185; in *A Common-vvealth or Nothing*, 223; in *The Remonstrance of the Noble-men*, 223

Anti-monarchists of 1659–1660: distributive vision of, 235

Apologetick for the Sequestred Clergie of the Church of England, An, 129, 133

Arendt, Hannah, 200

Aristotle: on genres, 13, 15; three types of audiences, 14; on epideictic narrations and proofs, 15

Armada, 91

Army: attempts to control printing, 10; as disrupter of county life, 85; opponent of Charles I, 87; Independents and radicals attracted to, 88; view of Charles's actions as proof of God's opposition to him, 95; Parliament pressured by to stop Treaty of Newport, 98;

warned against by the Charles of *Eikon Basilike*, 108; attempt of Rump to purge a failure, 165; Committee of Safety established, 165; interruption of Rump in October 1659, 165; Lambert's leadership of, 165; petitions to Rump for reforms and pay, 165; reforms for prevented by Haslerigg's quarrel with Vane, 165; mutiny of on February 1, 1660, 166; Rump's demand for reducing size of, 166; Rump supported by, 166; arrears in pay and Charles II's Declaration of Breda, 167; restructuring of urged by Vane, 204; hypocrisy of decried in radical tracts of 1659, 208; in *To His Excellency the Lord Fleetwood*, 210; in *Huc Ades, Haec Animae* and *The Remonstrance of the Apprentices*, 210–11; in *To the Officers and Souldiers* and *The Remonstrance of the Noble-men*, 218

Army grandees, 165, 168, 203, 208, 209

Arrangement: to Neo-Ramists, 24

Articles of Impeachment of the Five Members, 171

Ascham, Anthony, 202

Assizes, 85

Attempt on the Five Members: generally, 60–64; as pivotal event of the revolution, 60; Charles I's speech to Parliament, 70; defense of the Five Members as parliamentarian self-defense, 71–72; speeches of defense attributed to the Five Members, 71; struggle to

255